DIRK GENTLY'S HOLISTIC DETECTIVE AGENCY

The Salmon of Doubt

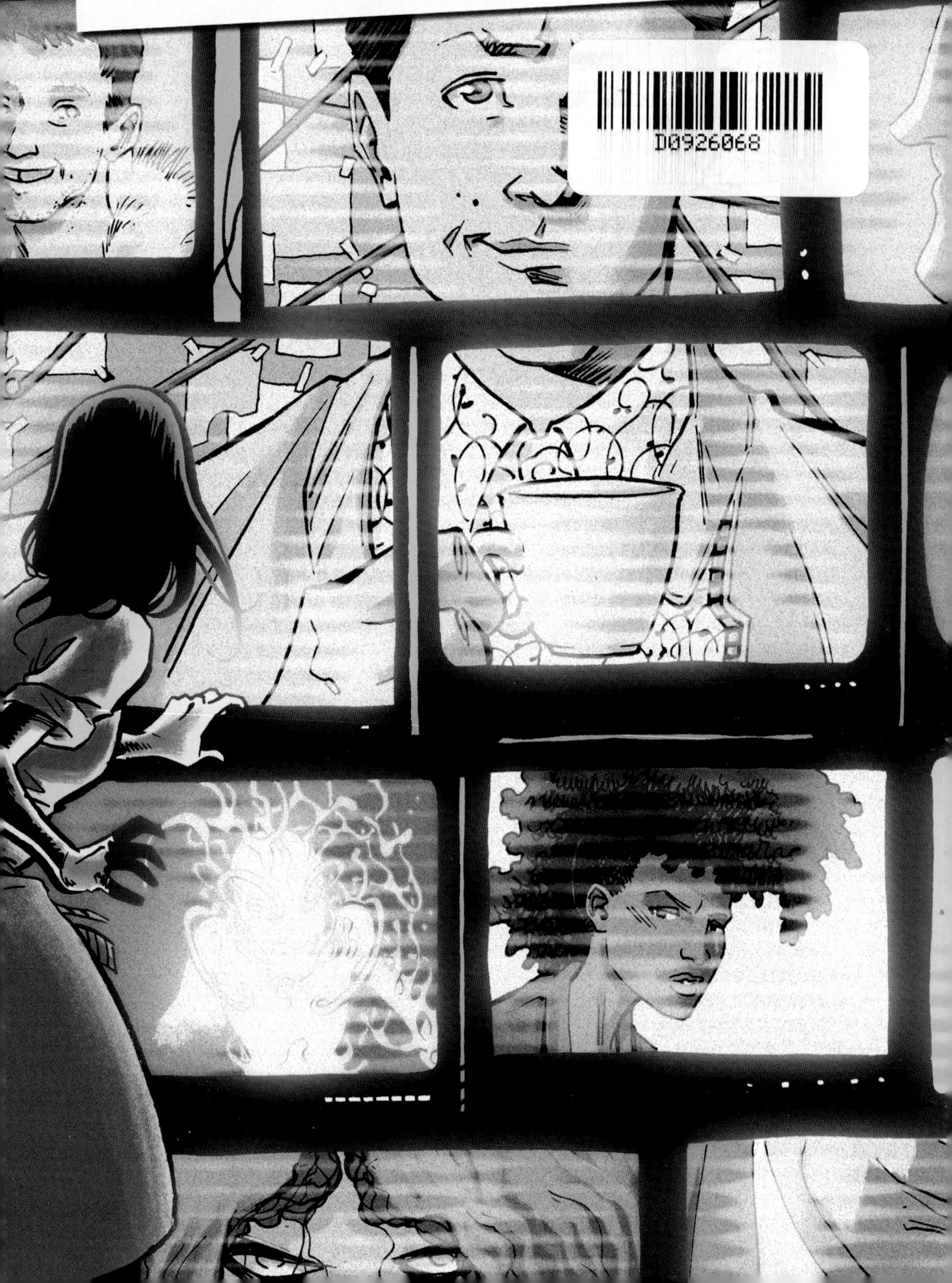

Written by **Arvind Ethan David**
Art by **Ilias Kyriazis**
Colors by **Charlie Kirchoff**
Letters by **Shawn Lee,**
Robbie Robbins, Chris Mowry,
and **Tom B. Long**

Series Edits by
Denton J. Tipton
Executive Producer
Max Landis

Collection Edits by
Justin Eisinger and
Alonzo Simon
Collection Design by
Tom B. Long
Publisher: **Ted Adams**

Dirk Gently's
Holistic Detective
Agency created
by **Douglas Adams**

Special thanks to
Devon Byers,
Mpho Koaho,
and Fiona Dourif.

ISBN: 978-1-63140-877-9
20 19 18 17   1 2 3 4

DIRK GENTLY'S HOLISTIC DETECTIVE AGENCY: THE SALMON OF DOUBT, VOLUME 1.
MAY 2017. FIRST PRINTING. © Completely Unexpected Productions. All Rights
Reserved. © 2017 AMC Film Holdings LLC. All Rights Reserved. The IDW logo is
registered in the U.S. Patent and Trademark Office. IDW Publishing, a division of
Idea and Design Works, LLC. Editorial offices: 2765 Truxtun Road, San Diego, CA
92106. Any similarities to persons living or dead are purely coincidental. With the
exception of artwork used for review purposes, none of the contents of this
publication may be reprinted without the permission of Idea and Design Works, LLC.
Printed in Canada.
IDW Publishing does not read or accept unsolicited submissions of ideas, stories,
or artwork.

Originally published as DIRK GENTLY'S HOLISTIC DETECTIVE AGENCY:
THE SALMON OF DOUBT issues #1–5.

IDW®

TED ADAMS,
CEO & Publisher
GREG GOLDSTEIN,
President & COO
ROBBIE ROBBINS,
EVP/Sr. Graphic Artist
CHRIS RYALL,
Chief Creative Officer
DAVID HEDGECOCK,
Editor-in-Chief
LAURIE WINDROW,
Senior Vice President of
Sales & Marketing
MATTHEW RUZICKA, CPA,
Chief Financial Officer
LORELEI BUNJES,
VP of Digital Services
JERRY BENNINGTON,
VP of New Product Development

BECOMING BART

I first learned about Douglas Adams while reading *Hitchhiker's Guide to the Galaxy* when I was 19. It had me hooked — I wouldn't leave the house until I'd finished. I probably haven't been as lost in a book since. Adams' strangeness is unlike any other, with a weirdly profound quality that transports you into his world.

Imagine my surprise years later when I got to play a character in one of those worlds! And it's not like characters like Bart come around often. The breakdown read "a character on the scale of Jack Sparrow and Beetlejuice!" Let me tell you, in Hollywood I usually get to play different versions of "quick-witted cop" or "nurse with a heart of gold." So I was really, really excited to play Bart.

But more than simply "playing" Bart, Max (Landis) and Arvind (Ethan David) encouraged weird. I was told to explore impulse and take crazy risks. I've never enjoyed creating a character so much. My regular preparation includes a lot of thinking about where I am coming from and why I'm doing what I'm doing; the motivations for my character. I end up building a whole world inside my head, so what I'm doing makes sense (at least to me!). That part of the process is actually my favorite, and with Bart there was so much to figure out because her world is unlike anyone else's. I got to be really, really imaginative, which was just so much fun. I reveled in it.

What's been interesting is watching fan reaction. To me, Bart is an innocent child. I love her and want to protect her, so it's weird to see other characters think of her as a villain. When reading the comics, I end up yelling at the pages "It's not Bart's fault!, she's just doing what she absolutely has to!" So this has been a very fun ride. Not to mention I receive a steady stream of fan art, from girls covering their Barbie dolls in mud (which I find particularly satisfying), to really detailed portraits of action sequences. It's just fun to see people love her as much as I do! Chucky fans are as devoted but I feel closer to Bart. I helped create her.

Hopefully anyone reading this has tuned in to watch the show because... it's really good! I couldn't love a show more, as it has some of the most imaginative characters on television. There is even more to explore in seasons to come. Take Bart, she's never felt like a girl, or really understands that the world sees a difference between the two genders. I'd be interested to explore her world with that twist thrust on me (might I say I dare them). Maybe it will happen; It is a wild, magical world unlike any other, and that only someone like Douglas Adams could inspire.

— Fiona Dourif

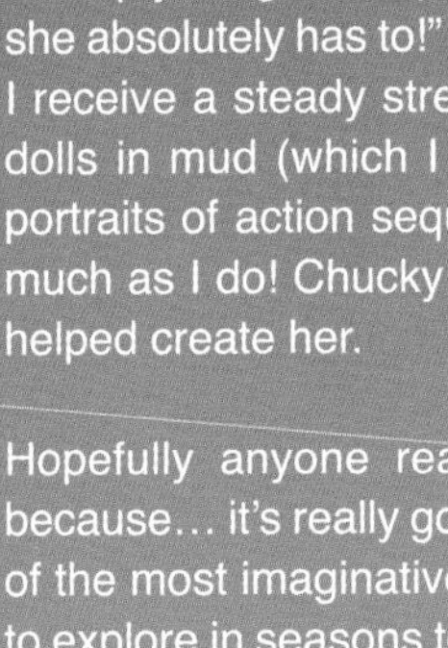

Fiona Dourif plays Bart on Dirk Gently's Holistic Detective Agency *and is also well known for the role of Nica Pierce in the* Child's Play *Franchise. She lives in Los Angeles and has considerably better personal hygiene than Bart.*

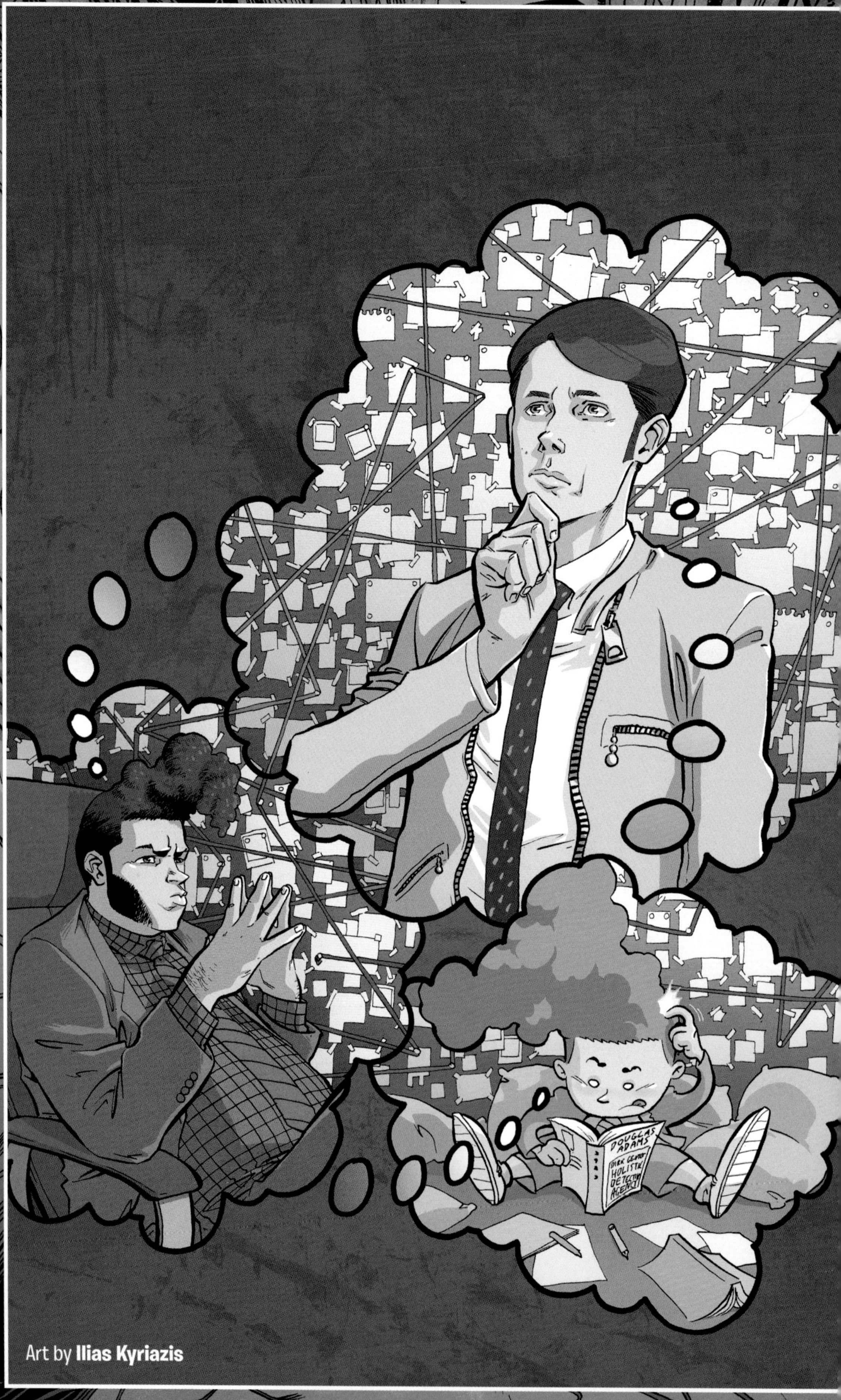
DOUGLAS
ADAMS

Art by **Ilias Kyriazis**

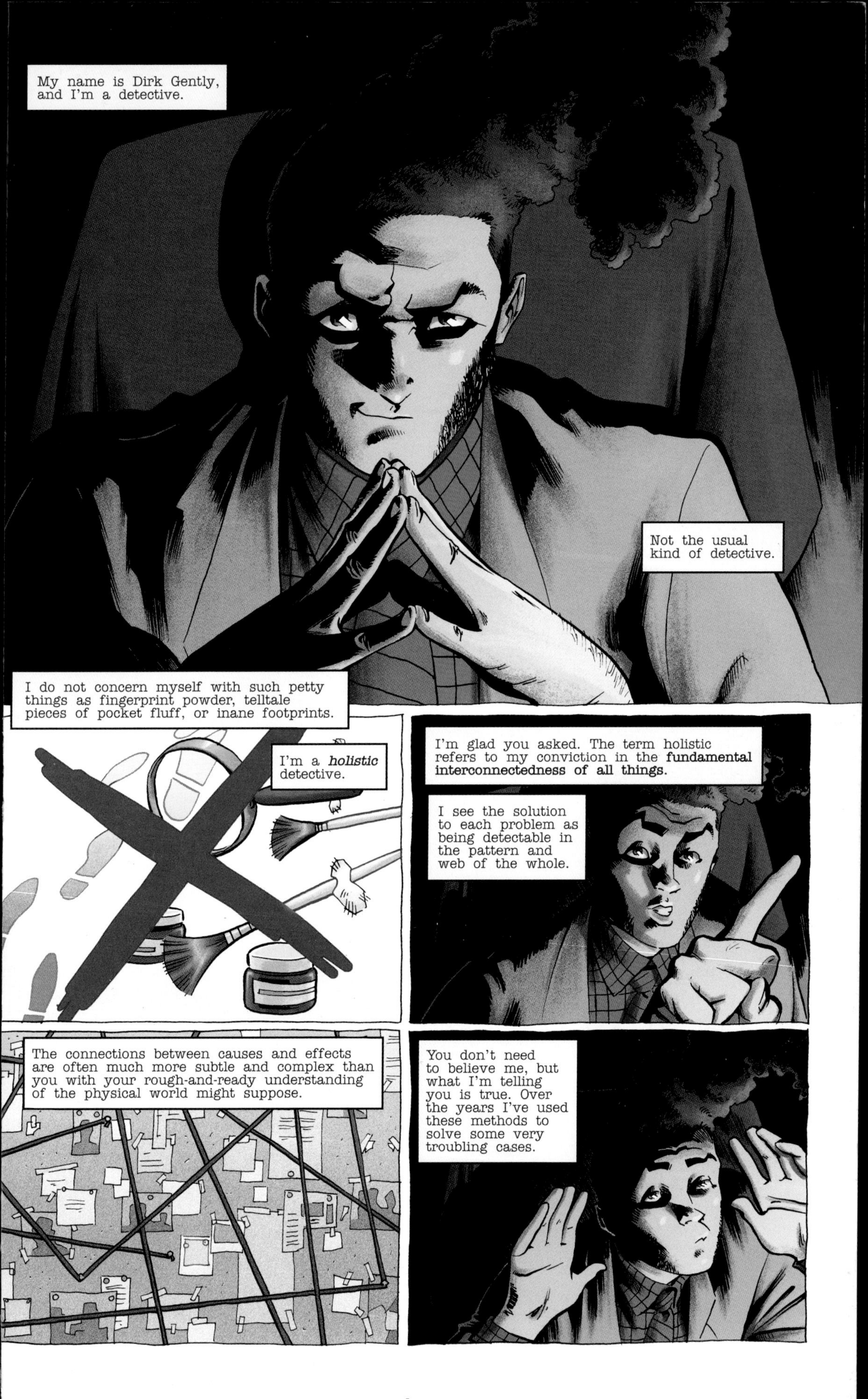
My name is Dirk Gently, and I'm a detective.
Not the usual kind of detective.
I do not concern myself with such petty things as fingerprint powder, telltale pieces of pocket fluff, or inane footprints.
I'm a ***holistic*** detective.
I'm glad you asked. The term holistic refers to my conviction in the **fundamental interconnectedness of all things.**
I see the solution to each problem as being detectable in the pattern and web of the whole.
The connections between causes and effects are often much more subtle and complex than you with your rough-and-ready understanding of the physical world might suppose.
You don't need to believe me, but what I'm telling you is true. Over the years I've used these methods to solve some very troubling cases.

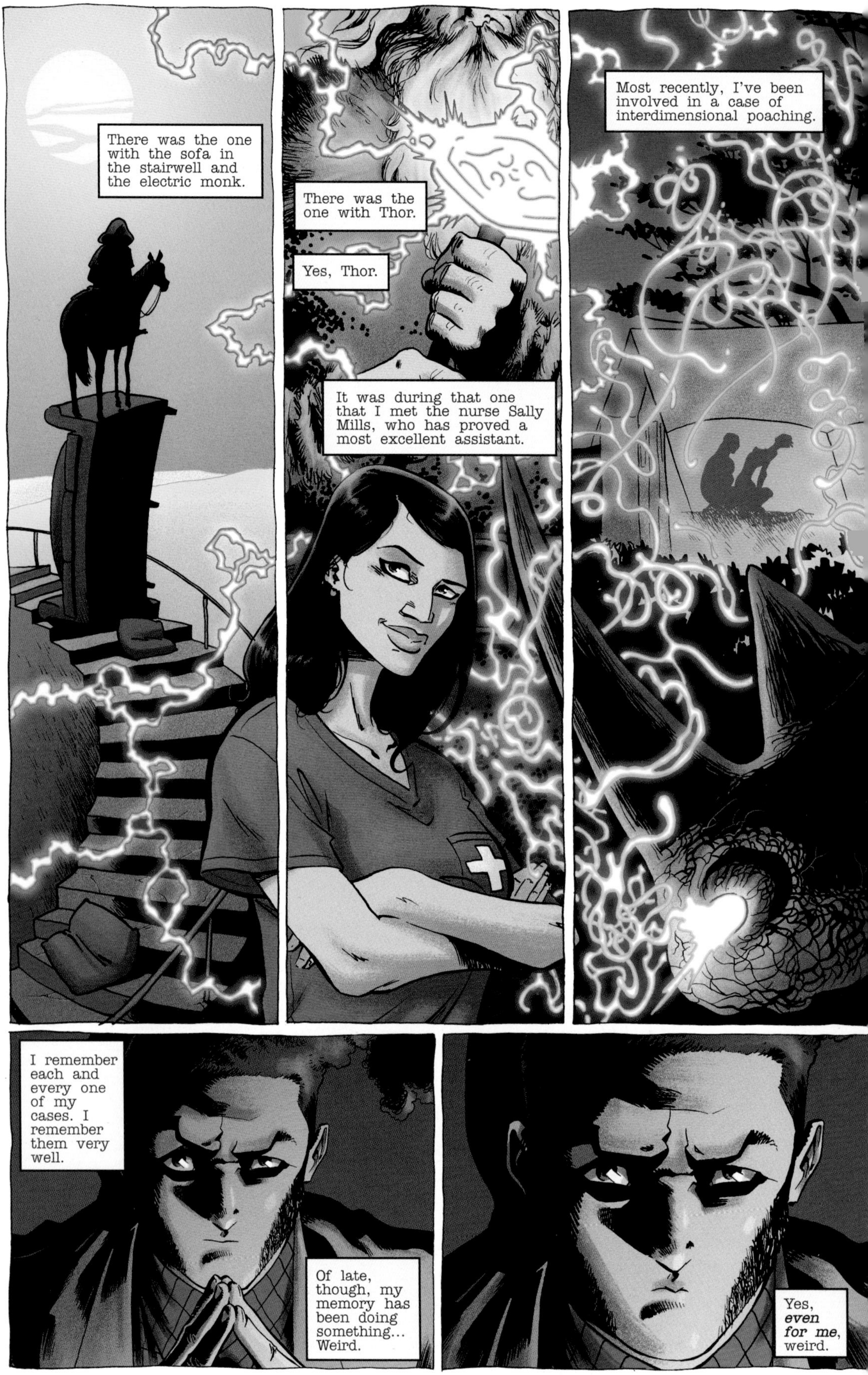
There was the one with the sofa in the stairwell and the electric monk.
There was the one with Thor.
Yes, Thor.
It was during that one that I met the nurse Sally Mills, who has proved a most excellent assistant.
Most recently, I've been involved in a case of interdimensional poaching.
I remember each and every one of my cases. I remember them very well.
Of late, though, my memory has been doing something... Weird.
Yes, *even for me*, weird.

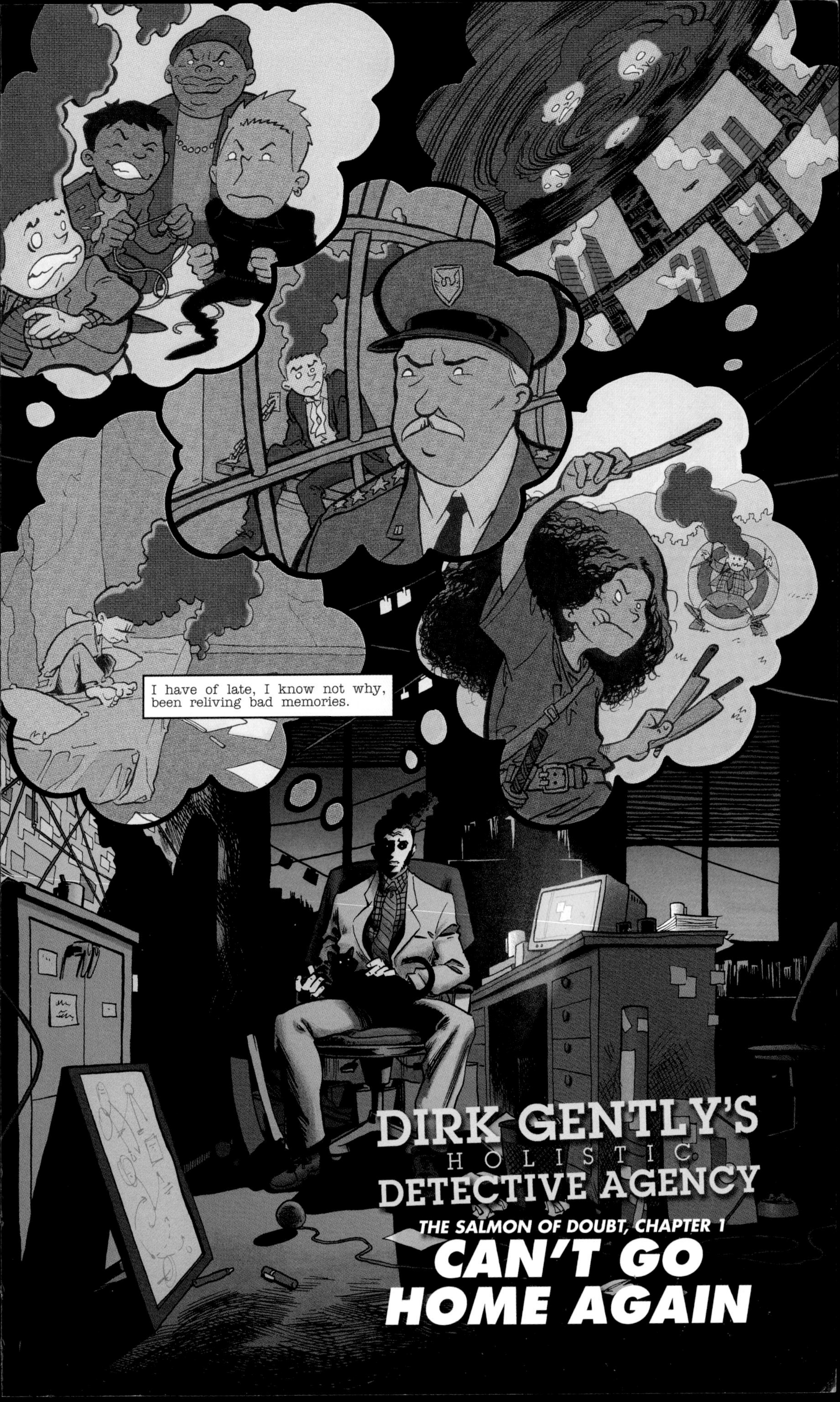
I have of late, I know not why, been reliving bad memories.
DIRK GENTLY'S
HOLISTIC
DETECTIVE AGENCY
THE SALMON OF DOUBT, CHAPTER 1
CAN'T GO HOME AGAIN

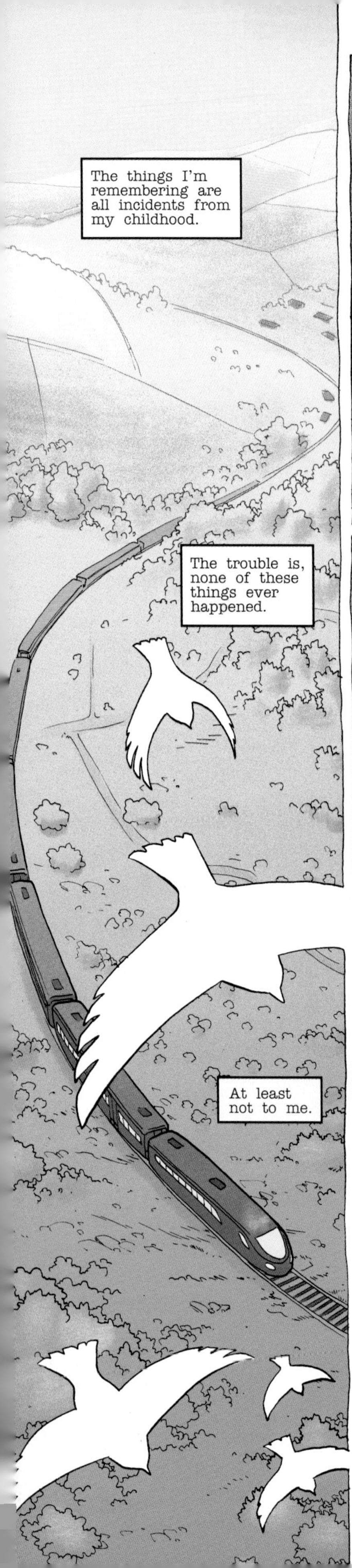
The things I'm remembering are all incidents from my childhood.
The trouble is, none of these things ever happened.
At least not to me.

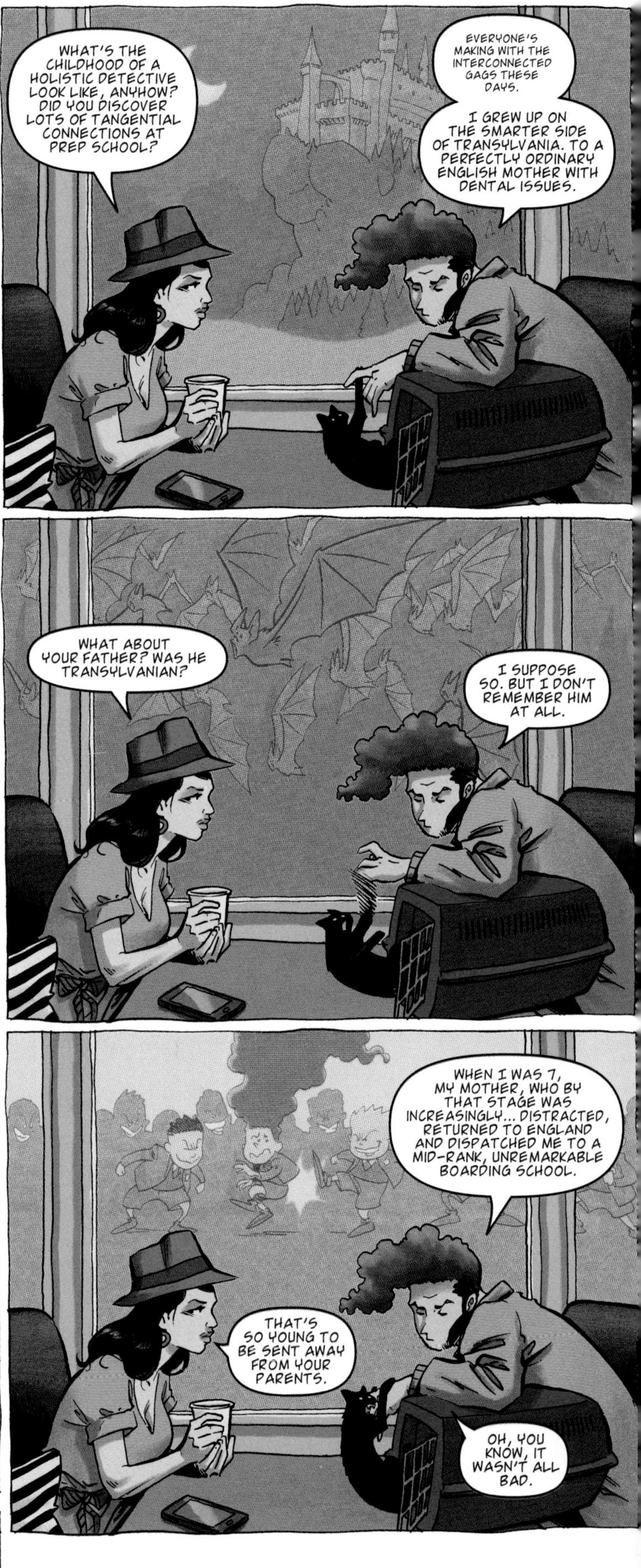
WHAT'S THE CHILDHOOD OF A HOLISTIC DETECTIVE LOOK LIKE, ANYHOW? DID YOU DISCOVER LOTS OF TANGENTIAL CONNECTIONS AT PREP SCHOOL?
EVERYONE'S MAKING WITH THE INTERCONNECTED GAGS THESE DAYS.
I GREW UP ON THE SMARTER SIDE OF TRANSYLVANIA. TO A PERFECTLY ORDINARY ENGLISH MOTHER WITH DENTAL ISSUES.
WHAT ABOUT YOUR FATHER? WAS HE TRANSYLVANIAN?
I SUPPOSE SO. BUT I DON'T REMEMBER HIM AT ALL.
WHEN I WAS 7, MY MOTHER, WHO BY THAT STAGE WAS INCREASINGLY... DISTRACTED, RETURNED TO ENGLAND AND DISPATCHED ME TO A MID-RANK, UNREMARKABLE BOARDING SCHOOL.
THAT'S SO YOUNG TO BE SENT AWAY FROM YOUR PARENTS.
OH, YOU KNOW, IT WASN'T ALL BAD.

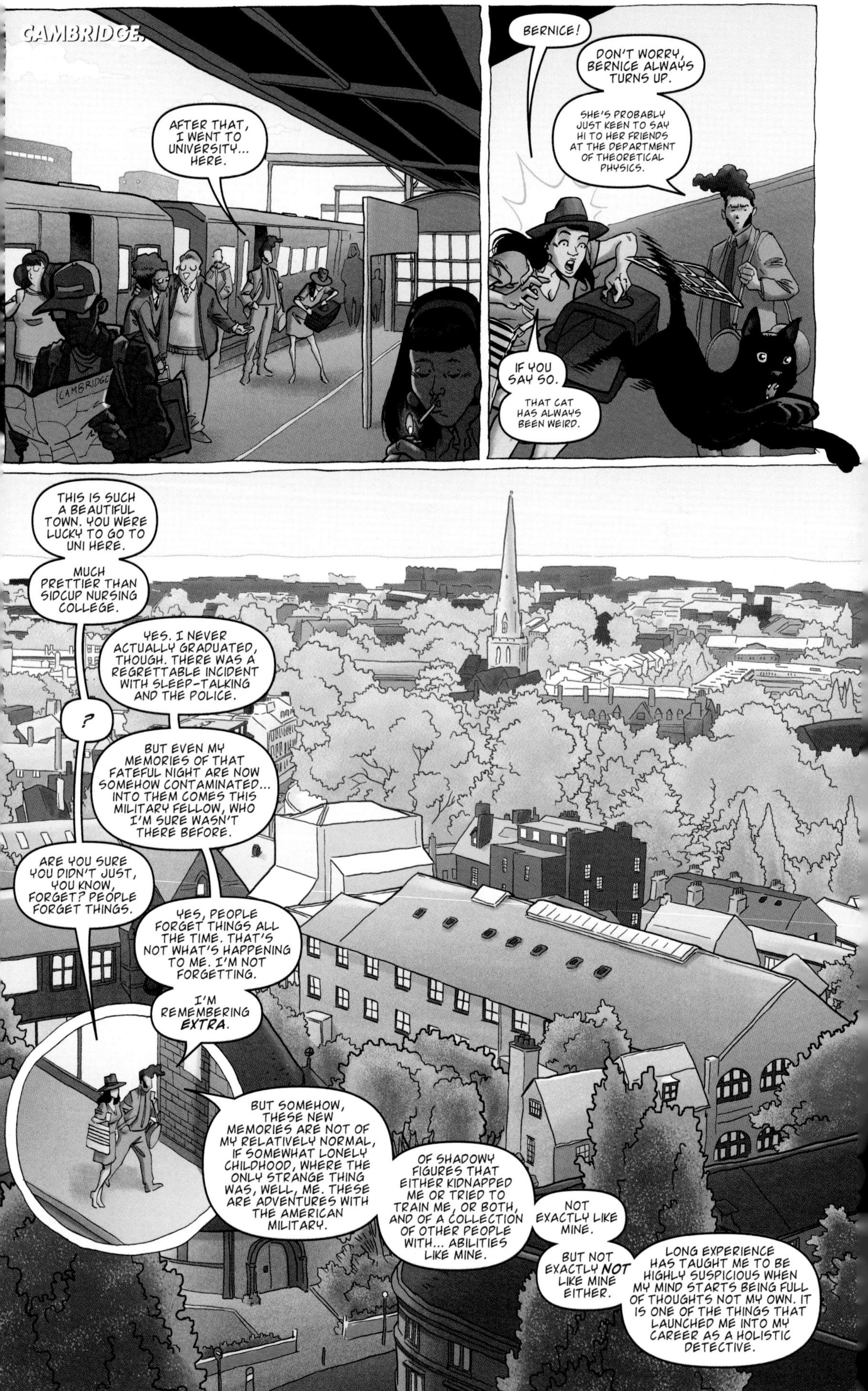
CAMBRIDGE.
AFTER THAT, I WENT TO UNIVERSITY... HERE.
CAMBRIDGE
BERNICE!
DON'T WORRY, BERNICE ALWAYS TURNS UP.
SHE'S PROBABLY JUST KEEN TO SAY HI TO HER FRIENDS AT THE DEPARTMENT OF THEORETICAL PHYSICS.
IF YOU SAY SO.
THAT CAT HAS ALWAYS BEEN WEIRD.
THIS IS SUCH A BEAUTIFUL TOWN. YOU WERE LUCKY TO GO TO UNI HERE.
MUCH PRETTIER THAN SIDCUP NURSING COLLEGE.
YES. I NEVER ACTUALLY GRADUATED, THOUGH. THERE WAS A REGRETTABLE INCIDENT WITH SLEEP-TALKING AND THE POLICE.
?
BUT EVEN MY MEMORIES OF THAT FATEFUL NIGHT ARE NOW SOMEHOW CONTAMINATED... INTO THEM COMES THIS MILITARY FELLOW, WHO I'M SURE WASN'T THERE BEFORE.
ARE YOU SURE YOU DIDN'T JUST, YOU KNOW, FORGET? PEOPLE FORGET THINGS.
YES, PEOPLE FORGET THINGS ALL THE TIME. THAT'S NOT WHAT'S HAPPENING TO ME. I'M NOT FORGETTING.
I'M REMEMBERING *EXTRA*.
BUT SOMEHOW, THESE NEW MEMORIES ARE NOT OF MY RELATIVELY NORMAL, IF SOMEWHAT LONELY CHILDHOOD, WHERE THE ONLY STRANGE THING WAS, WELL, ME. THESE ARE ADVENTURES WITH THE AMERICAN MILITARY.
OF SHADOWY FIGURES THAT EITHER KIDNAPPED ME OR TRIED TO TRAIN ME, OR BOTH, AND OF A COLLECTION OF OTHER PEOPLE WITH... ABILITIES LIKE MINE.
NOT EXACTLY LIKE MINE.
BUT NOT EXACTLY *NOT* LIKE MINE EITHER.
LONG EXPERIENCE HAS TAUGHT ME TO BE HIGHLY SUSPICIOUS WHEN MY MIND STARTS BEING FULL OF THOUGHTS NOT MY OWN. IT IS ONE OF THE THINGS THAT LAUNCHED ME INTO MY CAREER AS A HOLISTIC DETECTIVE.

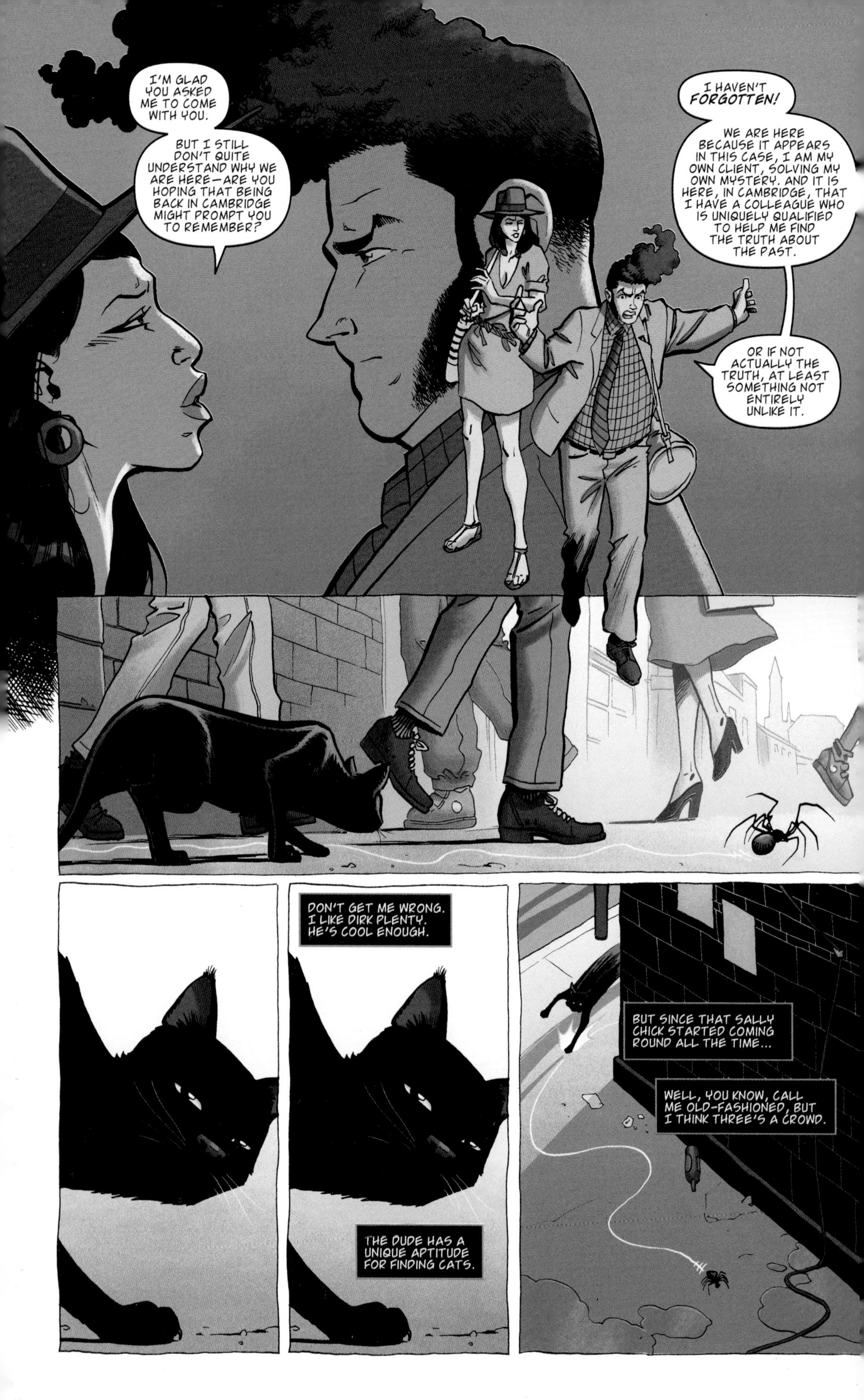
I'M GLAD YOU ASKED ME TO COME WITH YOU.
BUT I STILL DON'T QUITE UNDERSTAND WHY WE ARE HERE—ARE YOU HOPING THAT BEING BACK IN CAMBRIDGE MIGHT PROMPT YOU TO REMEMBER?
I HAVEN'T *FORGOTTEN!*
WE ARE HERE BECAUSE IT APPEARS IN THIS CASE, I AM MY OWN CLIENT, SOLVING MY OWN MYSTERY. AND IT IS HERE, IN CAMBRIDGE, THAT I HAVE A COLLEAGUE WHO IS UNIQUELY QUALIFIED TO HELP ME FIND THE TRUTH ABOUT THE PAST.
OR IF NOT ACTUALLY THE TRUTH, AT LEAST SOMETHING NOT ENTIRELY UNLIKE IT.
DON'T GET ME WRONG. I LIKE DIRK PLENTY. HE'S COOL ENOUGH.
THE DUDE HAS A UNIQUE APTITUDE FOR FINDING CATS.
BUT SINCE THAT SALLY CHICK STARTED COMING ROUND ALL THE TIME...
WELL, YOU KNOW, CALL ME OLD-FASHIONED, BUT I THINK THREE'S A CROWD.

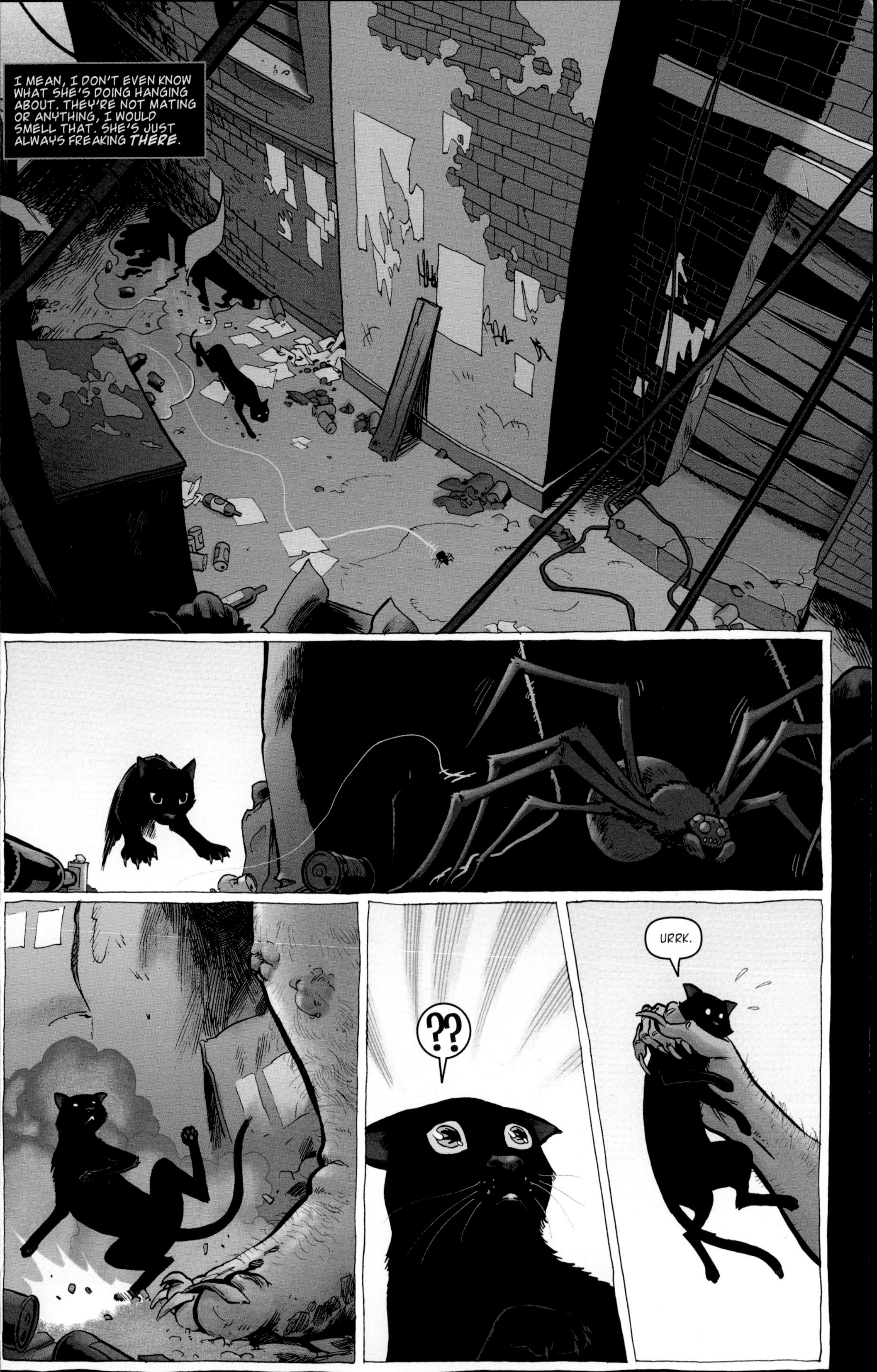
I MEAN, I DON'T EVEN KNOW WHAT SHE'S DOING HANGING ABOUT. THEY'RE NOT MATING OR ANYTHING, I WOULD SMELL THAT. SHE'S JUST ALWAYS FREAKING *THERE*.
??
URRK.

WHO'S A PRETTY LITTLE GIRL, THEN?

MEOW?

CHRIST IN A BUCKET. THEY SAID SEXUAL ASSAULT IN COLLEGE TOWNS WAS UP, BUT THIS IS RIDICULOUS.

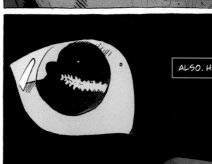

ALSO. HELP.

DIRK?

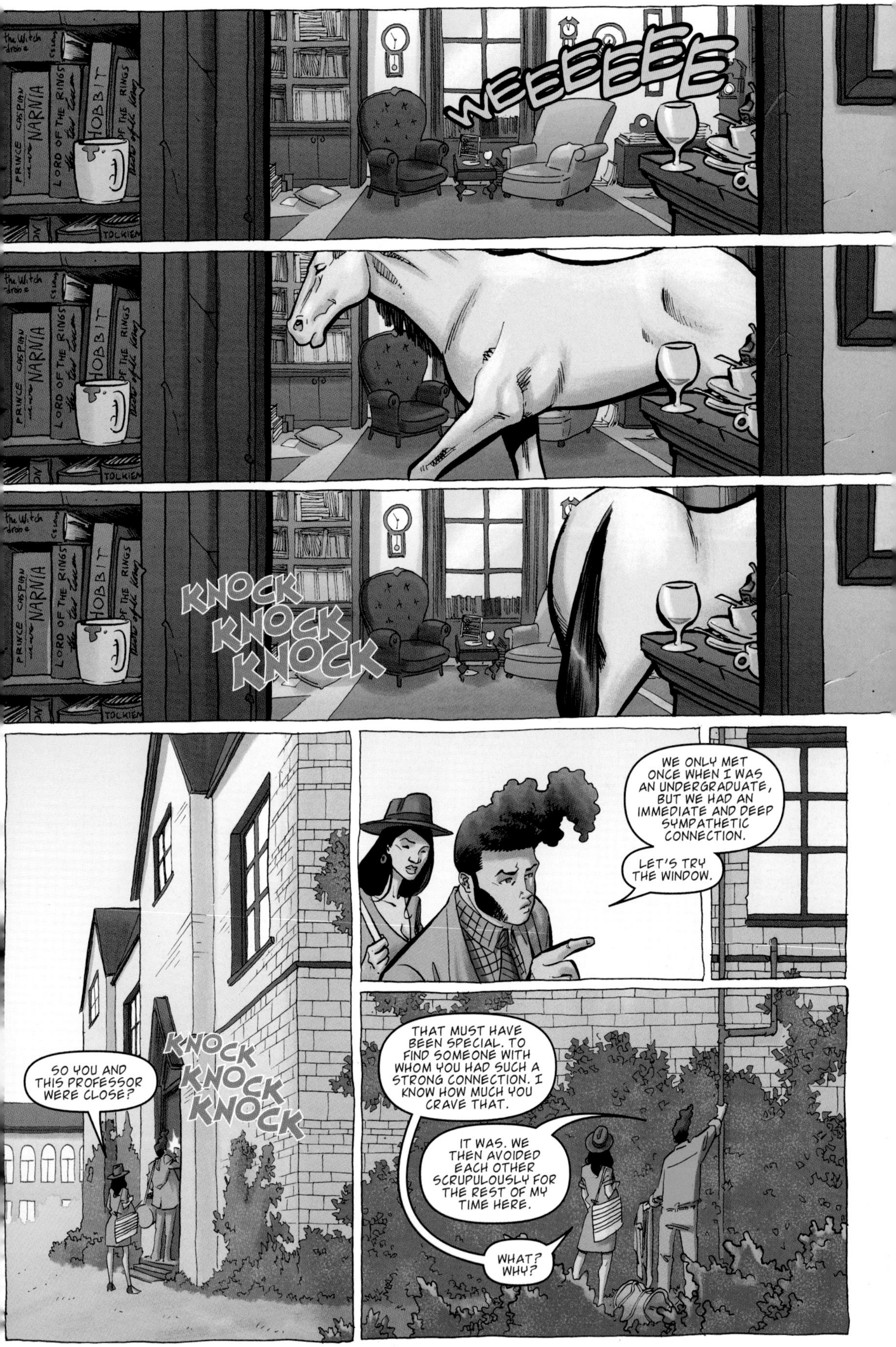
WEEEEEEE
KNOCK KNOCK KNOCK
SO YOU AND THIS PROFESSOR WERE CLOSE?
KNOCK KNOCK KNOCK
WE ONLY MET ONCE WHEN I WAS AN UNDERGRADUATE, BUT WE HAD AN IMMEDIATE AND DEEP SYMPATHETIC CONNECTION.
LET'S TRY THE WINDOW.
THAT MUST HAVE BEEN SPECIAL. TO FIND SOMEONE WITH WHOM YOU HAD SUCH A STRONG CONNECTION. I KNOW HOW MUCH YOU CRAVE THAT.
IT WAS. WE THEN AVOIDED EACH OTHER SCRUPULOUSLY FOR THE REST OF MY TIME HERE.
WHAT? WHY?

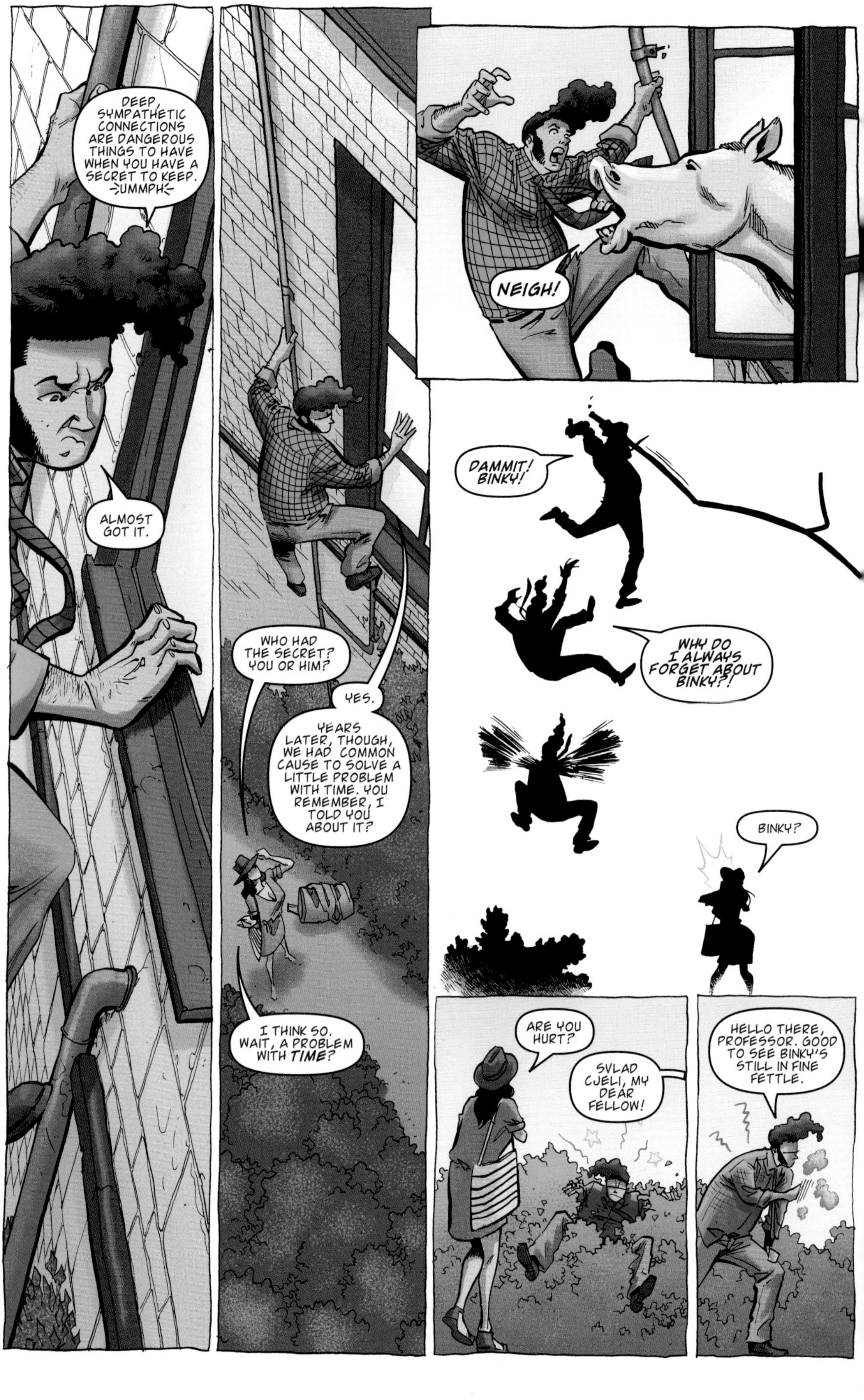
DEEP, SYMPATHETIC CONNECTIONS ARE DANGEROUS THINGS TO HAVE WHEN YOU HAVE A SECRET TO KEEP. -UMMPH-
ALMOST GOT IT.
WHO HAD THE SECRET? YOU OR HIM?
YES.
YEARS LATER, THOUGH, WE HAD COMMON CAUSE TO SOLVE A LITTLE PROBLEM WITH TIME. YOU REMEMBER, I TOLD YOU ABOUT IT?
I THINK SO. WAIT, A PROBLEM WITH TIME?
NEIGH!
DAMMIT! BINKY!
WHY DO I ALWAYS FORGET ABOUT BINKY?!
BINKY?
ARE YOU HURT?
SVLAD CJELI, MY DEAR FELLOW!
HELLO THERE, PROFESSOR. GOOD TO SEE BINKY'S STILL IN FINE FETTLE.

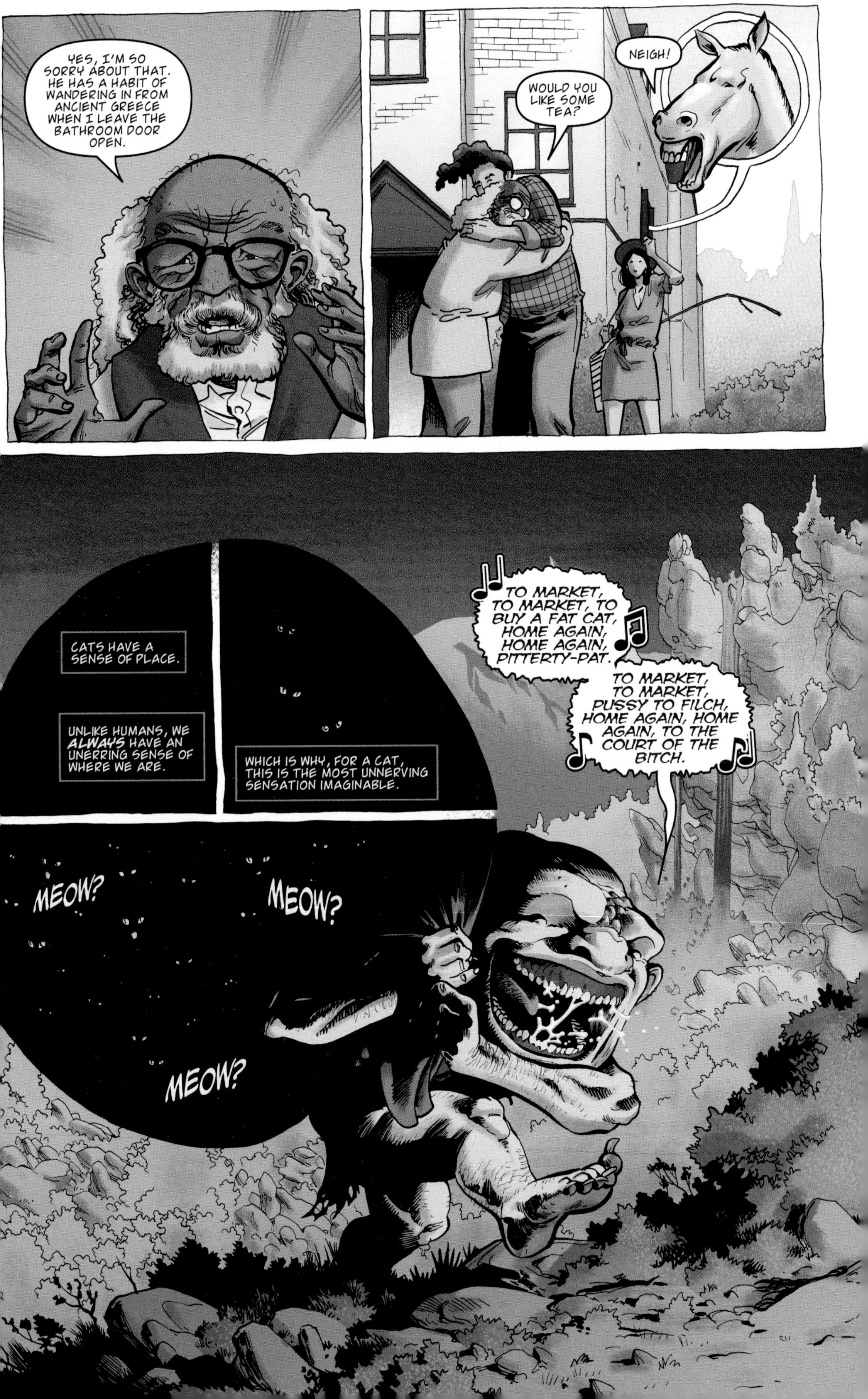
YES, I'M SO SORRY ABOUT THAT. HE HAS A HABIT OF WANDERING IN FROM ANCIENT GREECE WHEN I LEAVE THE BATHROOM DOOR OPEN.
NEIGH!
WOULD YOU LIKE SOME TEA?
CATS HAVE A SENSE OF PLACE.
UNLIKE HUMANS, WE ALWAYS HAVE AN UNERRING SENSE OF WHERE WE ARE.
WHICH IS WHY, FOR A CAT, THIS IS THE MOST UNNERVING SENSATION IMAGINABLE.
TO MARKET, TO MARKET, TO BUY A FAT CAT, HOME AGAIN, HOME AGAIN, PITTERTY-PAT.
TO MARKET, TO MARKET, PUSSY TO FILCH, HOME AGAIN, HOME AGAIN, TO THE COURT OF THE BITCH.
MEOW?
MEOW?
MEOW?

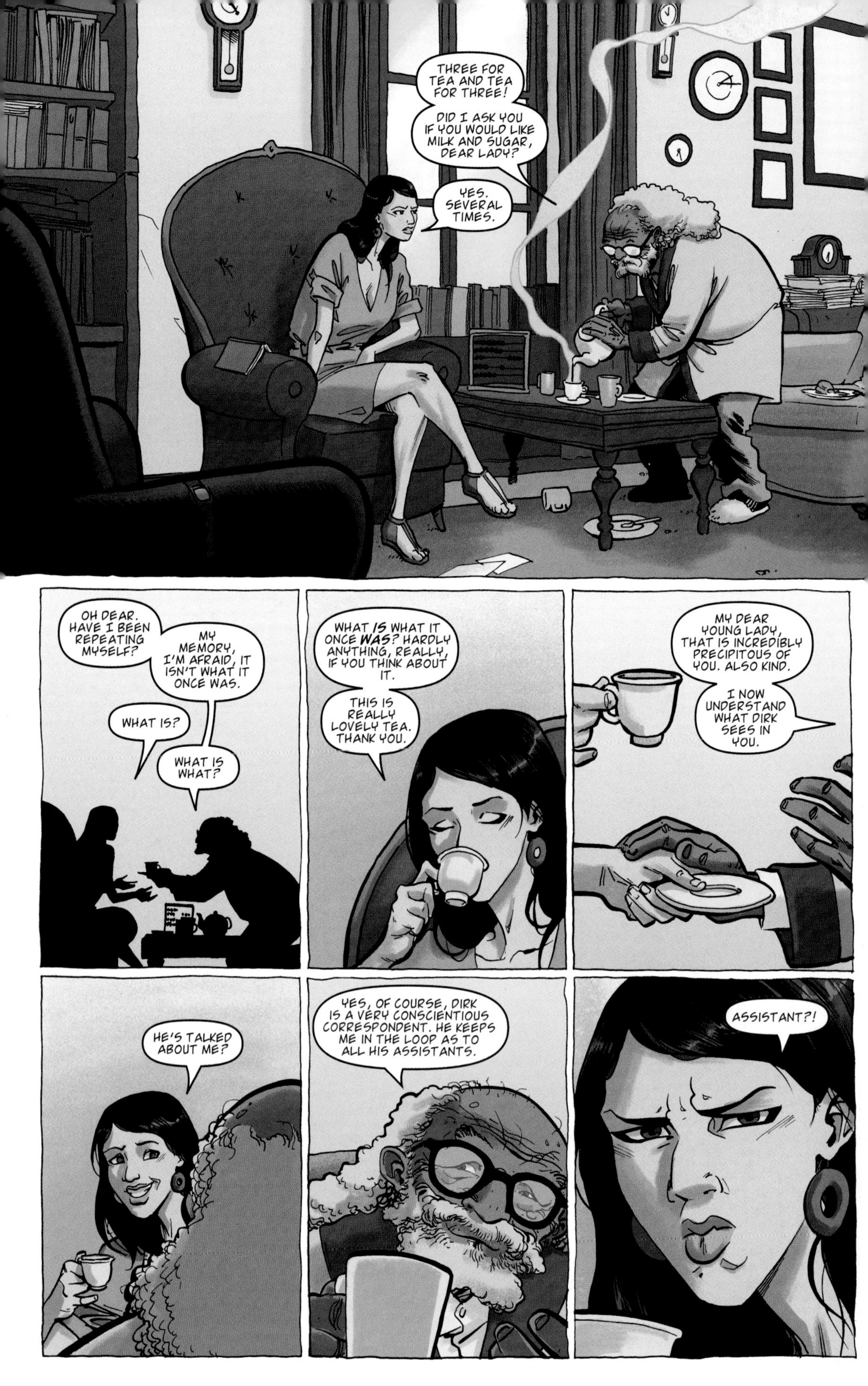
THREE FOR TEA AND TEA FOR THREE!
DID I ASK YOU IF YOU WOULD LIKE MILK AND SUGAR, DEAR LADY?
YES. SEVERAL TIMES.
OH DEAR. HAVE I BEEN REPEATING MYSELF?
MY MEMORY, I'M AFRAID, IT ISN'T WHAT IT ONCE WAS.
WHAT IS?
WHAT IS WHAT?
WHAT *IS* WHAT IT ONCE *WAS*? HARDLY ANYTHING, REALLY, IF YOU THINK ABOUT IT.
THIS IS REALLY LOVELY TEA. THANK YOU.
MY DEAR YOUNG LADY, THAT IS INCREDIBLY PRECIPITOUS OF YOU. ALSO KIND.
I NOW UNDERSTAND WHAT DIRK SEES IN YOU.
HE'S TALKED ABOUT ME?
YES, OF COURSE, DIRK IS A VERY CONSCIENTIOUS CORRESPONDENT. HE KEEPS ME IN THE LOOP AS TO ALL HIS ASSISTANTS.
ASSISTANT?!

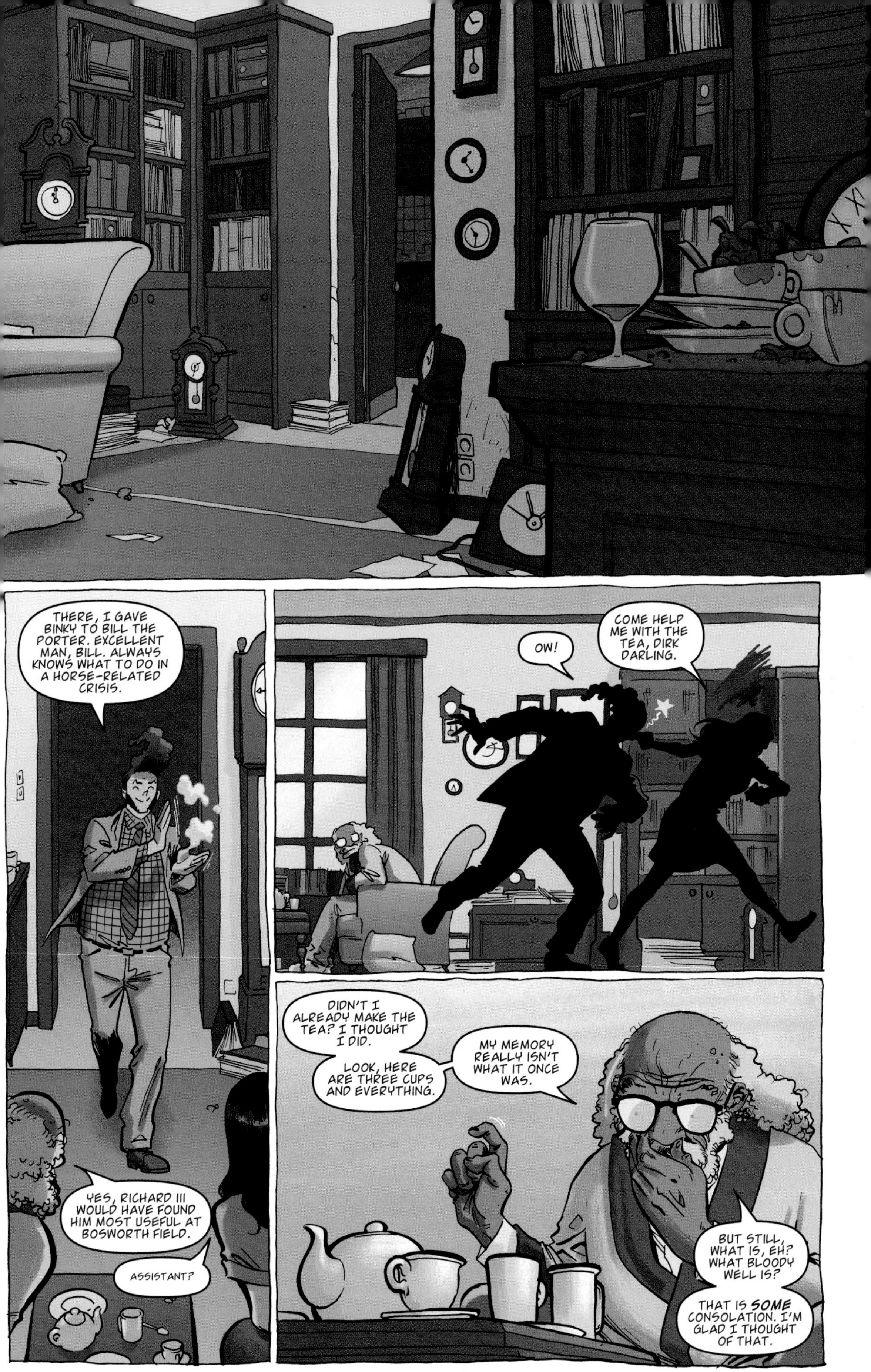
THERE, I GAVE BINKY TO BILL THE PORTER. EXCELLENT MAN, BILL. ALWAYS KNOWS WHAT TO DO IN A HORSE-RELATED CRISIS.
OW!
COME HELP ME WITH THE TEA, DIRK DARLING.
YES, RICHARD III WOULD HAVE FOUND HIM MOST USEFUL AT BOSWORTH FIELD.
ASSISTANT?
DIDN'T I ALREADY MAKE THE TEA? I THOUGHT I DID.
LOOK, HERE ARE THREE CUPS AND EVERYTHING.
MY MEMORY REALLY ISN'T WHAT IT ONCE WAS.
BUT STILL, WHAT IS, EH? WHAT BLOODY WELL IS?
THAT IS **SOME** CONSOLATION. I'M GLAD I THOUGHT OF THAT.

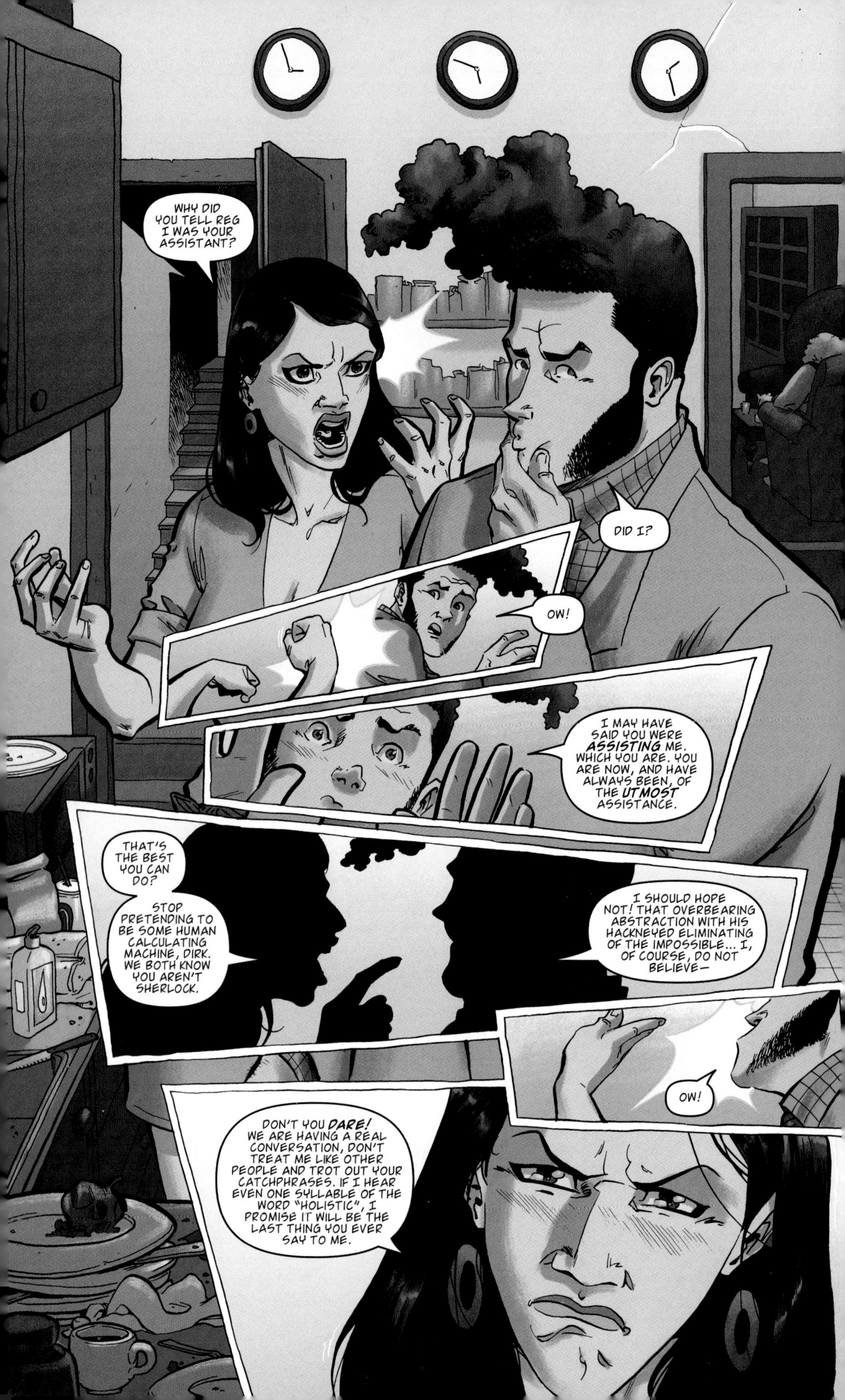
WHY DID YOU TELL REG I WAS YOUR ASSISTANT?
DID I?
OW!
I MAY HAVE SAID YOU WERE ASSISTING ME. WHICH YOU ARE. YOU ARE NOW, AND HAVE ALWAYS BEEN, OF THE UTMOST ASSISTANCE.
THAT'S THE BEST YOU CAN DO?
STOP PRETENDING TO BE SOME HUMAN CALCULATING MACHINE, DIRK. WE BOTH KNOW YOU AREN'T SHERLOCK.
I SHOULD HOPE NOT! THAT OVERBEARING ABSTRACTION WITH HIS HACKNEYED ELIMINATING OF THE IMPOSSIBLE... I, OF COURSE, DO NOT BELIEVE—
OW!
DON'T YOU DARE! WE ARE HAVING A REAL CONVERSATION, DON'T TREAT ME LIKE OTHER PEOPLE AND TROT OUT YOUR CATCHPHRASES. IF I HEAR EVEN ONE SYLLABLE OF THE WORD "HOLISTIC", I PROMISE IT WILL BE THE LAST THING YOU EVER SAY TO ME.

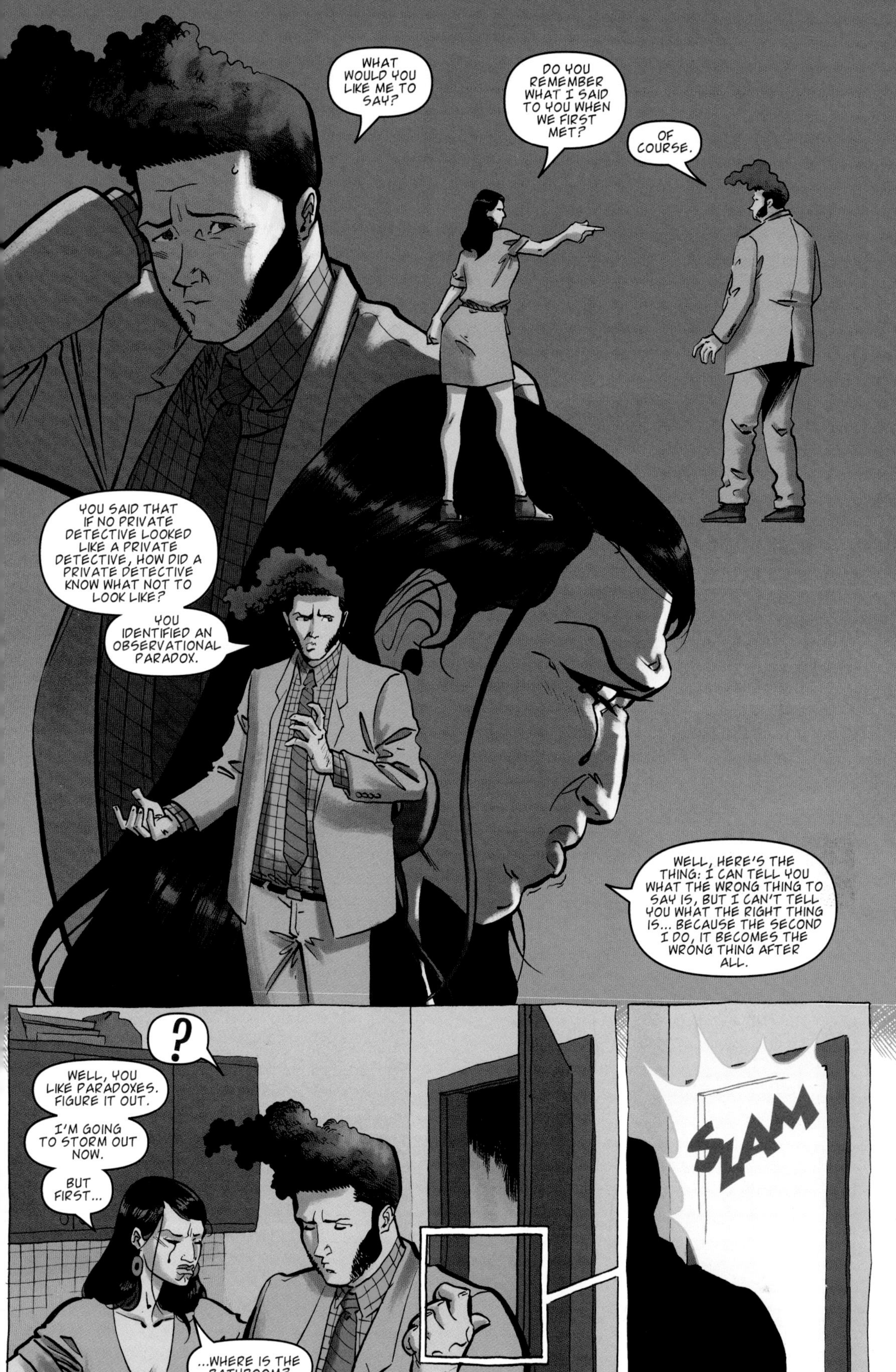
WHAT WOULD YOU LIKE ME TO SAY?
DO YOU REMEMBER WHAT I SAID TO YOU WHEN WE FIRST MET?
OF COURSE.
YOU SAID THAT IF NO PRIVATE DETECTIVE LOOKED LIKE A PRIVATE DETECTIVE, HOW DID A PRIVATE DETECTIVE KNOW WHAT NOT TO LOOK LIKE?
YOU IDENTIFIED AN OBSERVATIONAL PARADOX.
WELL, HERE'S THE THING: I CAN TELL YOU WHAT THE WRONG THING TO SAY IS, BUT I CAN'T TELL YOU WHAT THE RIGHT THING IS... BECAUSE THE SECOND I DO, IT BECOMES THE WRONG THING AFTER ALL.
?
WELL, YOU LIKE PARADOXES. FIGURE IT OUT.
I'M GOING TO STORM OUT NOW.
BUT FIRST...
...WHERE IS THE BATHROOM?
SLAM

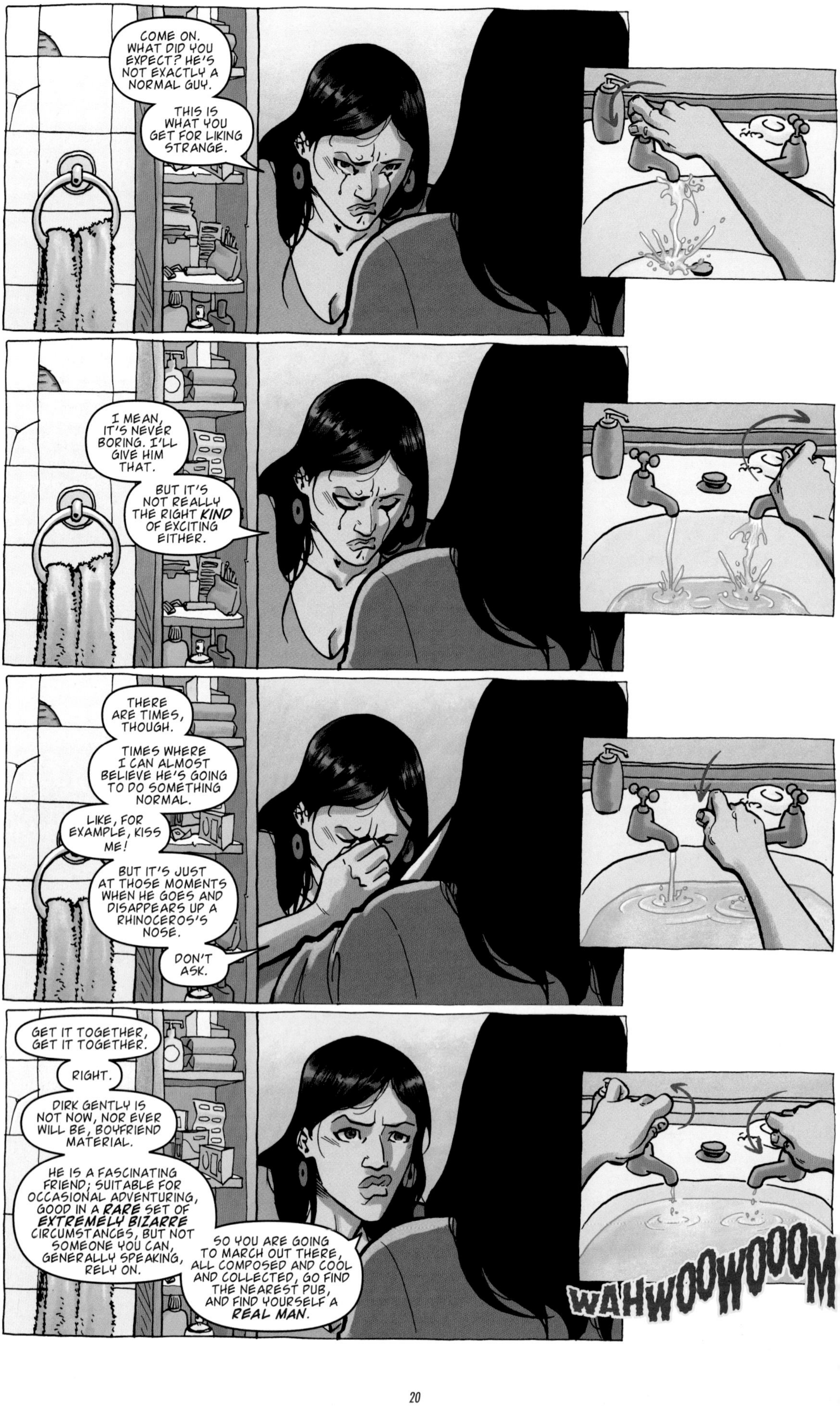
COME ON. WHAT DID YOU EXPECT? HE'S NOT EXACTLY A NORMAL GUY.
THIS IS WHAT YOU GET FOR LIKING STRANGE.
I MEAN, IT'S NEVER BORING. I'LL GIVE HIM THAT.
BUT IT'S NOT REALLY THE RIGHT KIND OF EXCITING EITHER.
THERE ARE TIMES, THOUGH.
TIMES WHERE I CAN ALMOST BELIEVE HE'S GOING TO DO SOMETHING NORMAL.
LIKE, FOR EXAMPLE, KISS ME!
BUT IT'S JUST AT THOSE MOMENTS WHEN HE GOES AND DISAPPEARS UP A RHINOCEROS'S NOSE.
DON'T ASK.
GET IT TOGETHER, GET IT TOGETHER.
RIGHT.
DIRK GENTLY IS NOT NOW, NOR EVER WILL BE, BOYFRIEND MATERIAL.
HE IS A FASCINATING FRIEND; SUITABLE FOR OCCASIONAL ADVENTURING, GOOD IN A RARE SET OF EXTREMELY BIZARRE CIRCUMSTANCES, BUT NOT SOMEONE YOU CAN, GENERALLY SPEAKING, RELY ON.
SO YOU ARE GOING TO MARCH OUT THERE, ALL COMPOSED AND COOL AND COLLECTED, GO FIND THE NEAREST PUB, AND FIND YOURSELF A REAL MAN.
WAHWOOWOOOM

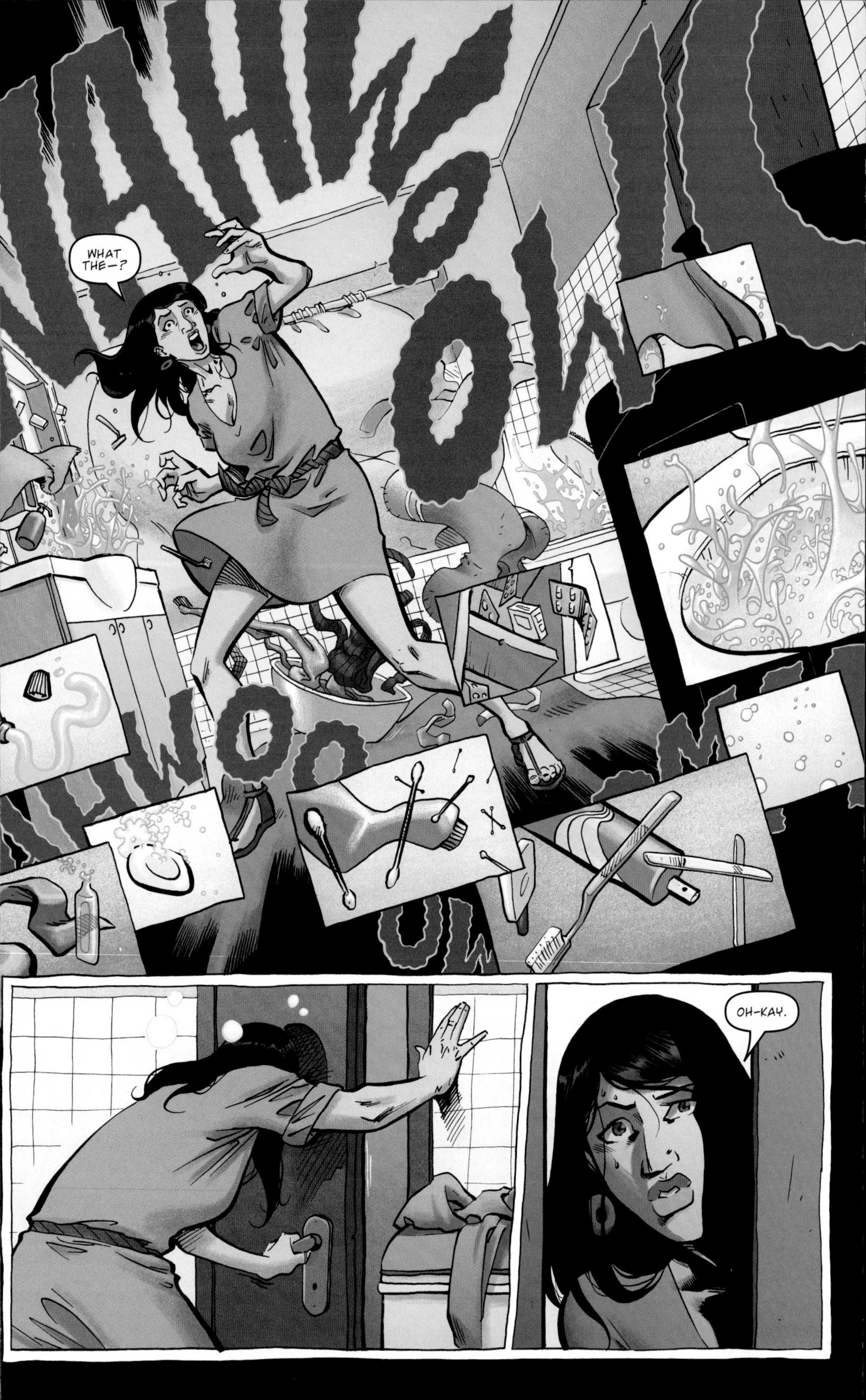
WHAT THE—?
OH-KAY.

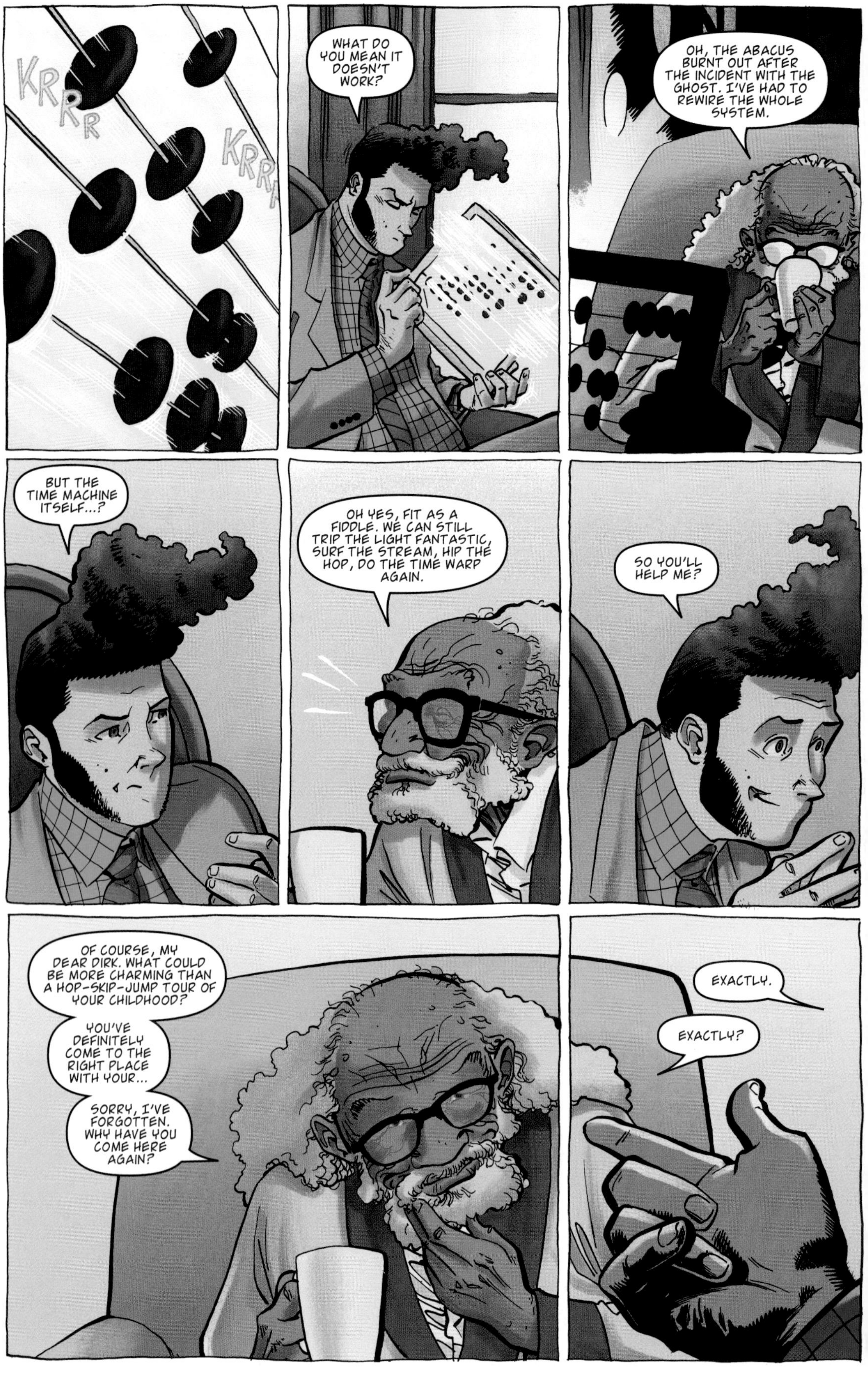
KRRR
KRRR
WHAT DO YOU MEAN IT DOESN'T WORK?
OH, THE ABACUS BURNT OUT AFTER THE INCIDENT WITH THE GHOST. I'VE HAD TO REWIRE THE WHOLE SYSTEM.
BUT THE TIME MACHINE ITSELF...?
OH YES, FIT AS A FIDDLE. WE CAN STILL TRIP THE LIGHT FANTASTIC, SURF THE STREAM, HIP THE HOP, DO THE TIME WARP AGAIN.
SO YOU'LL HELP ME?
OF COURSE, MY DEAR DIRK. WHAT COULD BE MORE CHARMING THAN A HOP-SKIP-JUMP TOUR OF YOUR CHILDHOOD?
YOU'VE DEFINITELY COME TO THE RIGHT PLACE WITH YOUR...
SORRY, I'VE FORGOTTEN. WHY HAVE YOU COME HERE AGAIN?
EXACTLY.
EXACTLY?

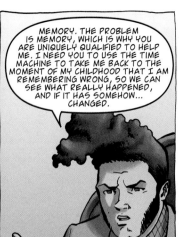

MEMORY. THE PROBLEM IS MEMORY, WHICH IS WHY YOU ARE UNIQUELY QUALIFIED TO HELP ME. I NEED YOU TO USE THE TIME MACHINE TO TAKE ME BACK TO THE MOMENT OF MY CHILDHOOD THAT I AM REMEMBERING WRONG, SO WE CAN SEE WHAT REALLY HAPPENED, AND IF IT HAS SOMEHOW... CHANGED.

BRILLIANT.

RIGHT. NOW WE'LL BE ABLE TO GET GOING AS SOON AS YOUR FRIEND FINISHES USING THE LOO.

OH. I DON'T THINK SALLY WILL BE COMING WITH US, ACTUALLY.

SHE'S, UM, UPSET.

OH. HOW UNFORTUNATE.

BUT NEVERTHELESS, WE STILL NEED HER TO FINISH USING THE LOO.

WHY?

BECAUSE THAT'S WHERE THE CONTROLS FOR THE TIME MACHINE ARE *NOW*. I REWIRED IT INTO THE PLUMBING. I CONTROL IT FROM THE SINK. MAKES IT TERRIBLY CONVENIENT IF I FORGET TO BRUSH MY TEETH AND NEED TO POP BACK TO THE NIGHT BEFORE TO DO IT.

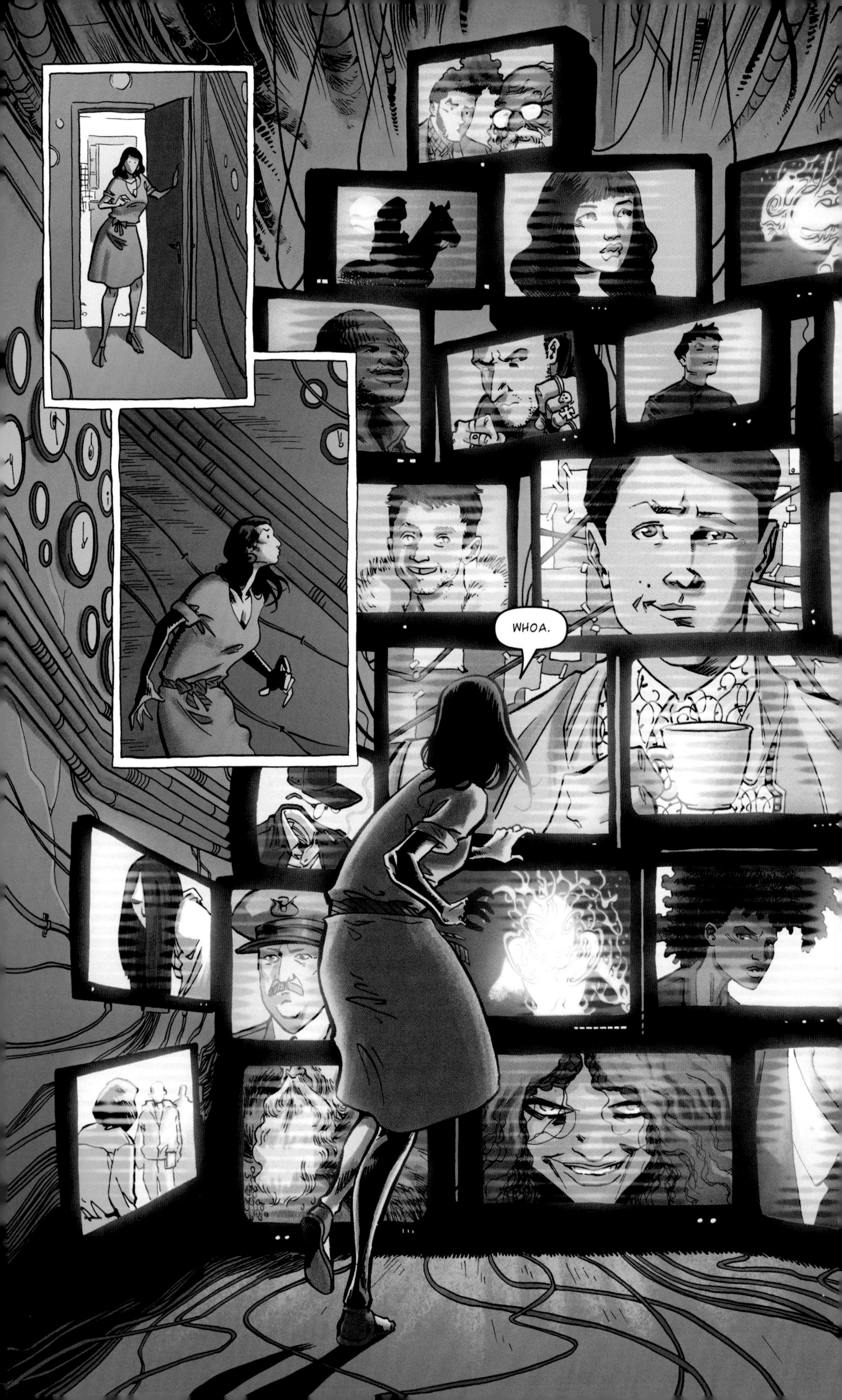
WHOA.

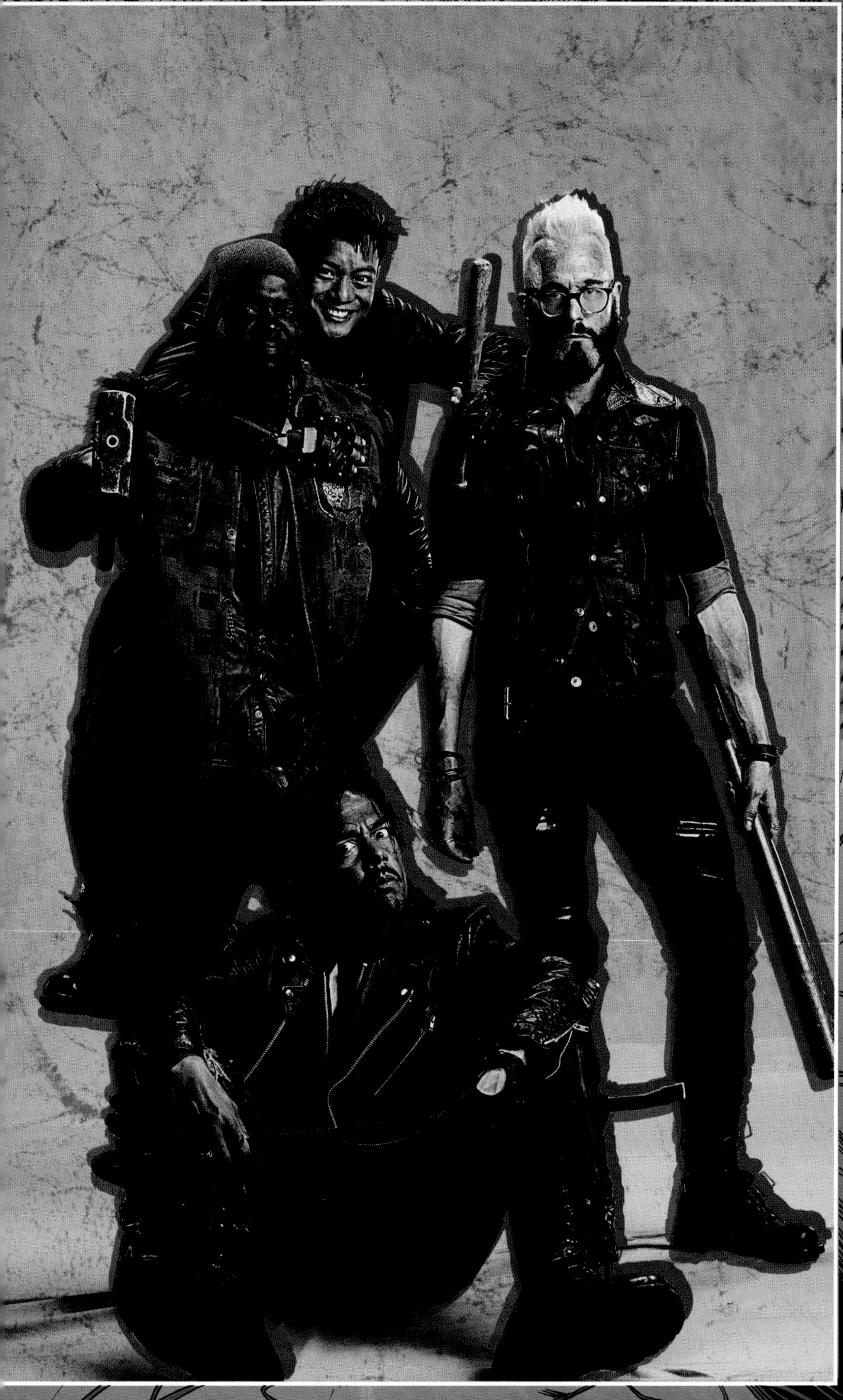

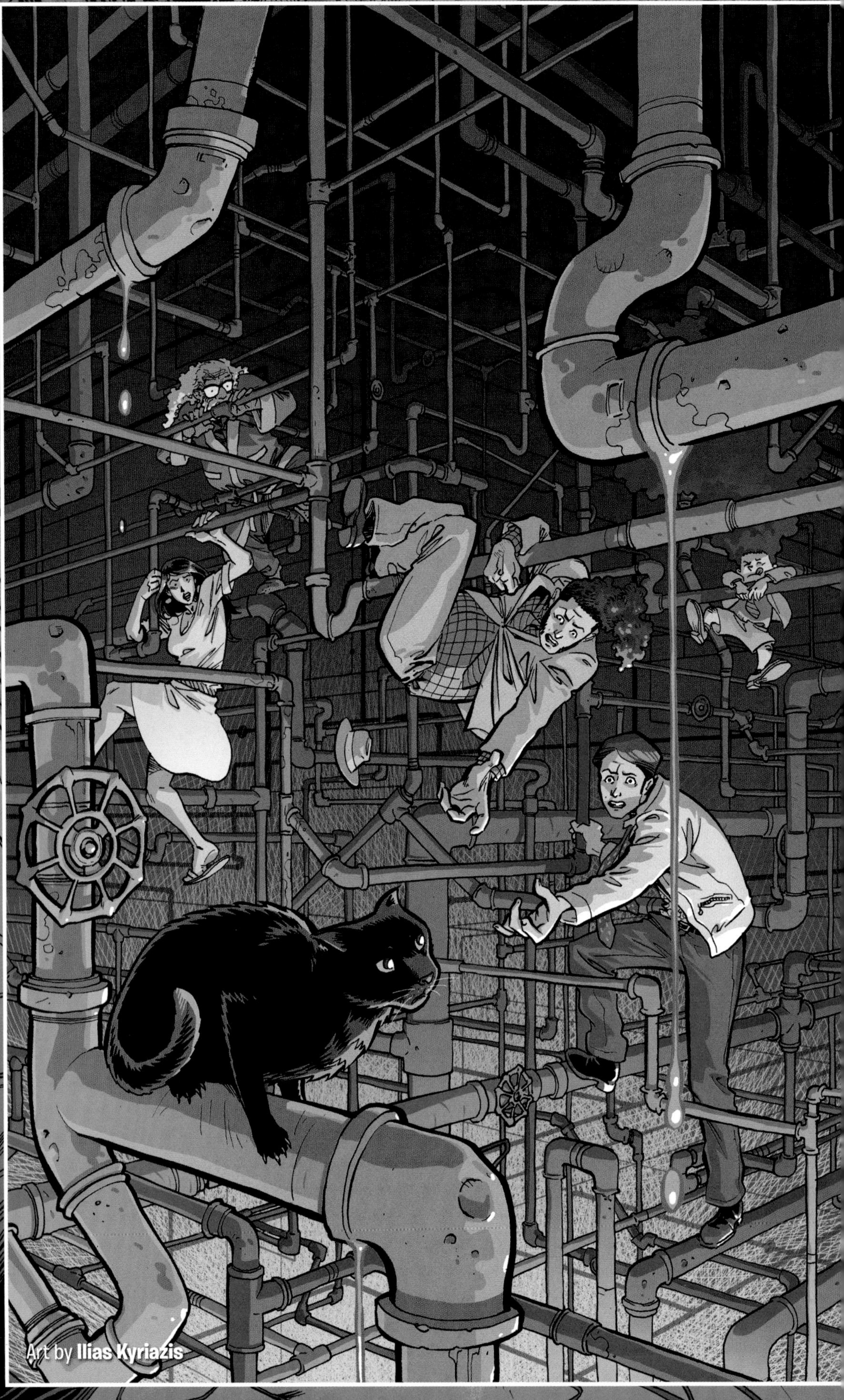
Art by Ilias Kyriazis

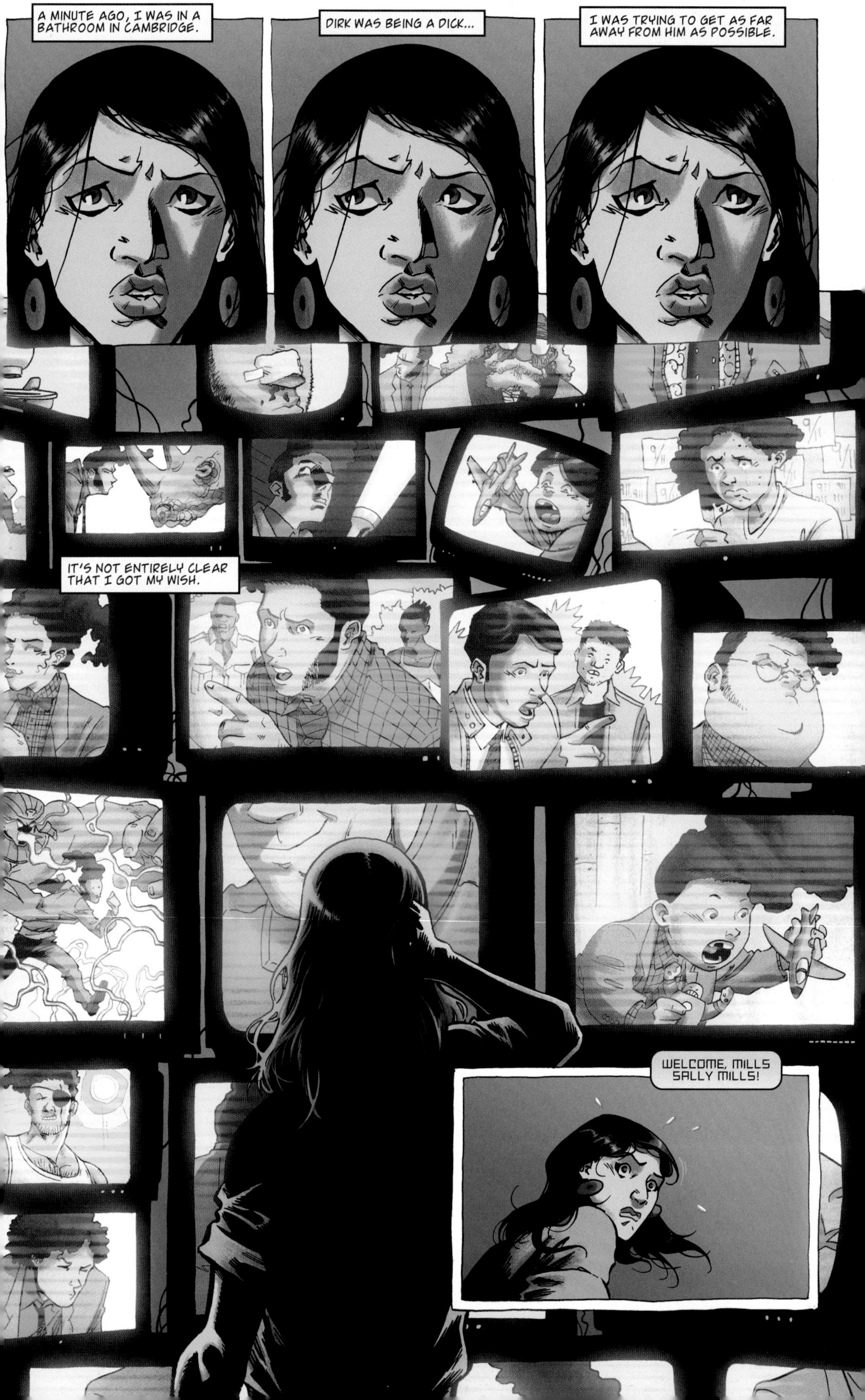

A MINUTE AGO, I WAS IN A BATHROOM IN CAMBRIDGE.
DIRK WAS BEING A DICK...
I WAS TRYING TO GET AS FAR AWAY FROM HIM AS POSSIBLE.
IT'S NOT ENTIRELY CLEAR THAT I GOT MY WISH.
WELCOME, MILLS SALLY MILLS!

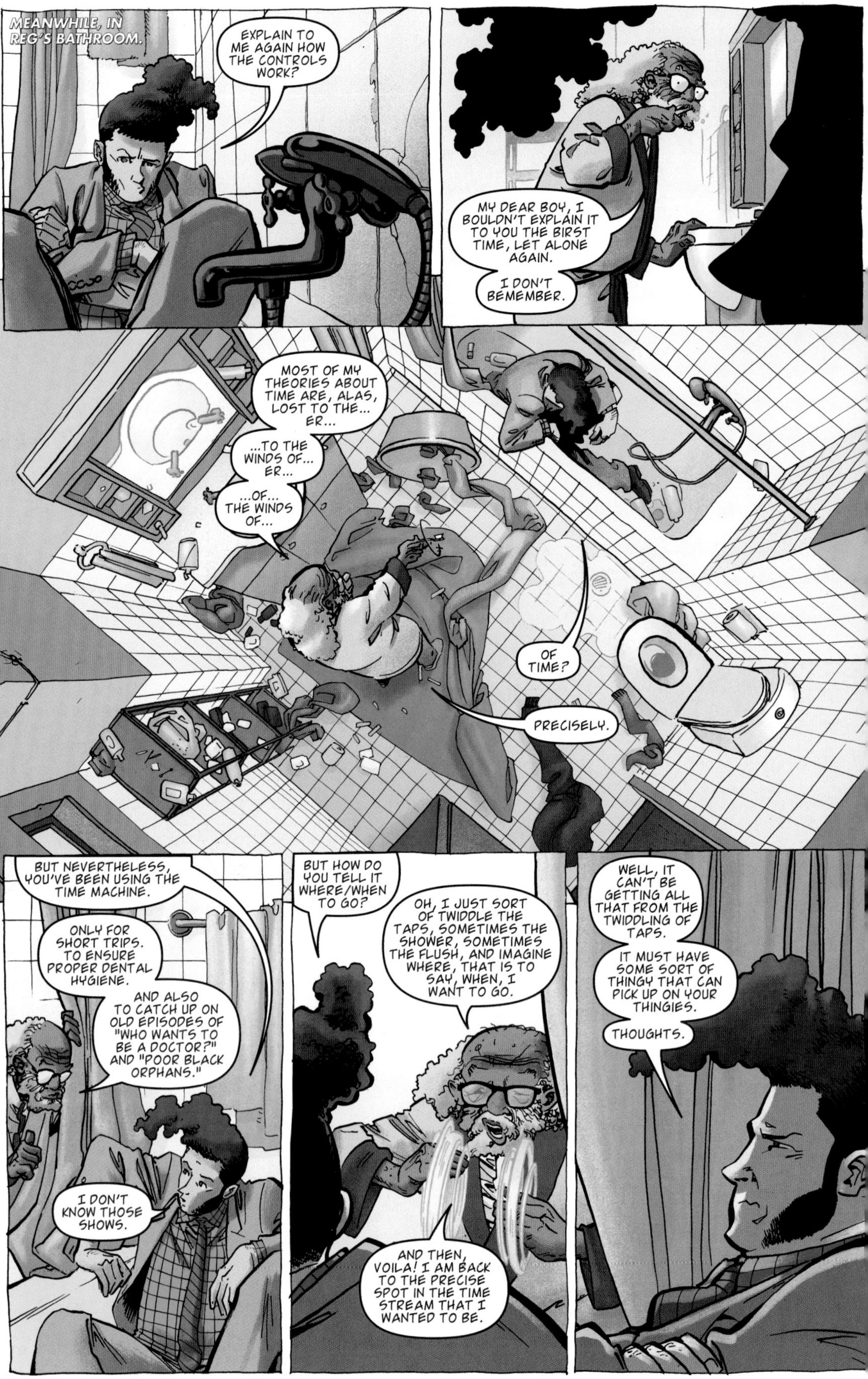
MEANWHILE, IN REG'S BATHROOM.
EXPLAIN TO ME AGAIN HOW THE CONTROLS WORK?
MY DEAR BOY, I BOULDN'T EXPLAIN IT TO YOU THE BIRST TIME, LET ALONE AGAIN.
I DON'T BEMEMBER.
MOST OF MY THEORIES ABOUT TIME ARE, ALAS, LOST TO THE... ER...
...TO THE WINDS OF... ER...
...OF... THE WINDS OF...
OF TIME?
PRECISELY.
BUT NEVERTHELESS, YOU'VE BEEN USING THE TIME MACHINE.
ONLY FOR SHORT TRIPS. TO ENSURE PROPER DENTAL HYGIENE.
AND ALSO TO CATCH UP ON OLD EPISODES OF "WHO WANTS TO BE A DOCTOR?" AND "POOR BLACK ORPHANS."
I DON'T KNOW THOSE SHOWS.
BUT HOW DO YOU TELL IT WHERE/WHEN TO GO?
OH, I JUST SORT OF TWIDDLE THE TAPS, SOMETIMES THE SHOWER, SOMETIMES THE FLUSH, AND IMAGINE WHERE, THAT IS TO SAY, WHEN, I WANT TO GO.
AND THEN, VOILA! I AM BACK TO THE PRECISE SPOT IN THE TIME STREAM THAT I WANTED TO BE.
WELL, IT CAN'T BE GETTING ALL THAT FROM THE TWIDDLING OF TAPS.
IT MUST HAVE SOME SORT OF THINGY THAT CAN PICK UP ON YOUR THINGIES.
THOUGHTS.

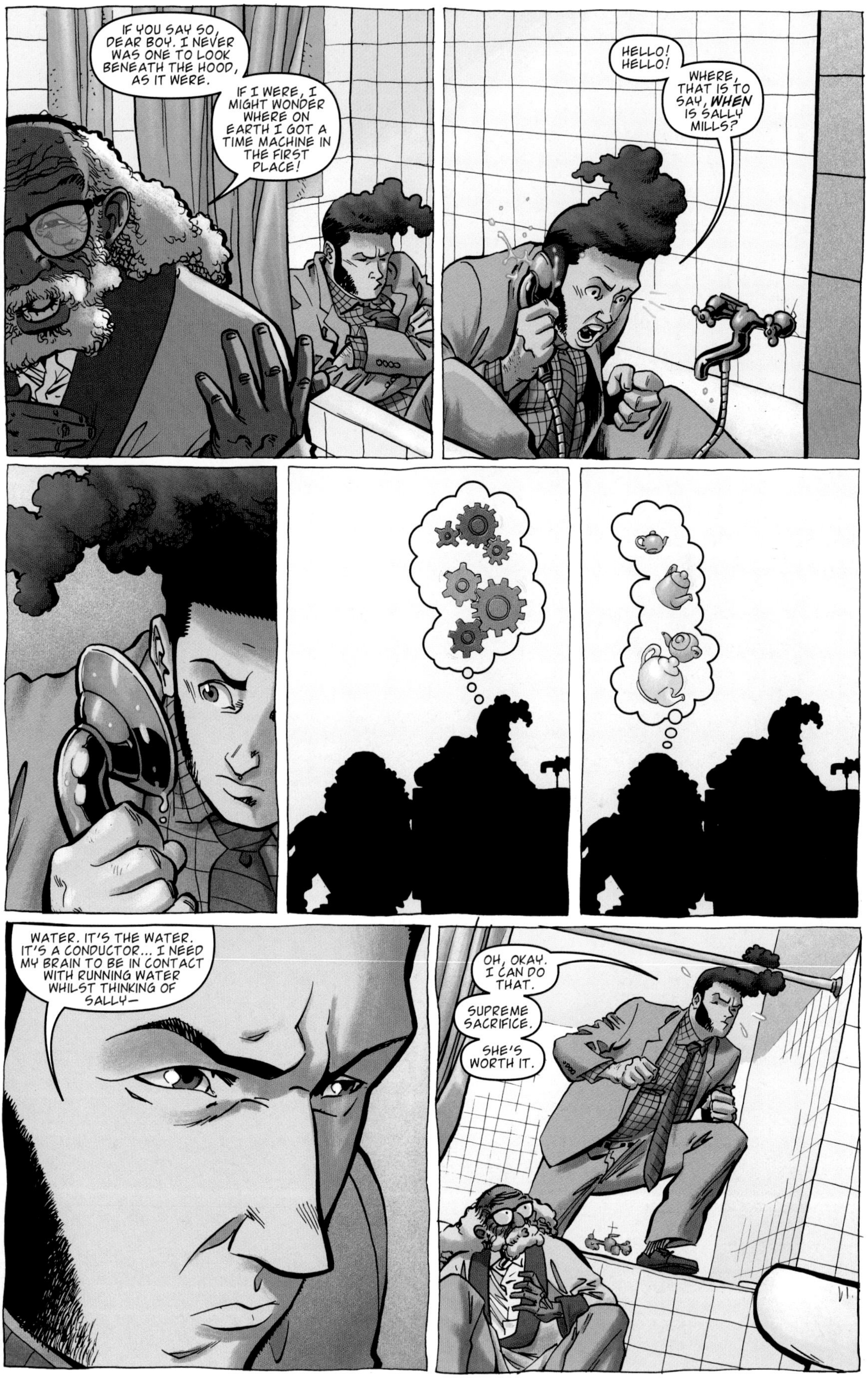
IF YOU SAY SO, DEAR BOY. I NEVER WAS ONE TO LOOK BENEATH THE HOOD, AS IT WERE.
IF I WERE, I MIGHT WONDER WHERE ON EARTH I GOT A TIME MACHINE IN THE FIRST PLACE!
HELLO! HELLO!
WHERE, THAT IS TO SAY, **WHEN** IS SALLY MILLS?
WATER. IT'S THE WATER. IT'S A CONDUCTOR... I NEED MY BRAIN TO BE IN CONTACT WITH RUNNING WATER WHILST THINKING OF SALLY—
OH, OKAY. I CAN DO THAT.
SUPREME SACRIFICE.
SHE'S WORTH IT.

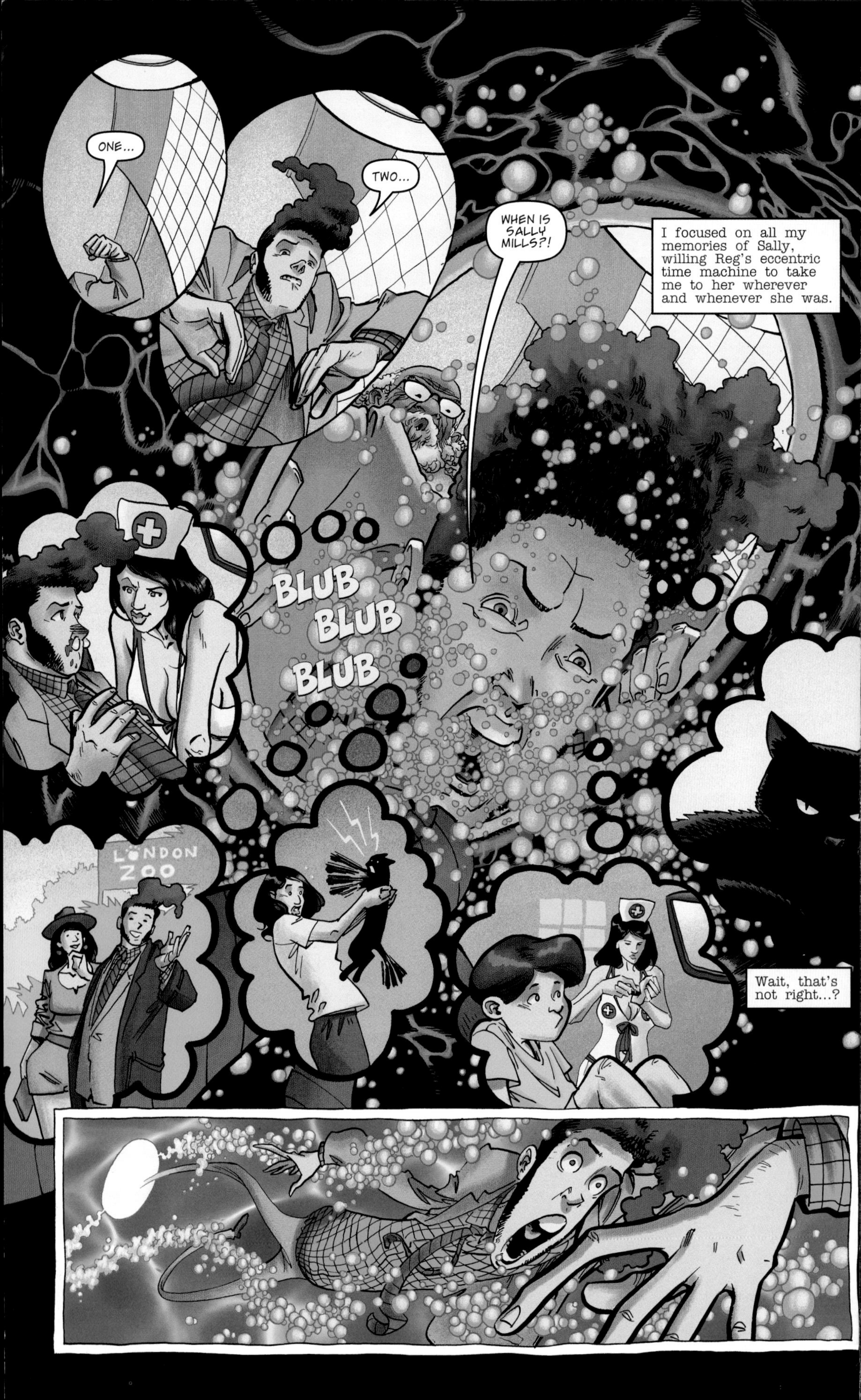
ONE...
TWO...
WHEN IS SALLY MILLS?!
I focused on all my memories of Sally, willing Reg's eccentric time machine to take me to her wherever and whenever she was.
BLUB
BLUB
BLUB
LONDON ZOO
Wait, that's not right...?

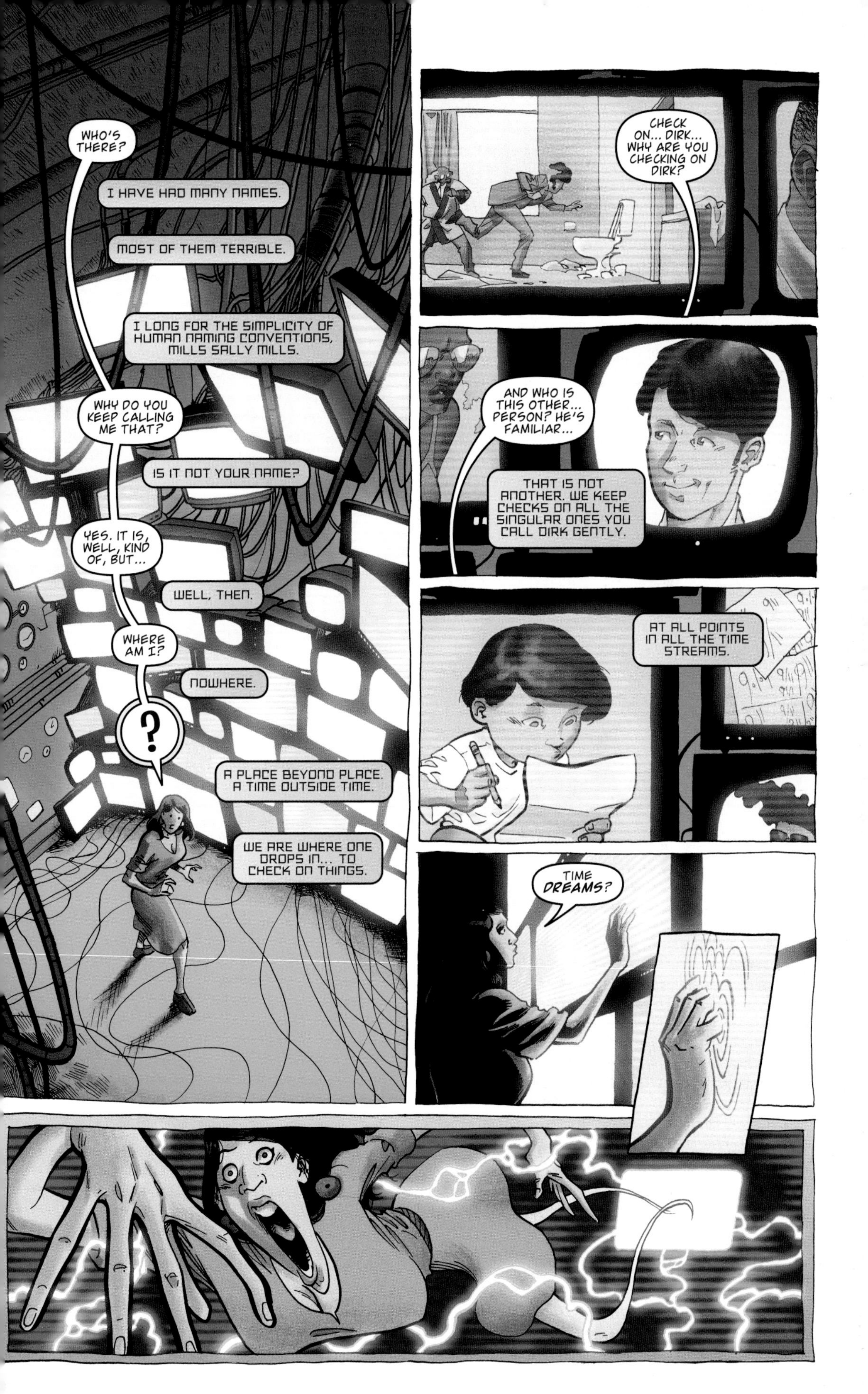
WHO'S THERE?
I HAVE HAD MANY NAMES.
MOST OF THEM TERRIBLE.
I LONG FOR THE SIMPLICITY OF HUMAN NAMING CONVENTIONS, MILLS SALLY MILLS.
WHY DO YOU KEEP CALLING ME THAT?
IS IT NOT YOUR NAME?
YES. IT IS, WELL, KIND OF, BUT...
WELL, THEN.
WHERE AM I?
NOWHERE.
?
A PLACE BEYOND PLACE. A TIME OUTSIDE TIME.
WE ARE WHERE ONE DROPS IN... TO CHECK ON THINGS.
CHECK ON... DIRK... WHY ARE YOU CHECKING ON DIRK?
AND WHO IS THIS OTHER... PERSON? HE'S FAMILIAR...
THAT IS NOT ANOTHER. WE KEEP CHECKS ON ALL THE SINGULAR ONES YOU CALL DIRK GENTLY.
AT ALL POINTS IN ALL THE TIME STREAMS.
TIME DREAMS?

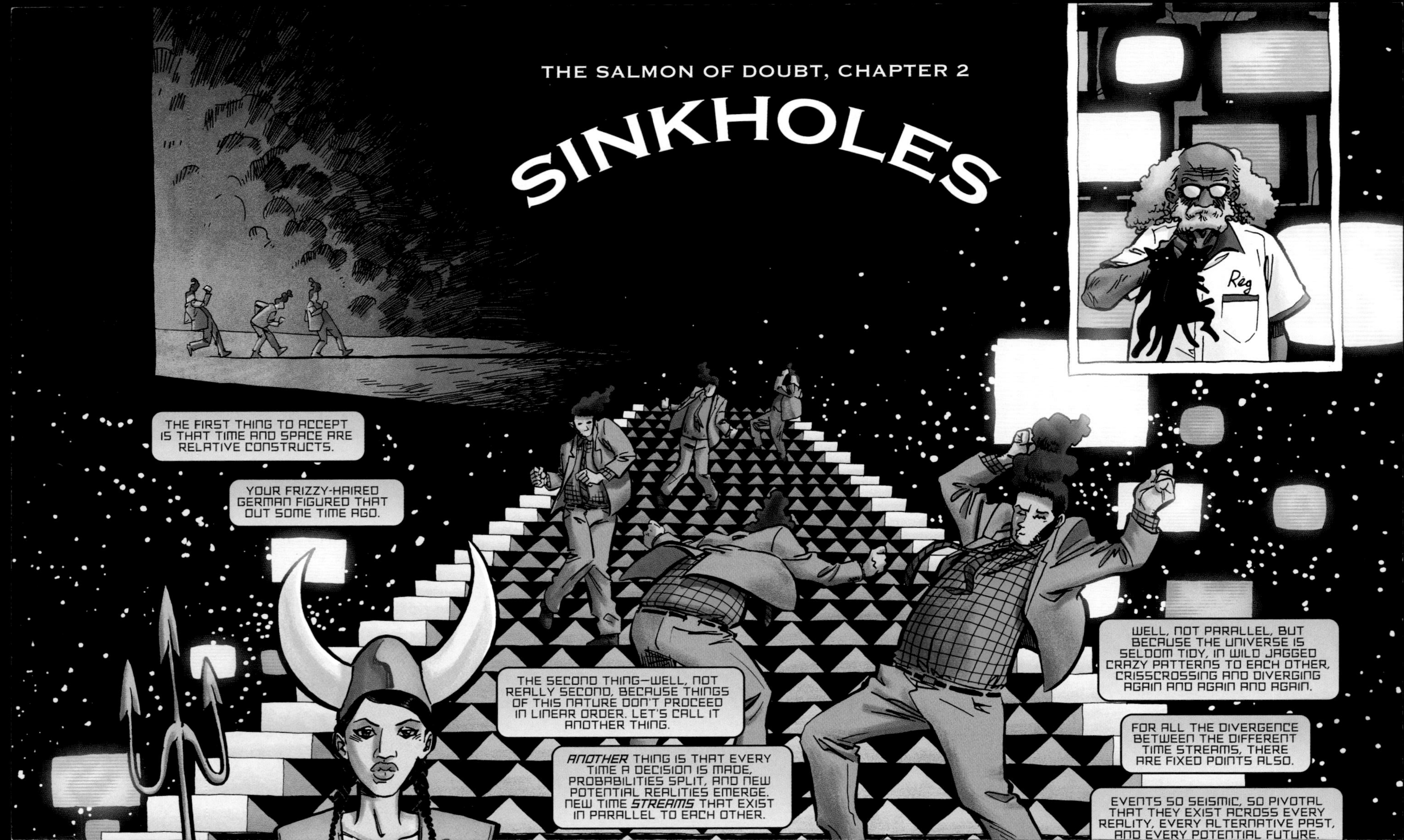
THE SALMON OF DOUBT, CHAPTER 2
SINKHOLES
Reg
THE FIRST THING TO ACCEPT IS THAT TIME AND SPACE ARE RELATIVE CONSTRUCTS.
YOUR FRIZZY-HAIRED GERMAN FIGURED THAT OUT SOME TIME AGO.
THE SECOND THING—WELL, NOT REALLY SECOND, BECAUSE THINGS OF THIS NATURE DON'T PROCEED IN LINEAR ORDER. LET'S CALL IT ANOTHER THING.
ANOTHER THING IS THAT EVERY TIME A DECISION IS MADE, PROBABILITIES SPLIT, AND NEW POTENTIAL REALITIES EMERGE. NEW TIME STREAMS THAT EXIST IN PARALLEL TO EACH OTHER.
WELL, NOT PARALLEL, BUT BECAUSE THE UNIVERSE IS SELDOM TIDY, IN WILD JAGGED CRAZY PATTERNS TO EACH OTHER, CRISSCROSSING AND DIVERGING AGAIN AND AGAIN AND AGAIN.
FOR ALL THE DIVERGENCE BETWEEN THE DIFFERENT TIME STREAMS, THERE ARE FIXED POINTS ALSO.
EVENTS SO SEISMIC, SO PIVOTAL THAT THEY EXIST ACROSS EVERY REALITY, EVERY ALTERNATIVE PAST, AND EVERY POTENTIAL FUTURE.

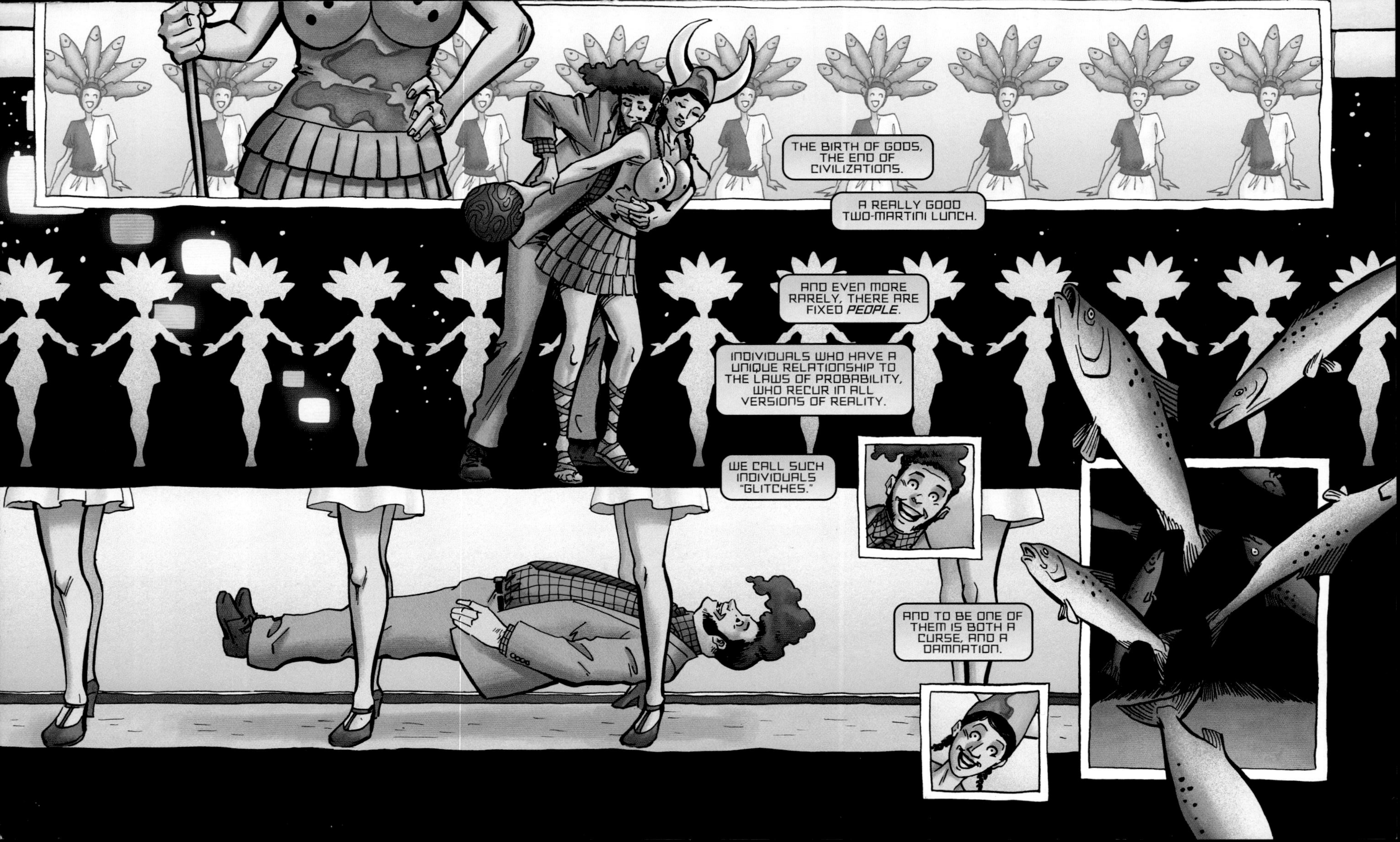
THE BIRTH OF GODS, THE END OF CIVILIZATIONS.
A REALLY GOOD TWO-MARTINI LUNCH.
AND EVEN MORE RARELY, THERE ARE FIXED *PEOPLE*.
INDIVIDUALS WHO HAVE A UNIQUE RELATIONSHIP TO THE LAWS OF PROBABILITY, WHO RECUR IN ALL VERSIONS OF REALITY.
WE CALL SUCH INDIVIDUALS "GLITCHES."
AND TO BE ONE OF THEM IS BOTH A CURSE, AND A DAMNATION.

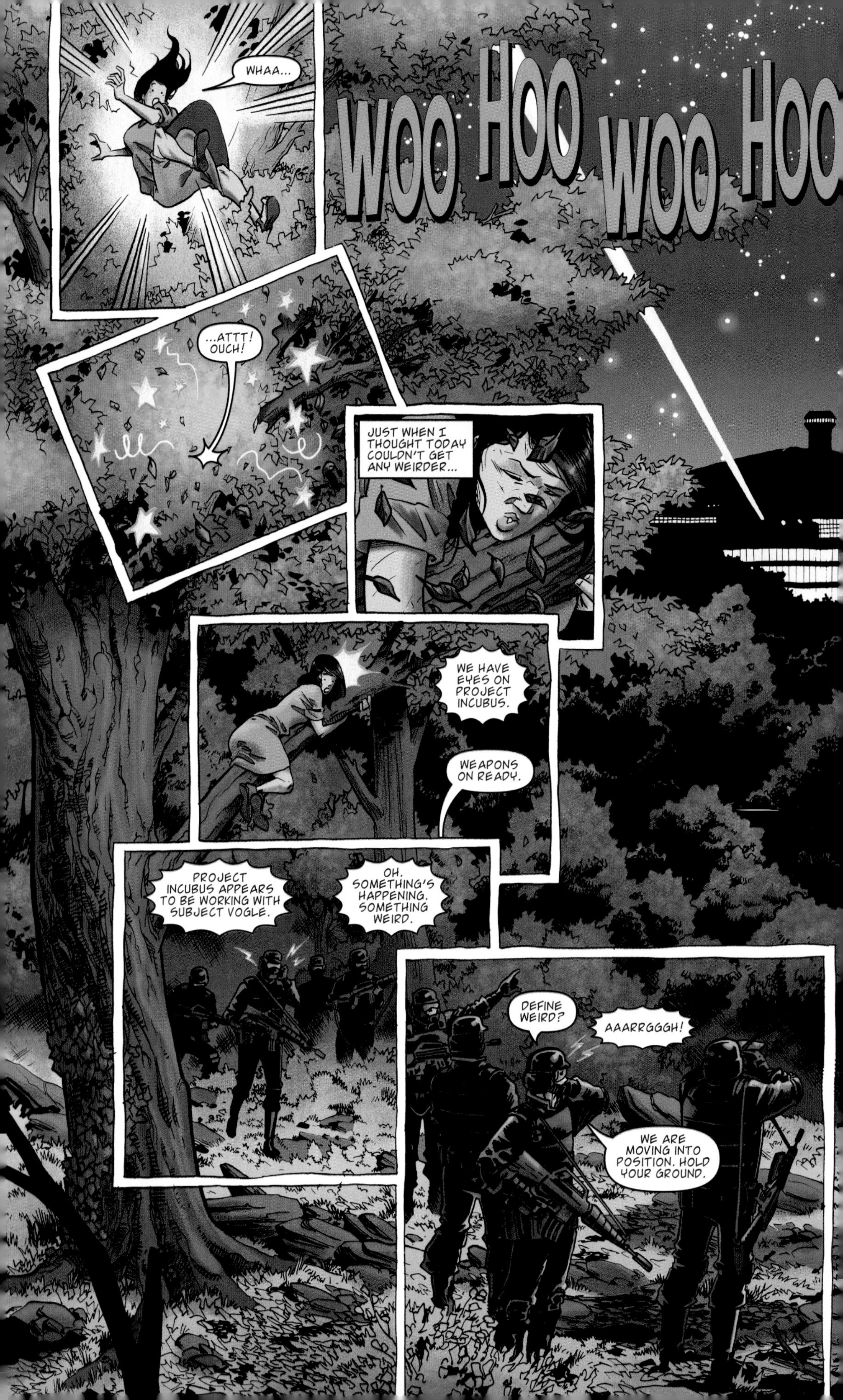

WHAA...
WOO HOO WOO HOO
...ATTT! OUCH!
JUST WHEN I THOUGHT TODAY COULDN'T GET ANY WEIRDER...
WE HAVE EYES ON PROJECT INCUBUS.
WEAPONS ON READY.
PROJECT INCUBUS APPEARS TO BE WORKING WITH SUBJECT VOGLE.
OH. SOMETHING'S HAPPENING. SOMETHING WEIRD.
DEFINE WEIRD?
AAARRGGGH!
WE ARE MOVING INTO POSITION. HOLD YOUR GROUND.

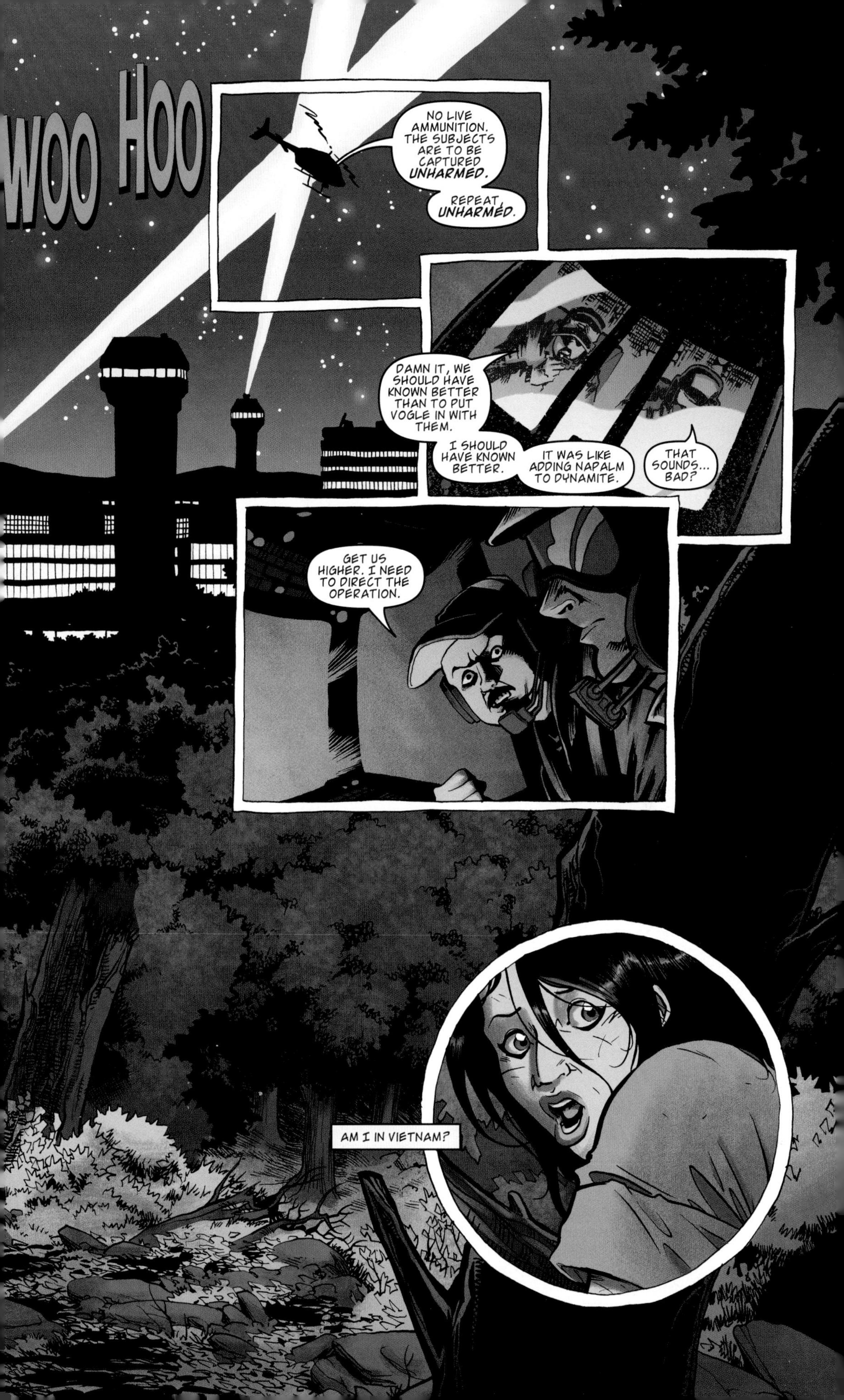
WOO HOO
NO LIVE AMMUNITION. THE SUBJECTS ARE TO BE CAPTURED UNHARMED.
REPEAT, UNHARMED.
DAMN IT, WE SHOULD HAVE KNOWN BETTER THAN TO PUT VOGLE IN WITH THEM.
I SHOULD HAVE KNOWN BETTER.
IT WAS LIKE ADDING NAPALM TO DYNAMITE.
THAT SOUNDS... BAD?
GET US HIGHER. I NEED TO DIRECT THE OPERATION.
AM I IN VIETNAM?

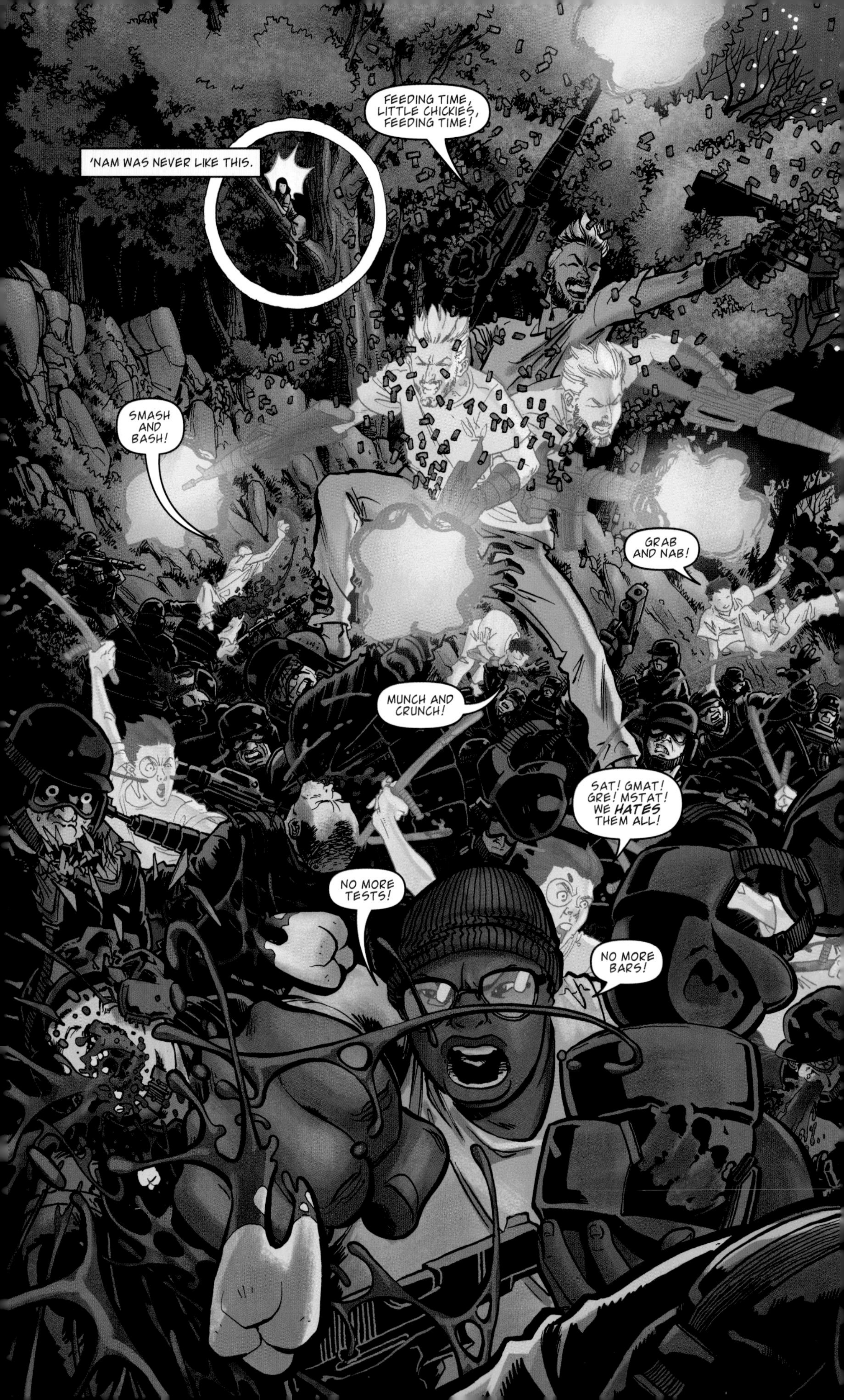
'NAM WAS NEVER LIKE THIS.
FEEDING TIME, LITTLE CHICKIES, FEEDING TIME!
SMASH AND BASH!
GRAB AND NAB!
MUNCH AND CRUNCH!
SAT! GMAT! GRE! MSTAT! WE HATES THEM ALL!
NO MORE TESTS!
NO MORE BARS!

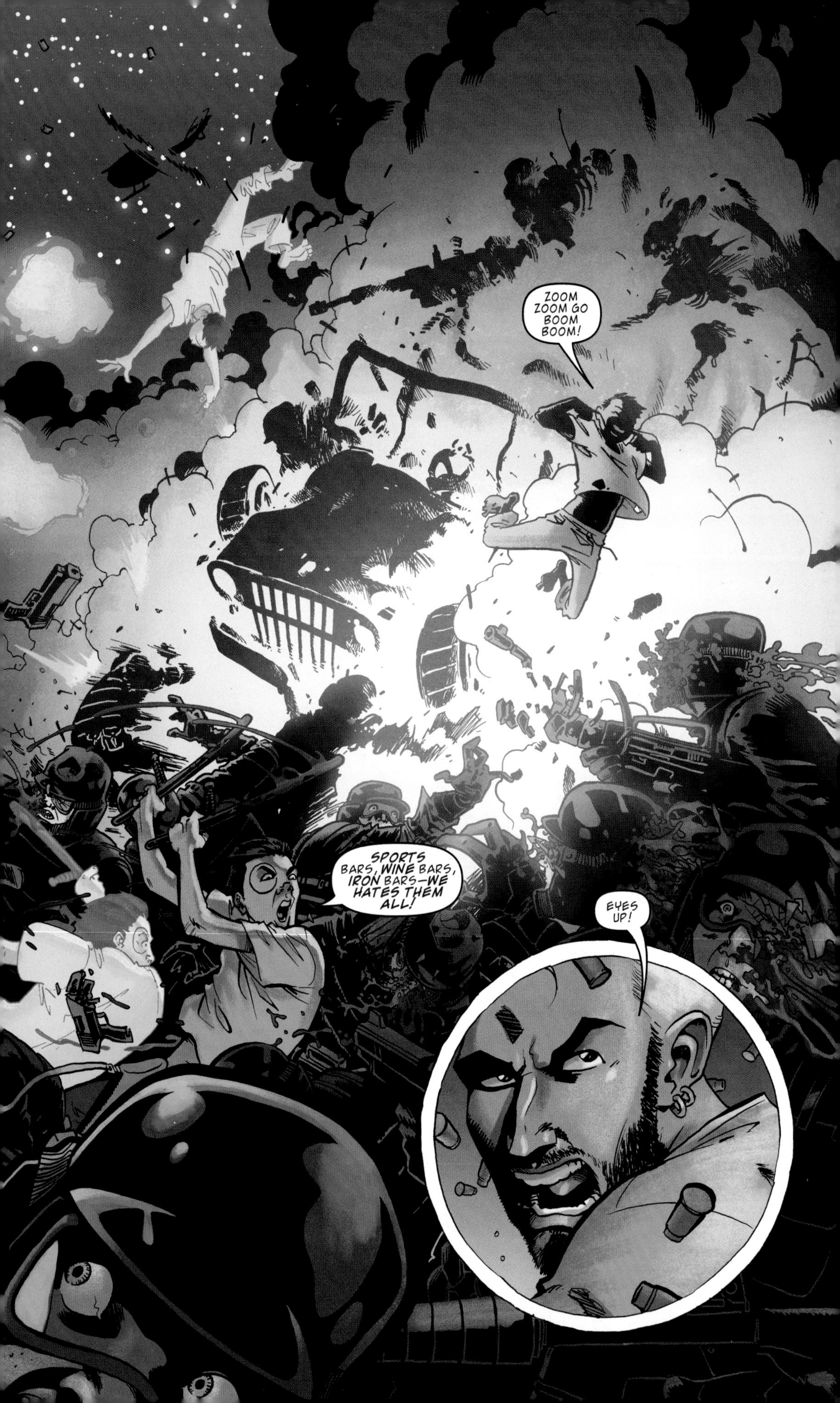
ZOOM ZOOM GO BOOM BOOM!
SPORTS BARS, WINE BARS, IRON BARS—WE HATES THEM ALL!
EYES UP!

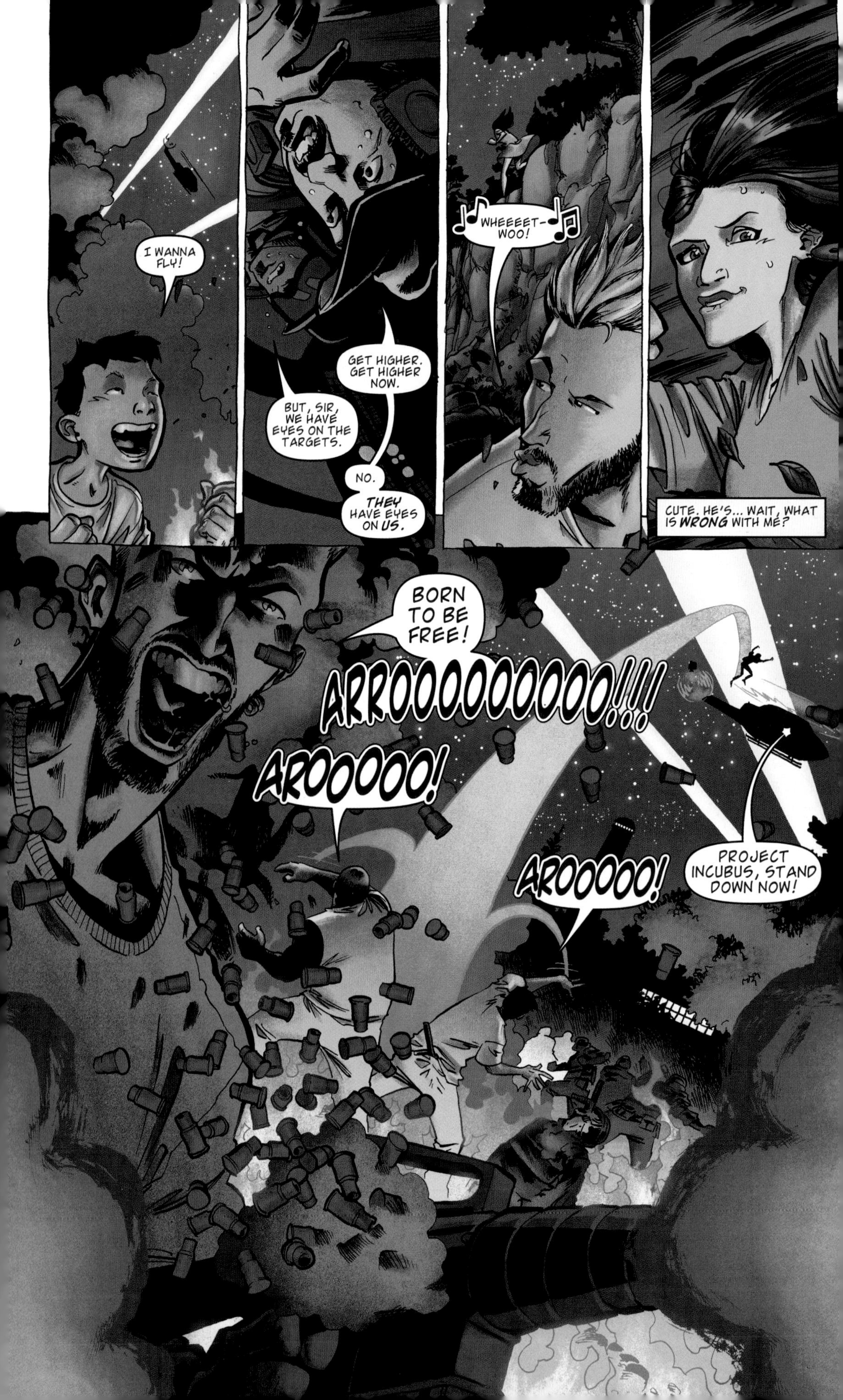

I WANNA FLY!
GET HIGHER. GET HIGHER NOW.
BUT, SIR, WE HAVE EYES ON THE TARGETS.
NO.
THEY HAVE EYES ON US.
WHEEEET-WOO!
CUTE. HE'S... WAIT, WHAT IS WRONG WITH ME?
BORN TO BE FREE!
ARROOOOOOOOOO!!!!
AROOOOO!
AROOOOO!
PROJECT INCUBUS, STAND DOWN NOW!

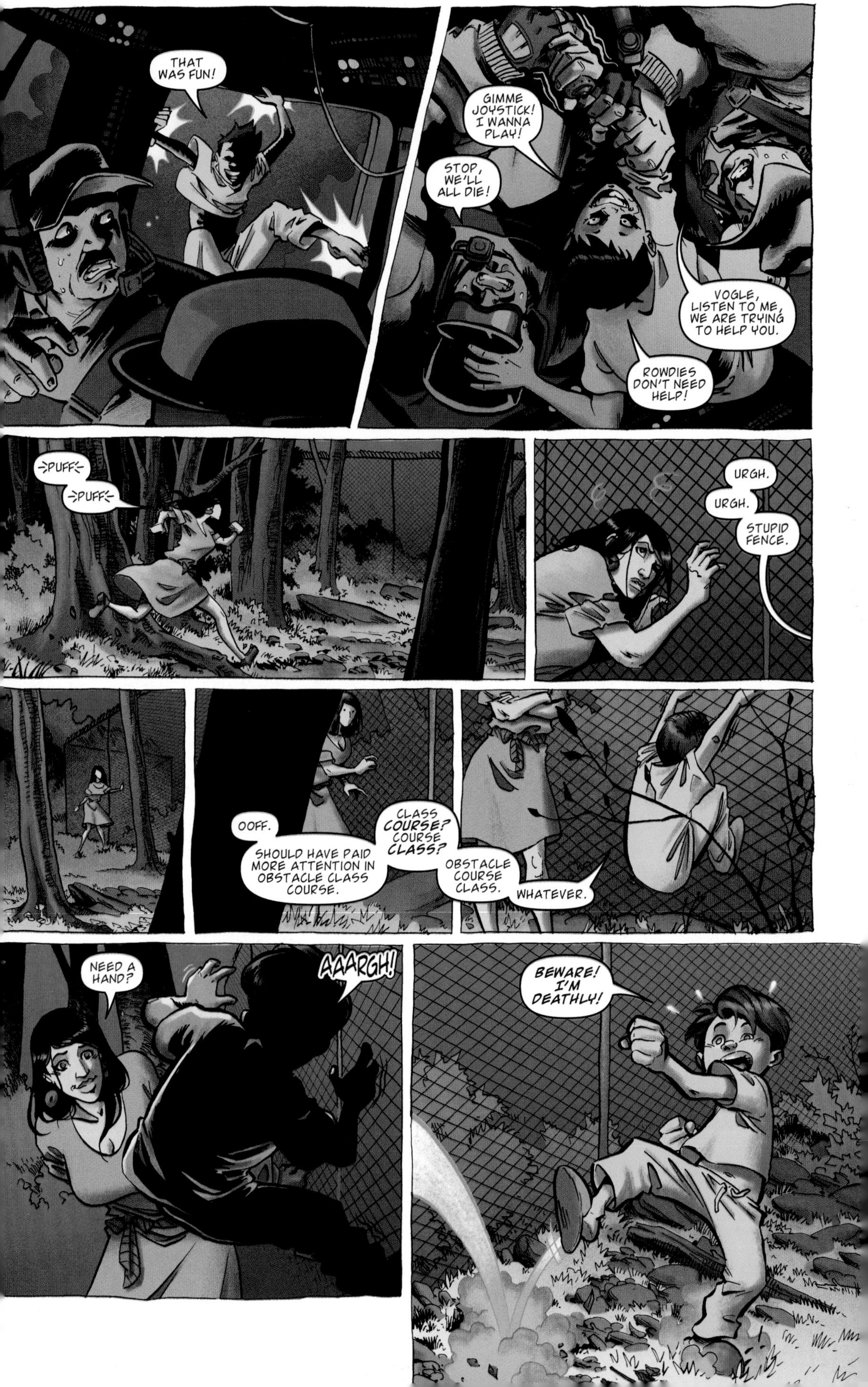

THAT WAS FUN!
GIMME JOYSTICK! I WANNA PLAY!
STOP, WE'LL ALL DIE!
VOGLE, LISTEN TO ME, WE ARE TRYING TO HELP YOU.
ROWDIES DON'T NEED HELP!
PUFF
PUFF
URGH.
URGH.
STUPID FENCE.
OOFF.
SHOULD HAVE PAID MORE ATTENTION IN OBSTACLE CLASS COURSE.
CLASS COURSE? COURSE CLASS?
OBSTACLE COURSE CLASS.
WHATEVER.
NEED A HAND?
AAARGH!
BEWARE! I'M DEATHLY!

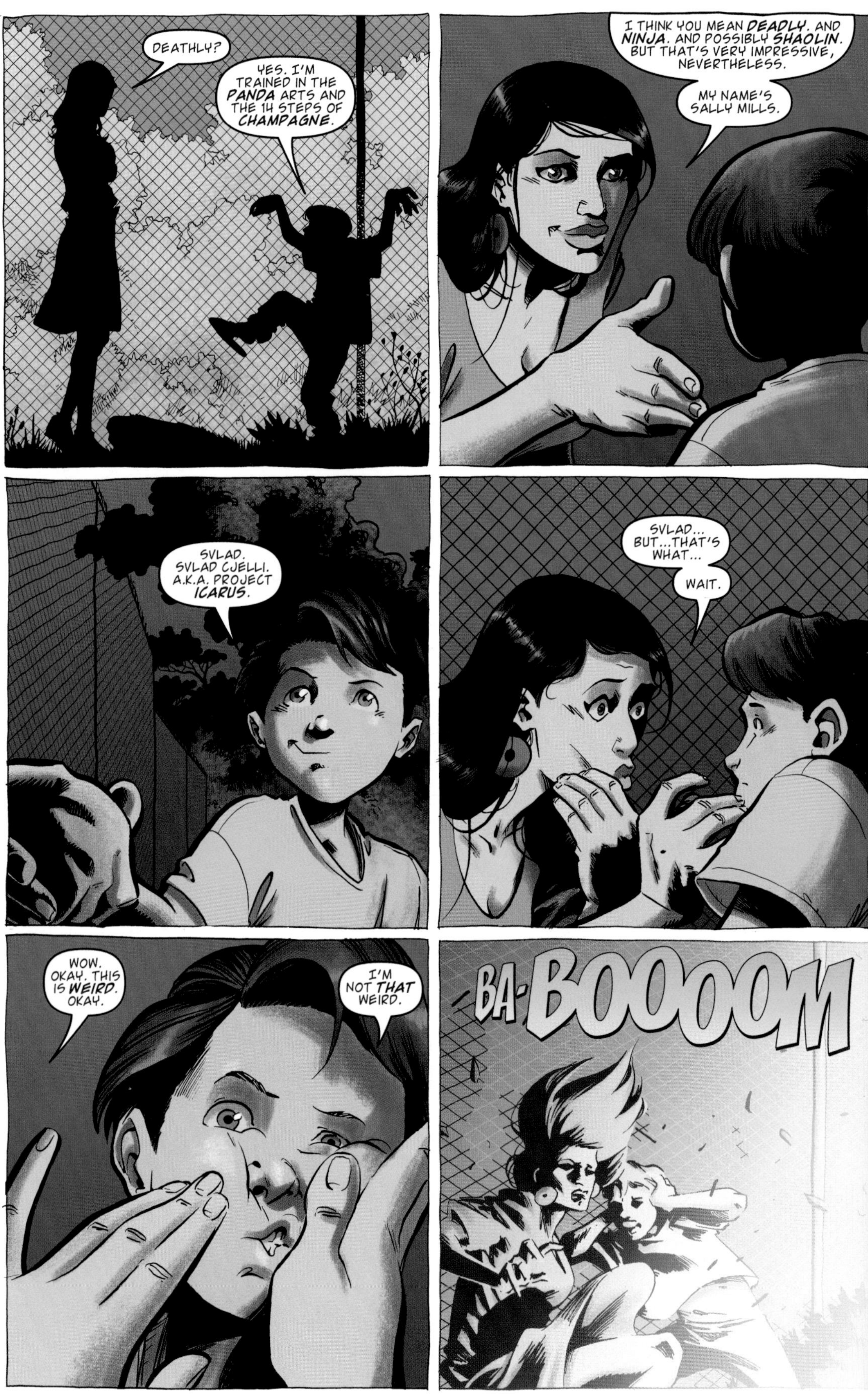
DEATHLY?
YES. I'M TRAINED IN THE PANDA ARTS AND THE 14 STEPS OF CHAMPAGNE.
I THINK YOU MEAN DEADLY. AND NINJA. AND POSSIBLY SHAOLIN. BUT THAT'S VERY IMPRESSIVE, NEVERTHELESS.
MY NAME'S SALLY MILLS.
SVLAD. SVLAD CJELLI. A.K.A. PROJECT ICARUS.
SVLAD... BUT...THAT'S WHAT...
WAIT.
WOW. OKAY. THIS IS WEIRD. OKAY.
I'M NOT THAT WEIRD.
BA-BOOOOM

WE NEED TO GET AWAY FROM HERE.

YES. YES.

WHAT IS THIS PLACE?

BLACKWING IS A SPECIAL FACILITY FOR THE TRAINING AND PROTECTION OF THE WORLD'S MOST UNUSUAL INDIVIDUALS, WHEREIN THEY CAN BEST REALIZE THEIR POTENTIAL OF THEIR GIFTS.

THAT'S WHAT THE COLONEL SAYS.

BART SAYS IT'S A SINKHOLE IN THE UNIVERSE'S COSMIC PLAN.

THEY WERE TRAINING ME TO BE A SPY.

I THOUGHT I WOULD LIKE TO BE SPY.

BUT IT TURNS OUT IT'S A BIT LONELY.

LOTS OF BEING LOCKED IN EMPTY ROOMS WITH BIG MIRRORS.

TOP SECRET

CA KEE

TRESPASSERS WILL BE SHOT

I HAVE A QUESTION.

ANGER

TO CRE

CA KEE

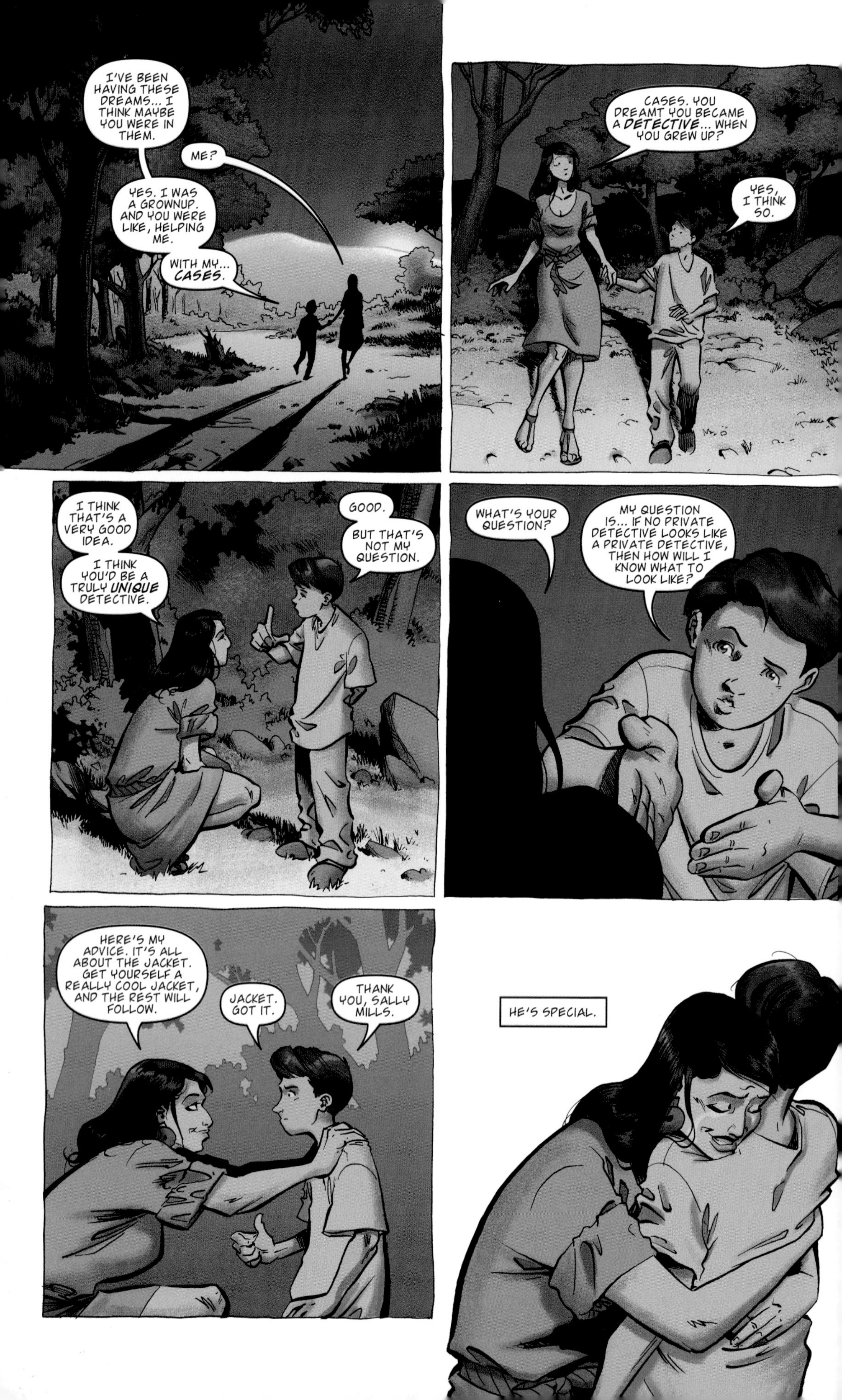

I'VE BEEN HAVING THESE DREAMS... I THINK MAYBE YOU WERE IN THEM.
ME?
YES. I WAS A GROWNUP. AND YOU WERE LIKE, HELPING ME.
WITH MY... CASES.
CASES. YOU DREAMT YOU BECAME A DETECTIVE... WHEN YOU GREW UP?
YES, I THINK SO.
I THINK THAT'S A VERY GOOD IDEA.
I THINK YOU'D BE A TRULY UNIQUE DETECTIVE.
GOOD.
BUT THAT'S NOT MY QUESTION.
WHAT'S YOUR QUESTION?
MY QUESTION IS... IF NO PRIVATE DETECTIVE LOOKS LIKE A PRIVATE DETECTIVE, THEN HOW WILL I KNOW WHAT TO LOOK LIKE?
HERE'S MY ADVICE. IT'S ALL ABOUT THE JACKET. GET YOURSELF A REALLY COOL JACKET, AND THE REST WILL FOLLOW.
JACKET. GOT IT.
THANK YOU, SALLY MILLS.
HE'S SPECIAL.

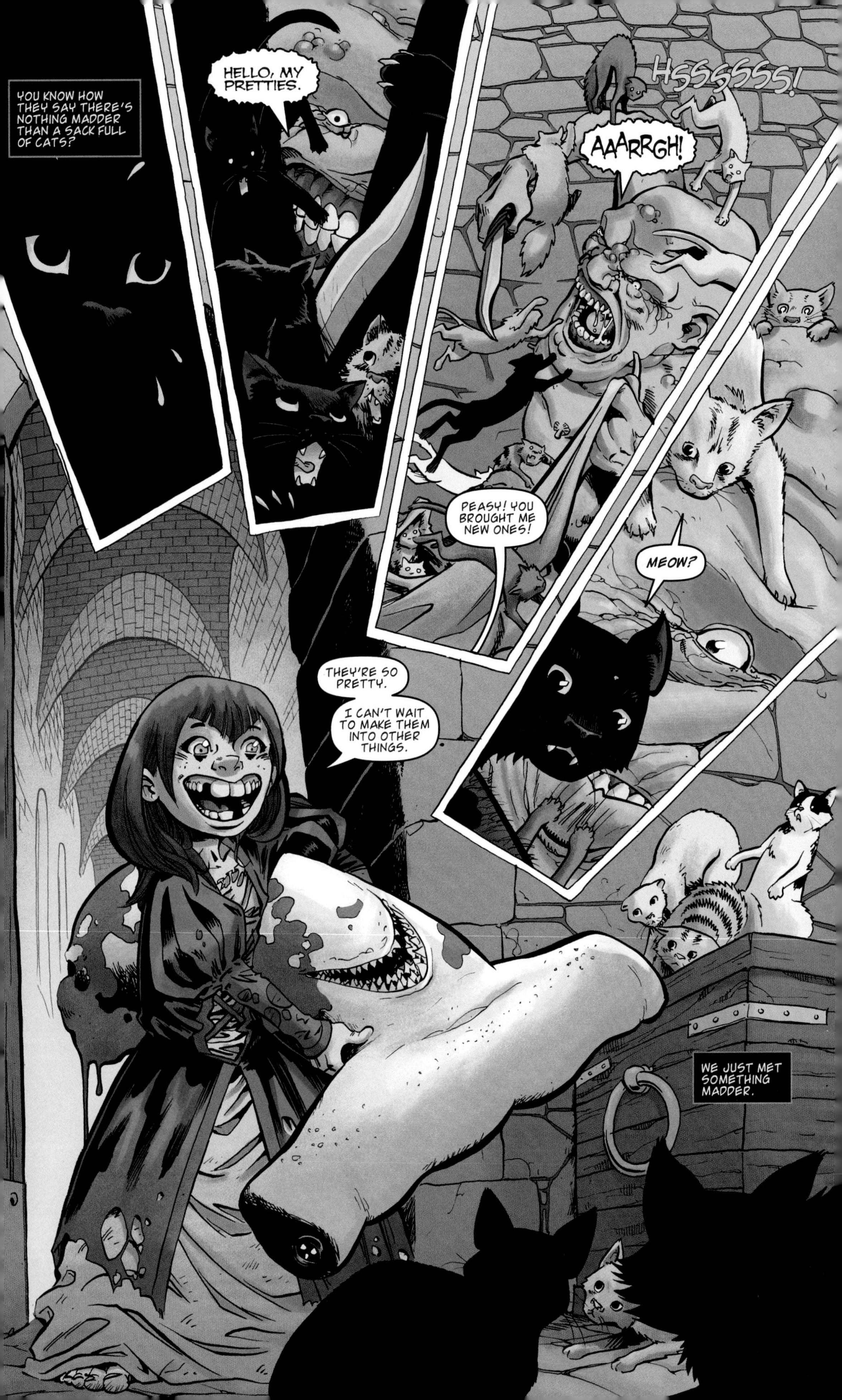

YOU KNOW HOW THEY SAY THERE'S NOTHING MADDER THAN A SACK FULL OF CATS?
HELLO, MY PRETTIES.
HSSSSSS!
AAARRGH!
PEASY! YOU BROUGHT ME NEW ONES!
MEOW?
THEY'RE SO PRETTY.
I CAN'T WAIT TO MAKE THEM INTO OTHER THINGS.
WE JUST MET SOMETHING MADDER.

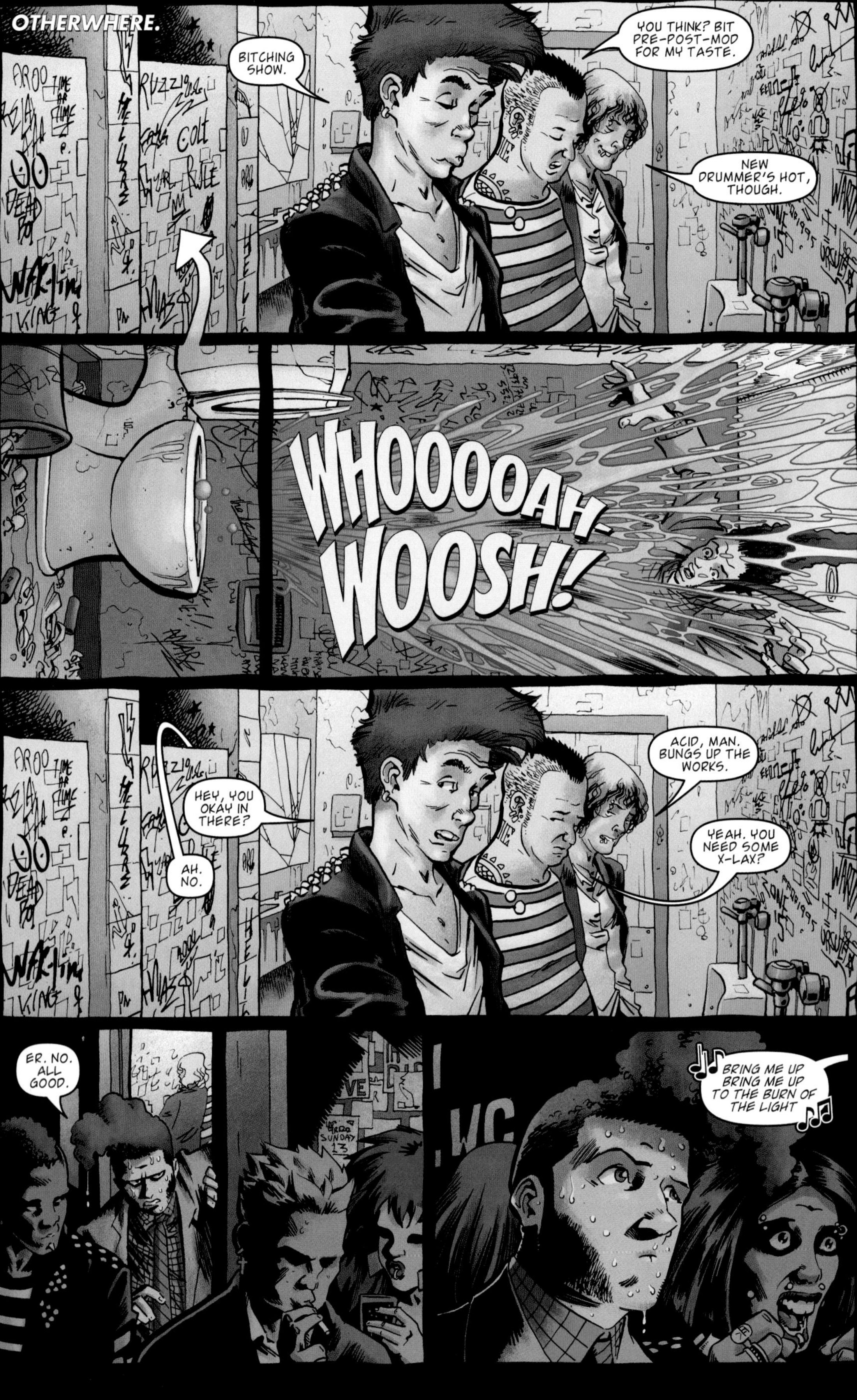
OTHERWHERE.
BITCHING SHOW.
YOU THINK? BIT PRE-POST-MOD FOR MY TASTE.
NEW DRUMMER'S HOT, THOUGH.
WHOOOOAH-WOOSH!
HEY, YOU OKAY IN THERE?
AH. NO.
ACID, MAN. BUNGS UP THE WORKS.
YEAH. YOU NEED SOME X-LAX?
ER. NO. ALL GOOD.
BRING ME UP BRING ME UP TO THE BURN OF THE LIGHT

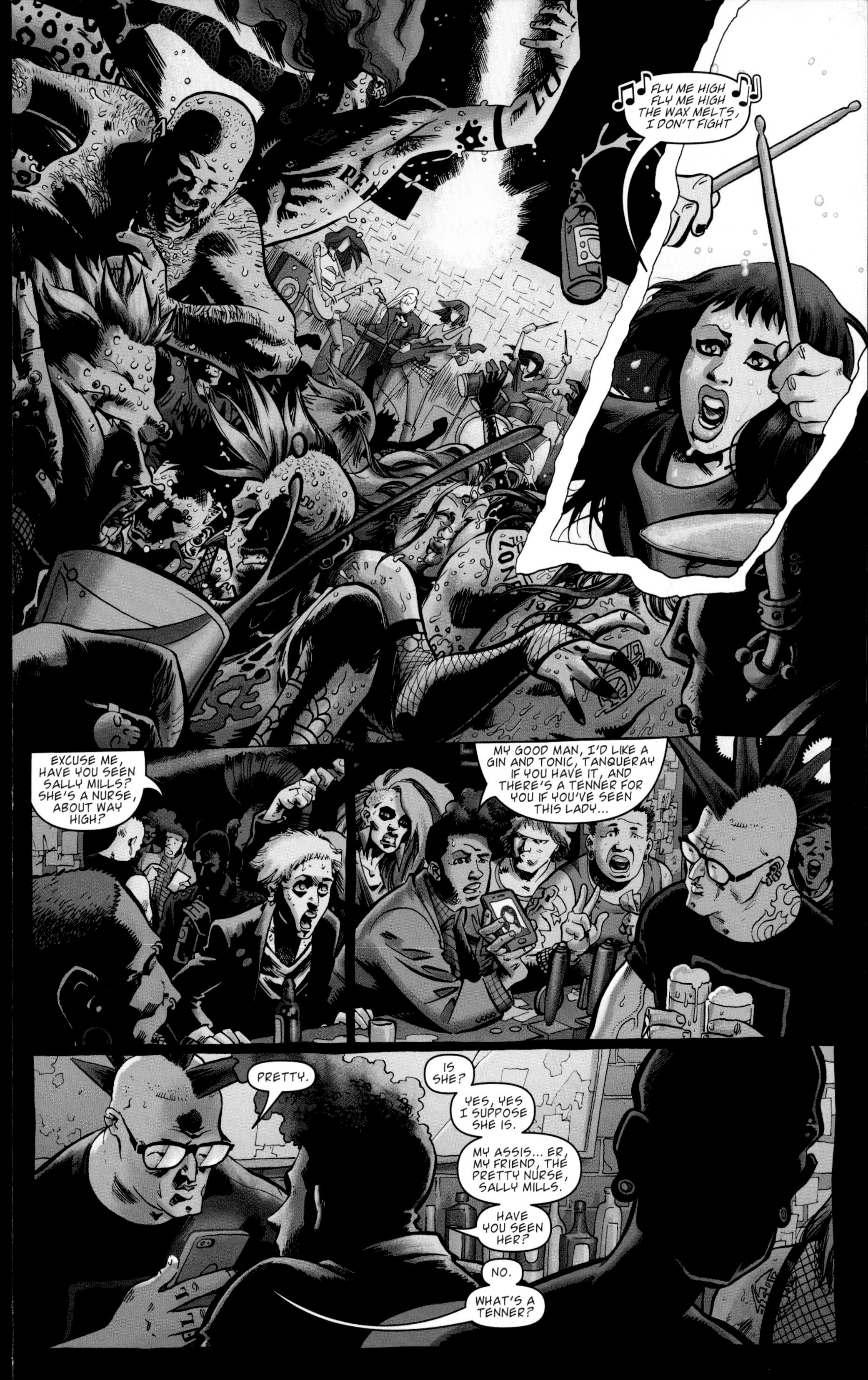
FLY ME HIGH
FLY ME HIGH
THE WAX MELTS,
I DON'T FIGHT
EXCUSE ME, HAVE YOU SEEN SALLY MILLS? SHE'S A NURSE, ABOUT WAY HIGH?
MY GOOD MAN, I'D LIKE A GIN AND TONIC, TANQUERAY IF YOU HAVE IT, AND THERE'S A TENNER FOR YOU IF YOU'VE SEEN THIS LADY...
PRETTY.
IS SHE?
YES, YES I SUPPOSE SHE IS.
MY ASSIS... ER, MY FRIEND, THE PRETTY NURSE, SALLY MILLS.
HAVE YOU SEEN HER?
NO.
WHAT'S A TENNER?

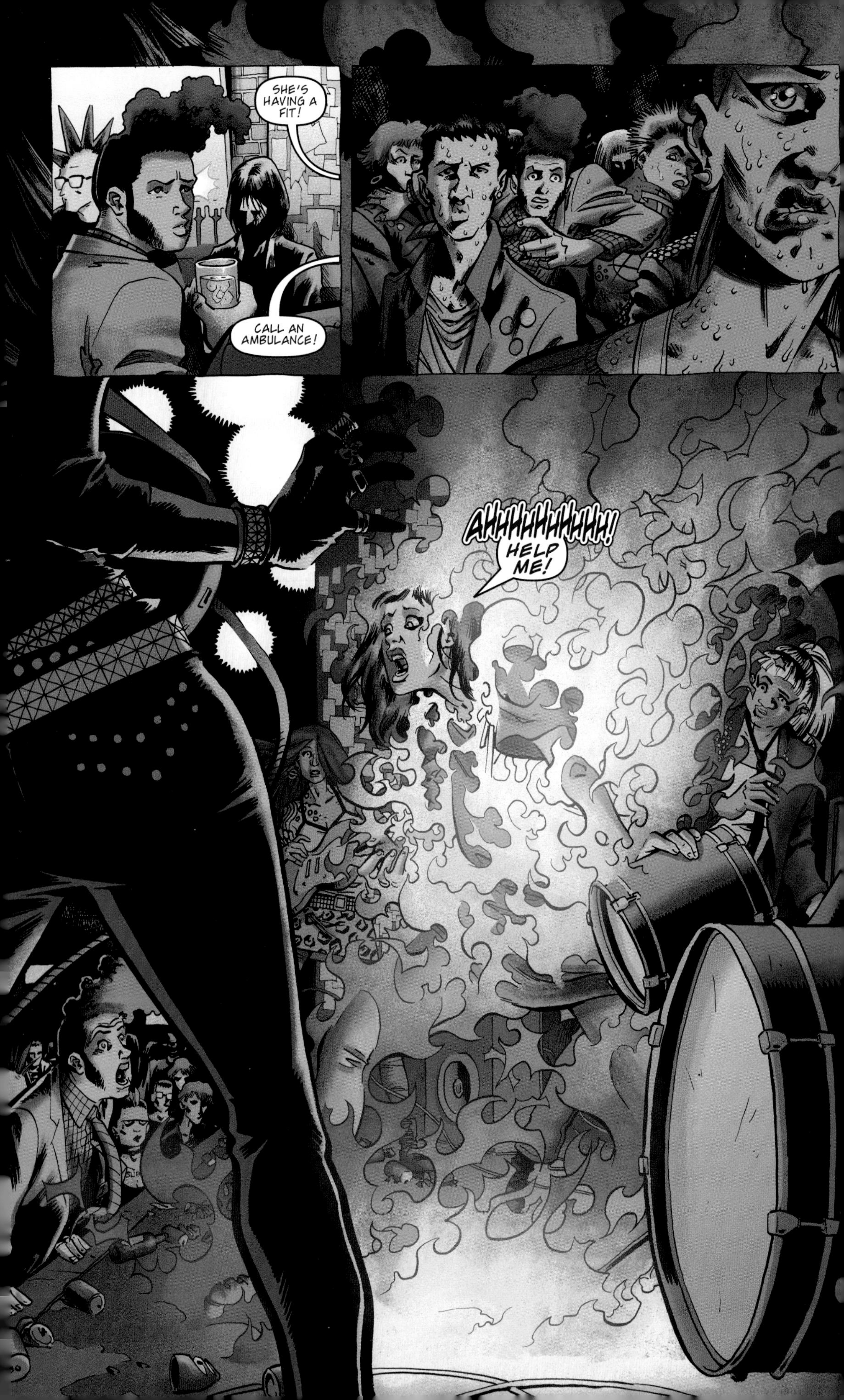
SHE'S HAVING A FIT!
CALL AN AMBULANCE!
AHHHHHHHHHH!
HELP ME!

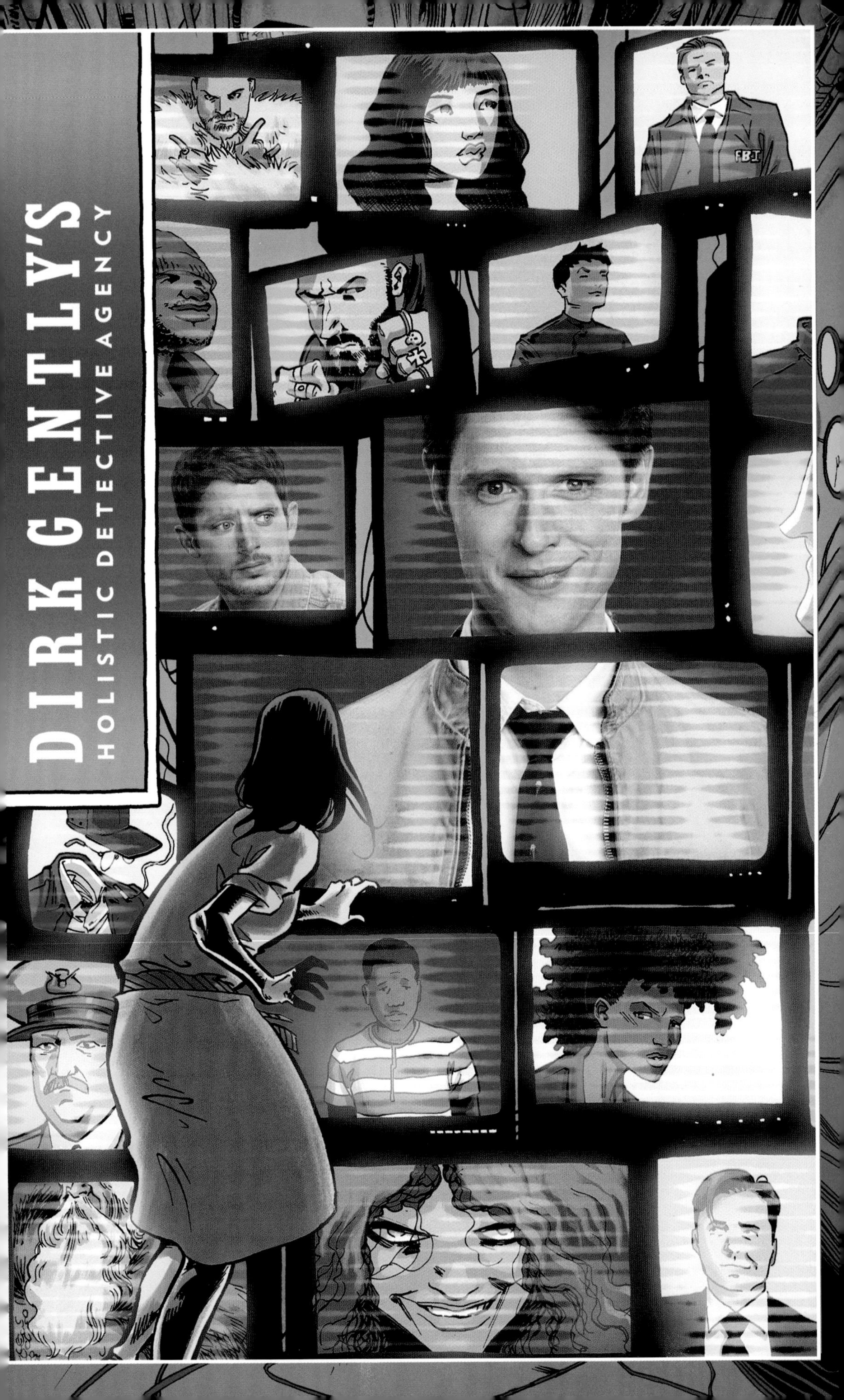
DIRK GENTLY'S
HOLISTIC DETECTIVE AGENCY
FBI

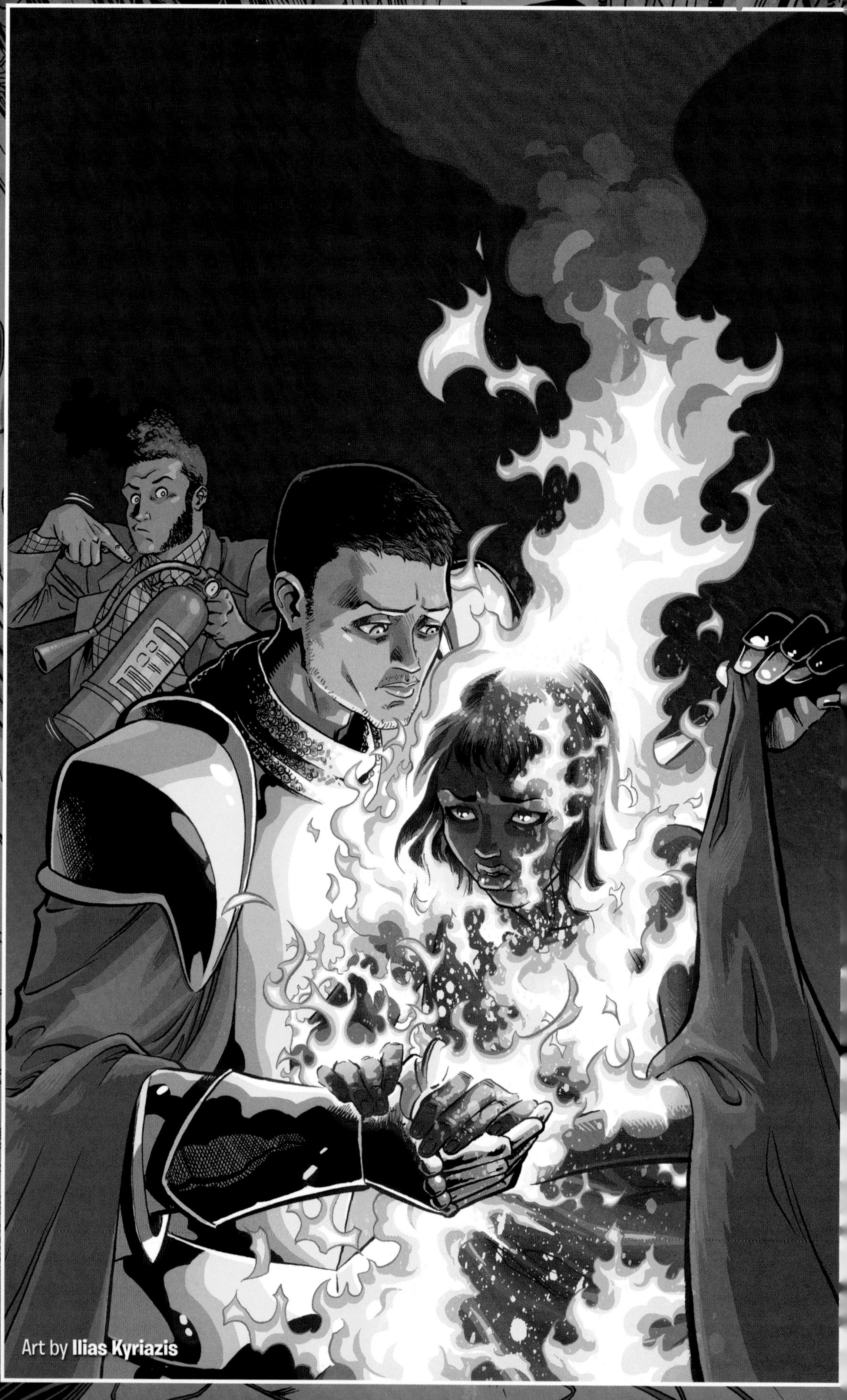

Art by **Ilias Kyriazis**

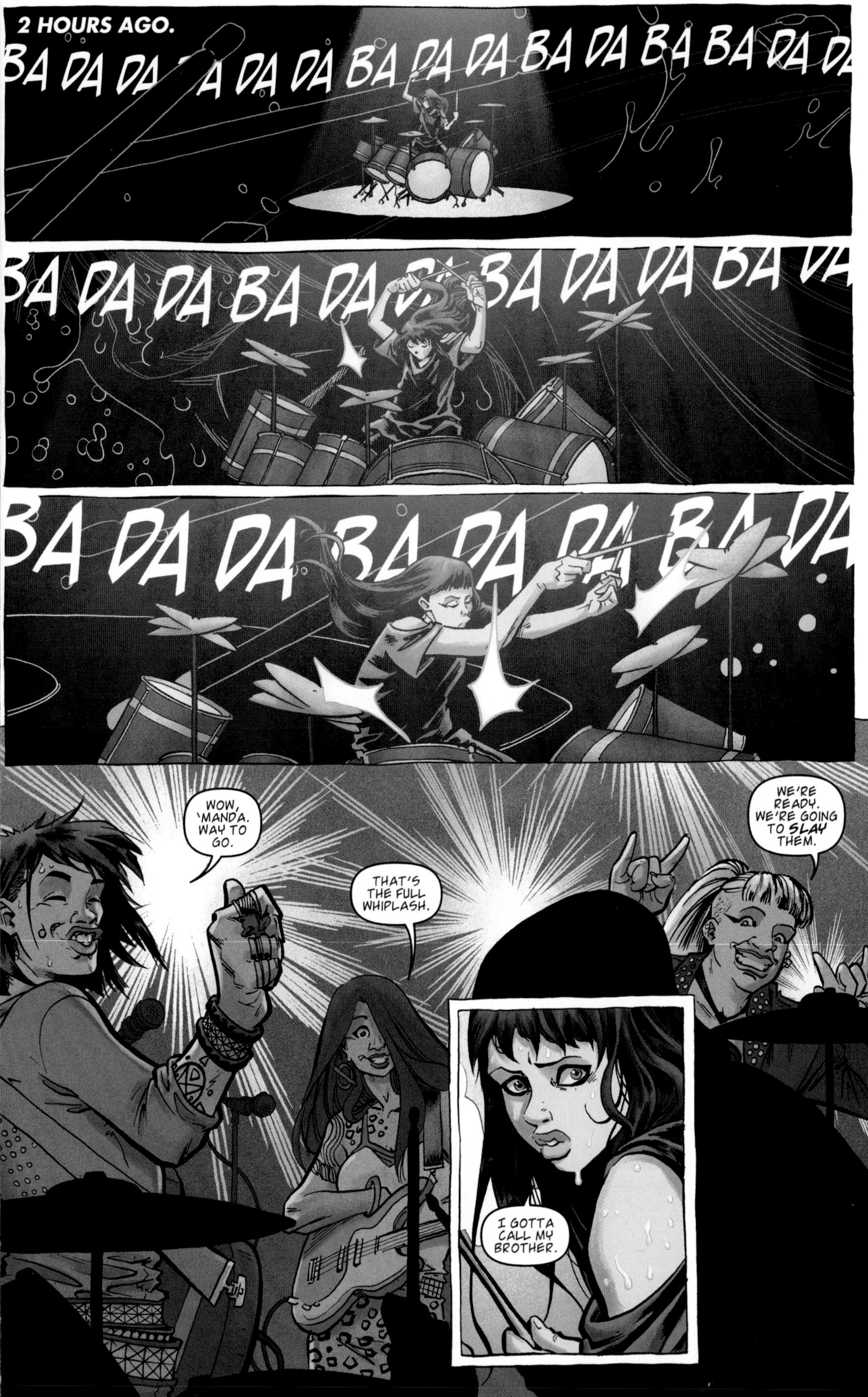
2 HOURS AGO.
BA DA DA BA DA DA BA DA DA BA DA BA BA DA DA
BA DA DA BA DA DA BA DA DA BA DA
BA DA DA BA DA DA BA DA
WOW, 'MANDA. WAY TO GO.
THAT'S THE FULL WHIPLASH.
WE'RE READY. WE'RE GOING TO SLAY THEM.
I GOTTA CALL MY BROTHER.

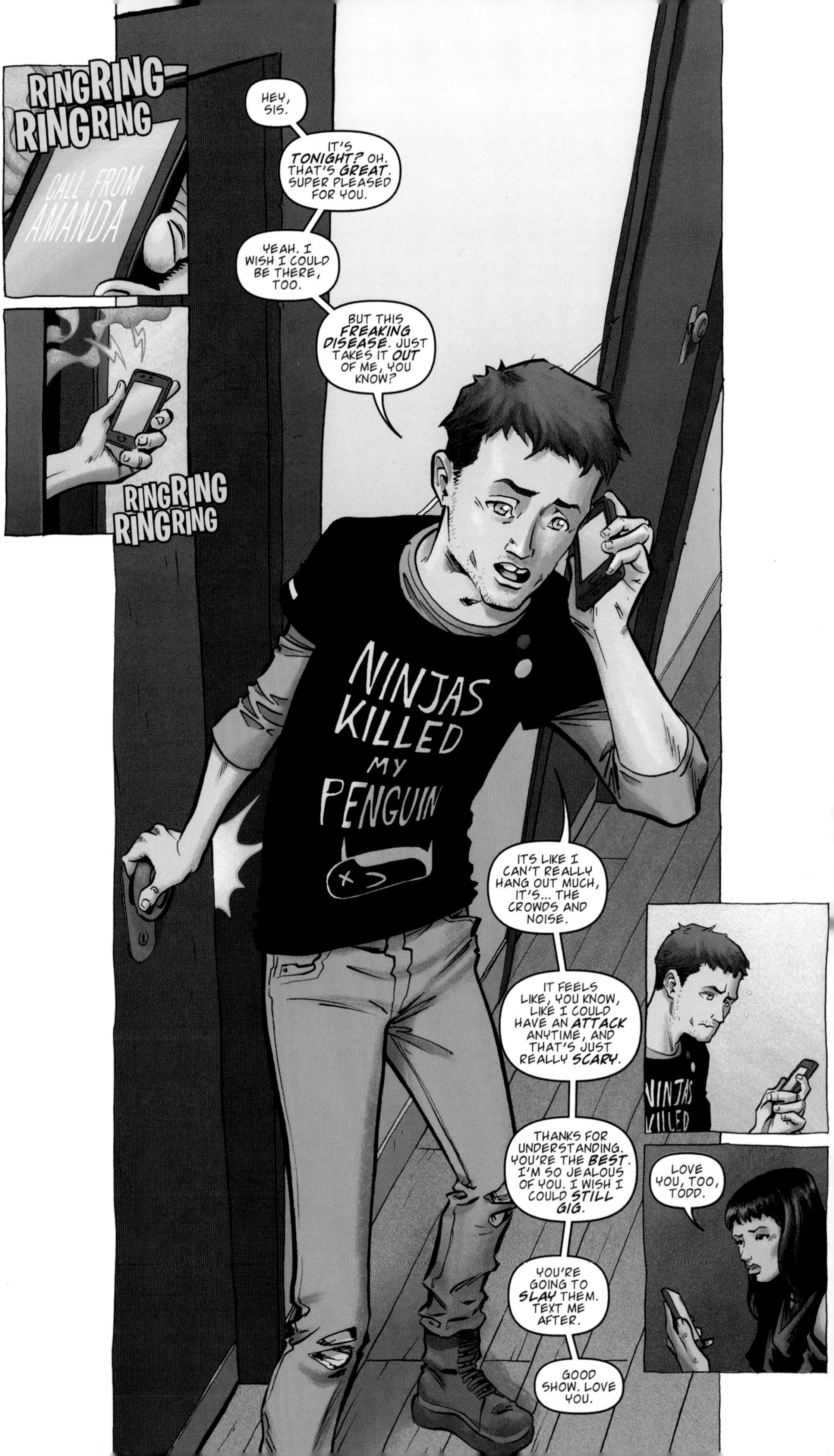
RINGRING RINGRING
CALL FROM AMANDA
RINGRING RINGRING
HEY, SIS.
IT'S TONIGHT? OH. THAT'S GREAT. SUPER PLEASED FOR YOU.
YEAH. I WISH I COULD BE THERE, TOO.
BUT THIS FREAKING DISEASE. JUST TAKES IT OUT OF ME, YOU KNOW?
NINJAS KILLED MY PENGUIN
ITS LIKE I CAN'T REALLY HANG OUT MUCH, IT'S... THE CROWDS AND NOISE.
IT FEELS LIKE, YOU KNOW, LIKE I COULD HAVE AN ATTACK ANYTIME, AND THAT'S JUST REALLY SCARY.
THANKS FOR UNDERSTANDING. YOU'RE THE BEST. I'M SO JEALOUS OF YOU. I WISH I COULD STILL GIG.
YOU'RE GOING TO SLAY THEM. TEXT ME AFTER.
GOOD SHOW. LOVE YOU.
LOVE YOU, TOO, TODD.

THE SALMON OF DOUBT, CHAPTER 3: PARARIBULITIS

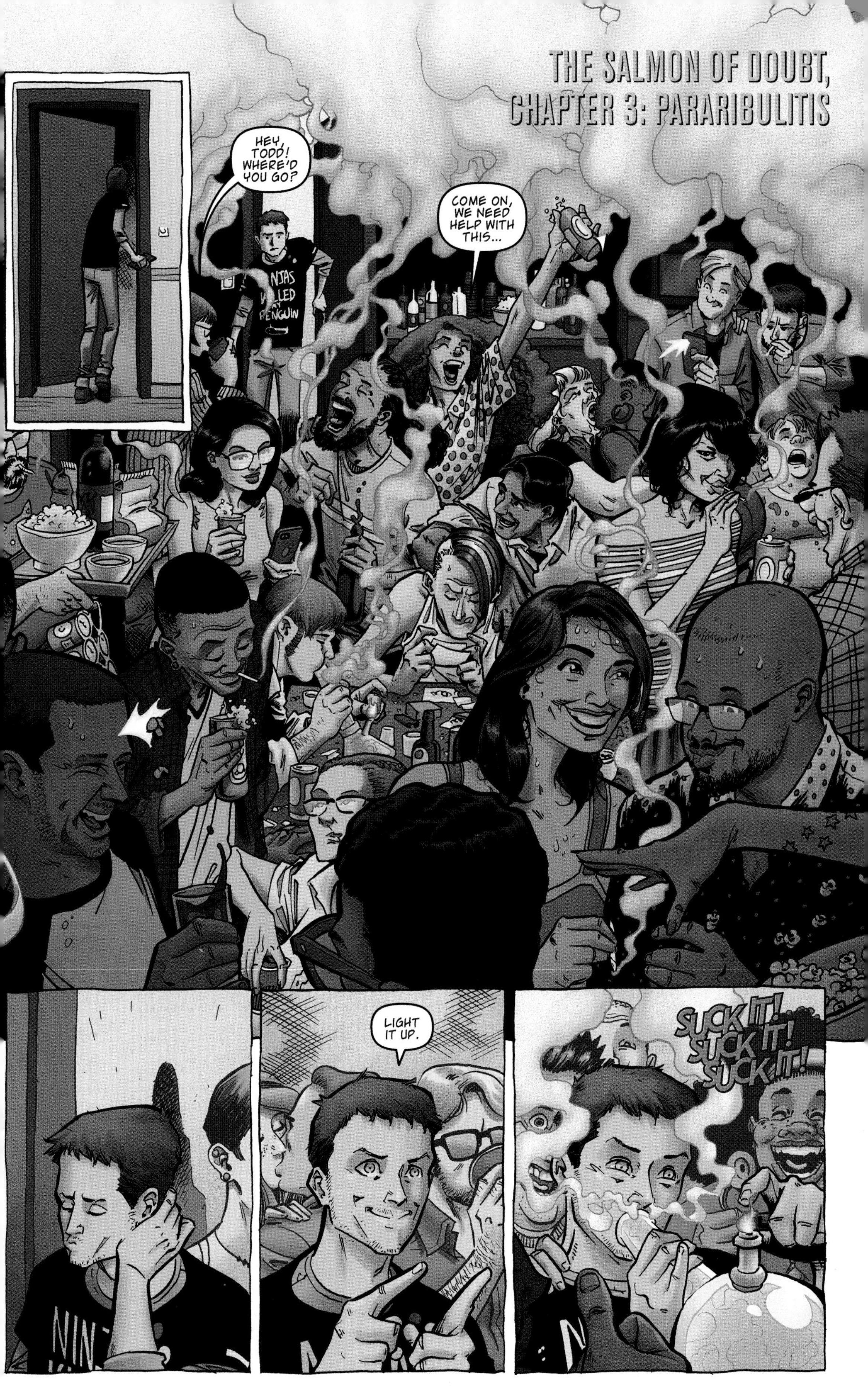
HEY, TODD! WHERE'D YOU GO?
COME ON, WE NEED HELP WITH THIS...
LIGHT IT UP.
SUCK IT! SUCK IT! SUCK IT!

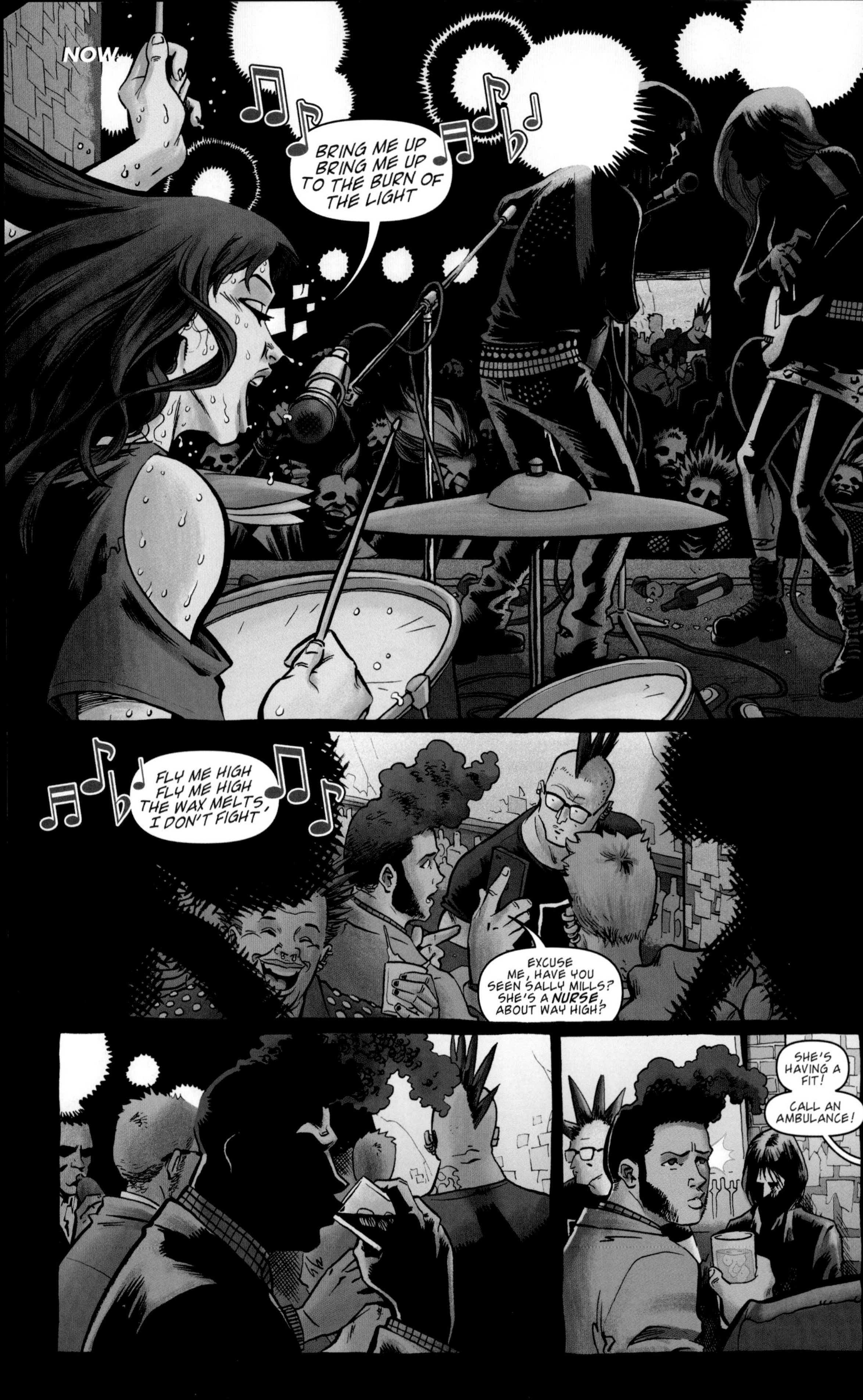
NOW
BRING ME UP
BRING ME UP
TO THE BURN OF
THE LIGHT
FLY ME HIGH
FLY ME HIGH
THE WAX MELTS,
I DON'T FIGHT
EXCUSE ME, HAVE YOU SEEN SALLY MILLS? SHE'S A NURSE, ABOUT WAY HIGH?
SHE'S HAVING A FIT!
CALL AN AMBULANCE!

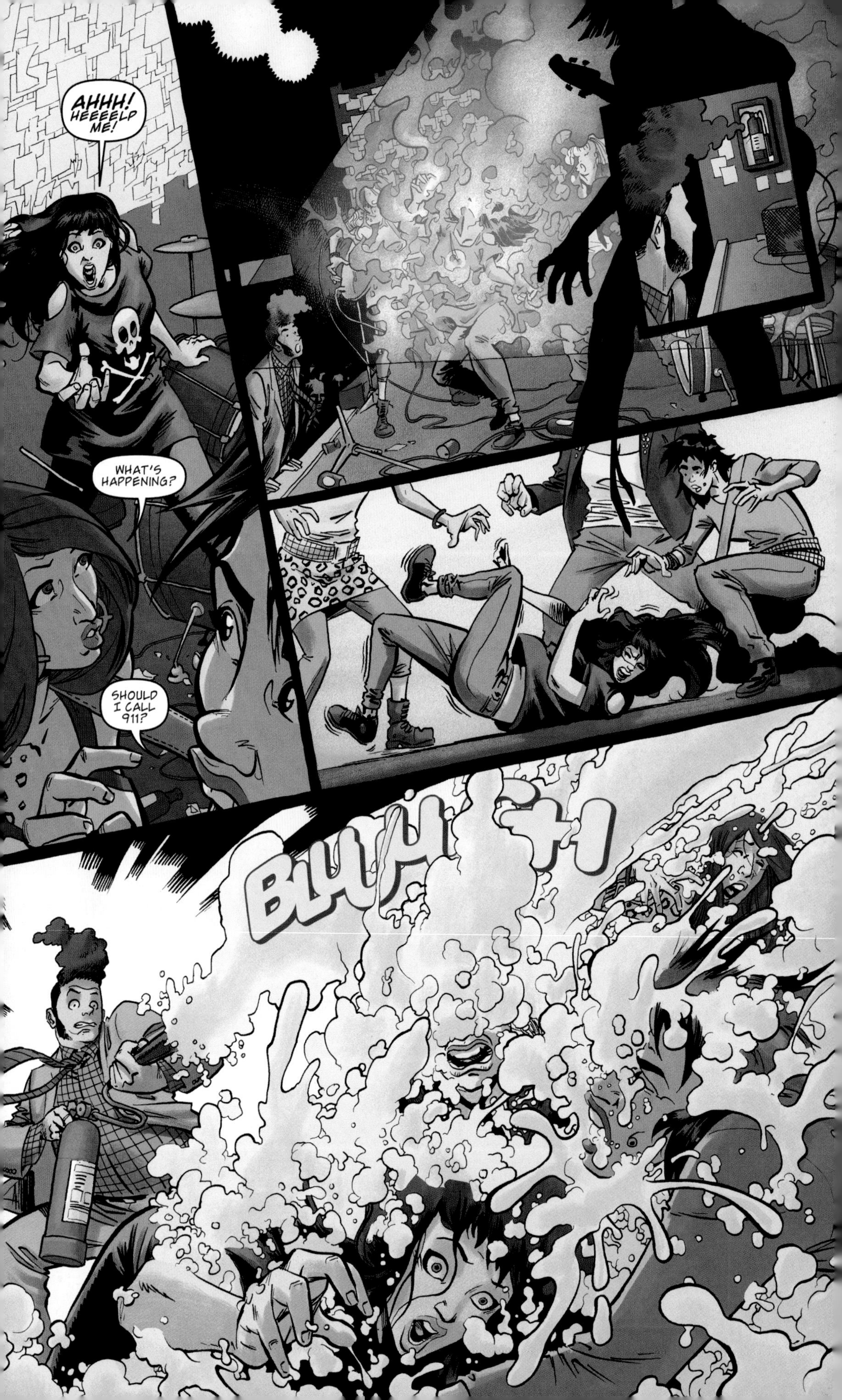
AHHH! HEEEELP ME!
WHAT'S HAPPENING?
SHOULD I CALL 911?
BLUUSH

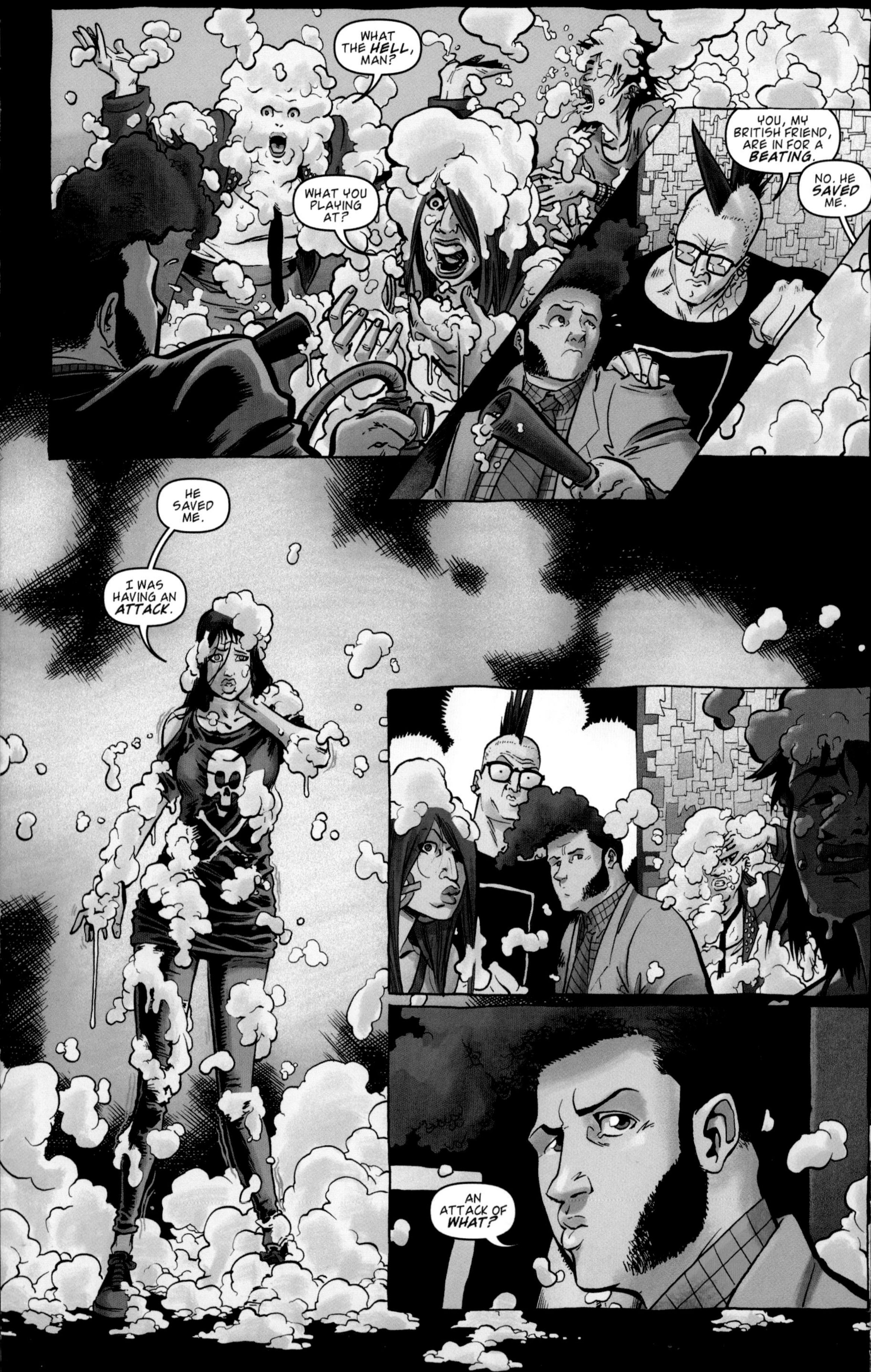

WHAT THE HELL, MAN?
WHAT YOU PLAYING AT?
YOU, MY BRITISH FRIEND, ARE IN FOR A BEATING.
NO. HE SAVED ME.
HE SAVED ME.
I WAS HAVING AN ATTACK.
AN ATTACK OF WHAT?

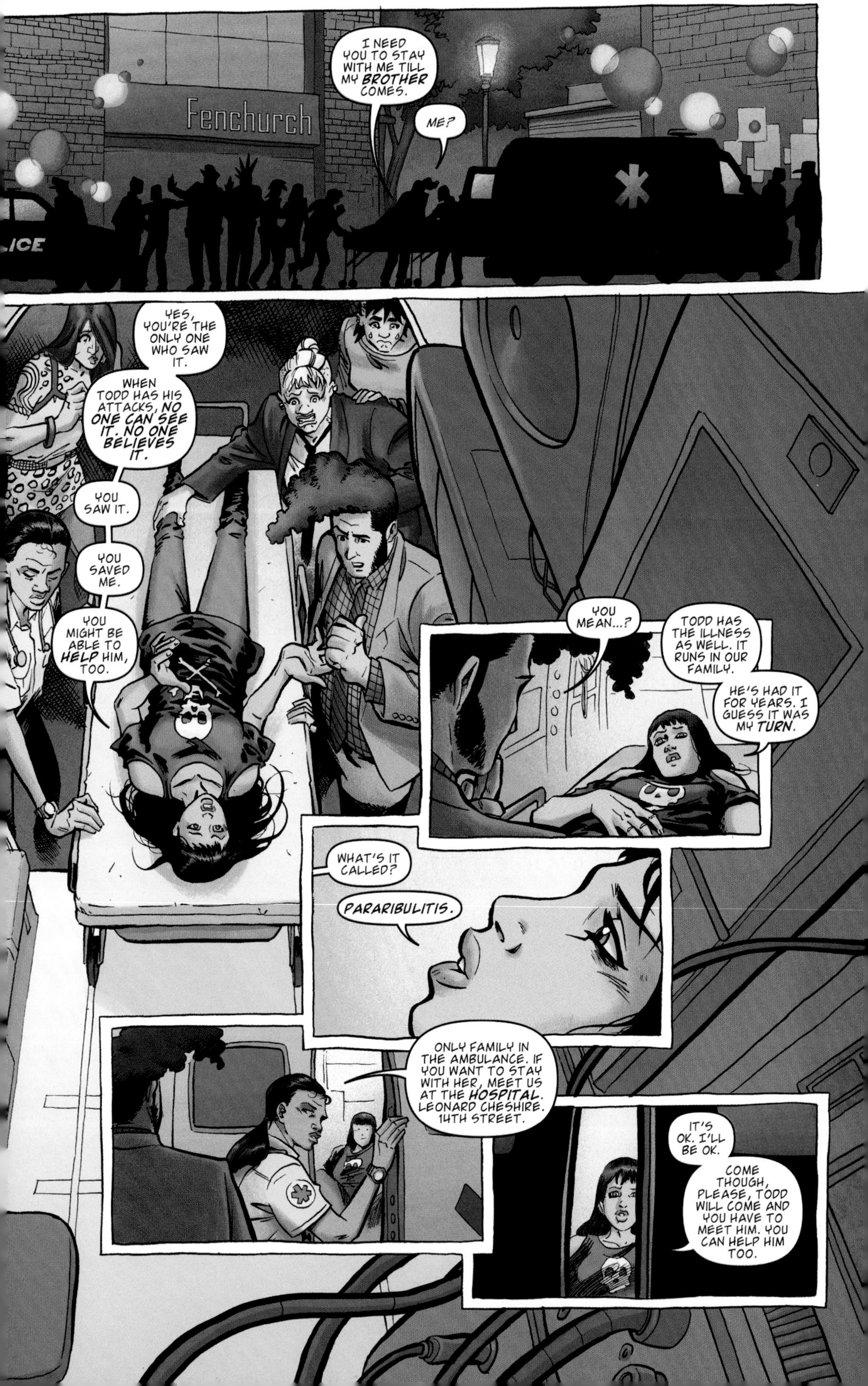
Fenchurch
ICE
I NEED YOU TO STAY WITH ME TILL MY BROTHER COMES.
ME?
YES, YOU'RE THE ONLY ONE WHO SAW IT.
WHEN TODD HAS HIS ATTACKS, NO ONE CAN SEE IT. NO ONE BELIEVES IT.
YOU SAW IT.
YOU SAVED ME.
YOU MIGHT BE ABLE TO HELP HIM, TOO.
YOU MEAN...?
TODD HAS THE ILLNESS AS WELL. IT RUNS IN OUR FAMILY.
HE'S HAD IT FOR YEARS. I GUESS IT WAS MY TURN.
WHAT'S IT CALLED?
PARARIBULITIS.
ONLY FAMILY IN THE AMBULANCE. IF YOU WANT TO STAY WITH HER, MEET US AT THE HOSPITAL. LEONARD CHESHIRE. 14TH STREET.
IT'S OK. I'LL BE OK.
COME THOUGH, PLEASE, TODD WILL COME AND YOU HAVE TO MEET HIM. YOU CAN HELP HIM TOO.

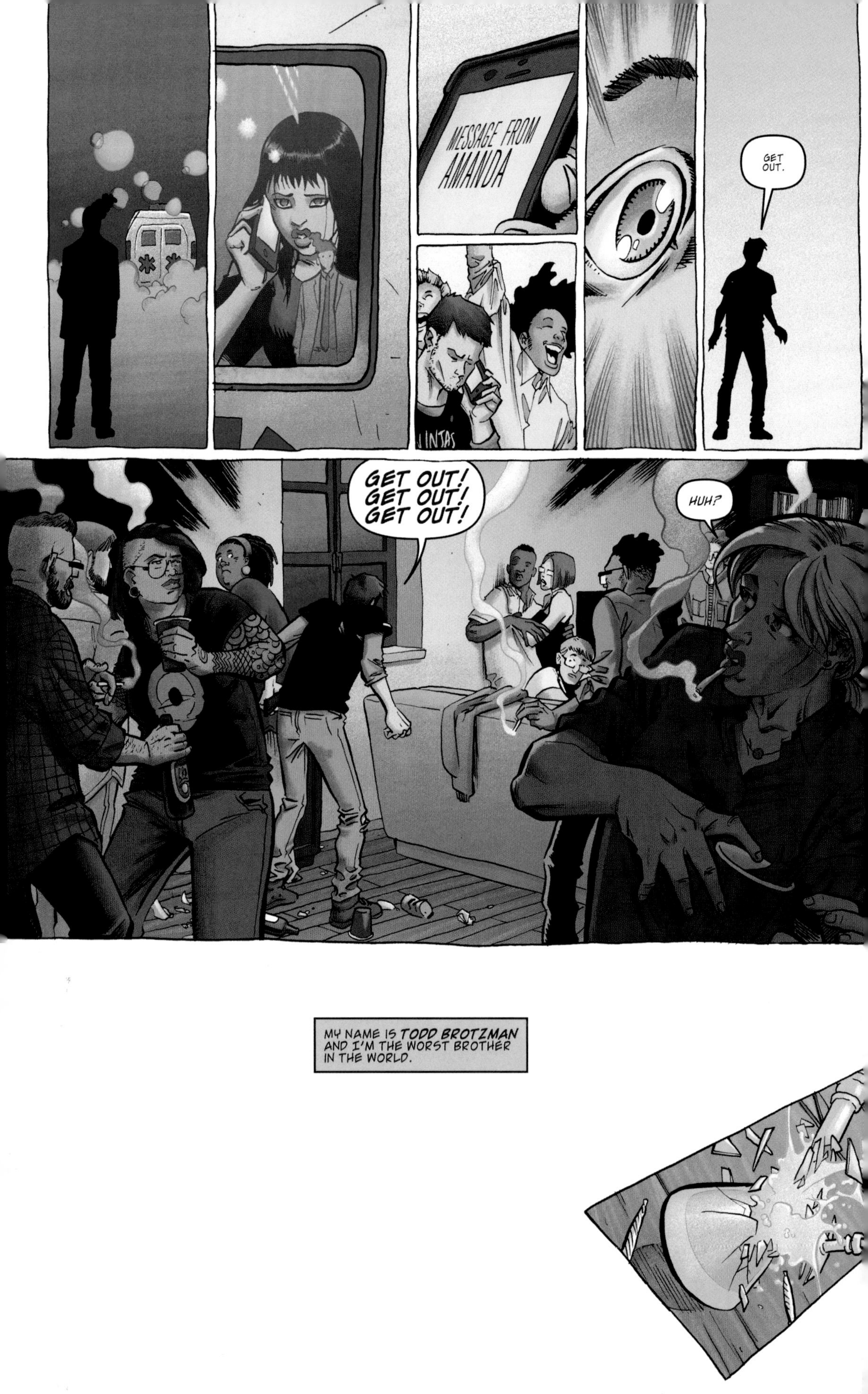
MESSAGE FROM AMANDA
GET OUT.
GET OUT! GET OUT! GET OUT!
HUH?
MY NAME IS TODD BROTZMAN AND I'M THE WORST BROTHER IN THE WORLD.

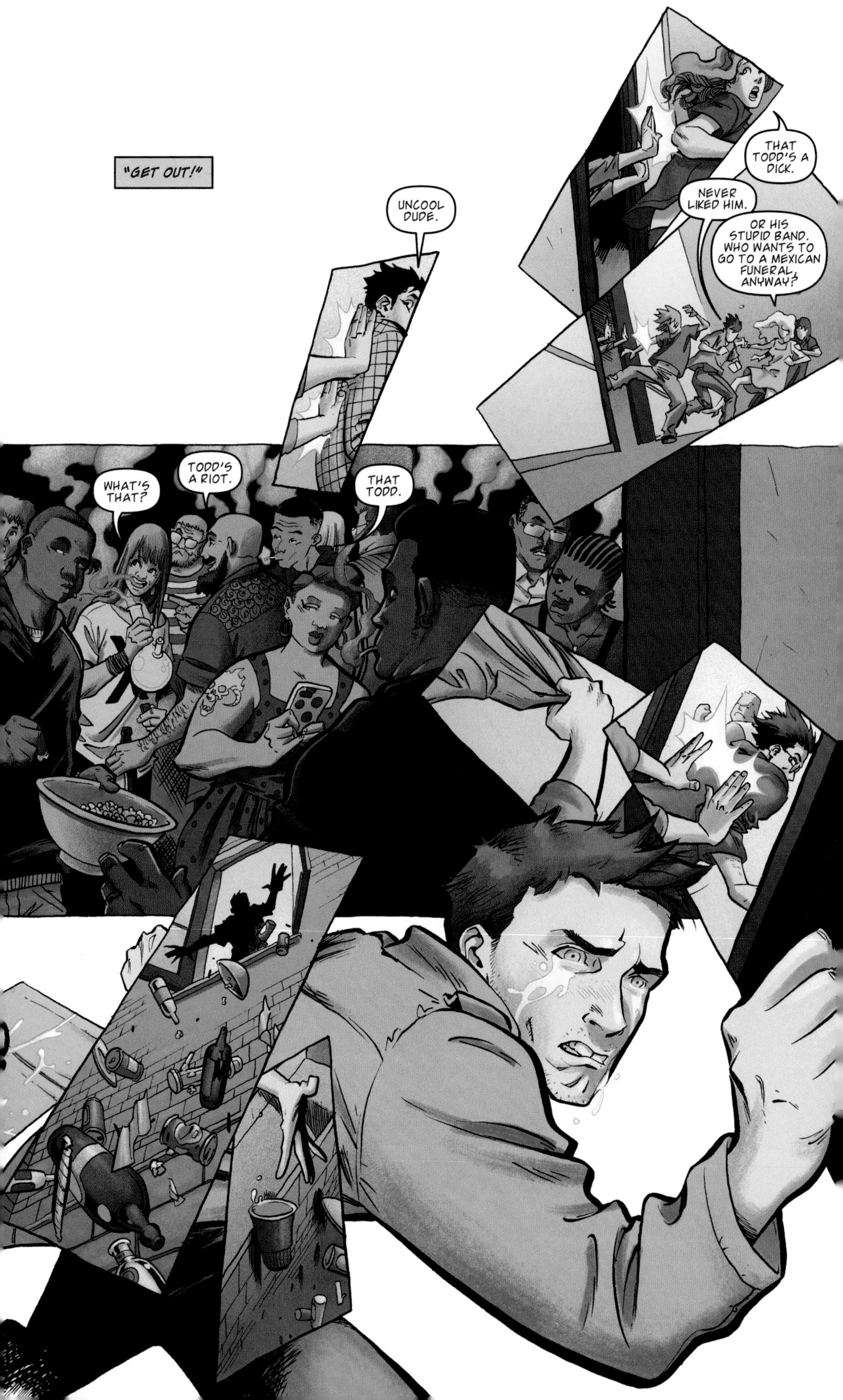
"GET OUT!"
UNCOOL DUDE.
THAT TODD'S A DICK.
NEVER LIKED HIM.
OR HIS STUPID BAND. WHO WANTS TO GO TO A MEXICAN FUNERAL ANYWAY?
WHAT'S THAT?
TODD'S A RIOT.
THAT TODD.

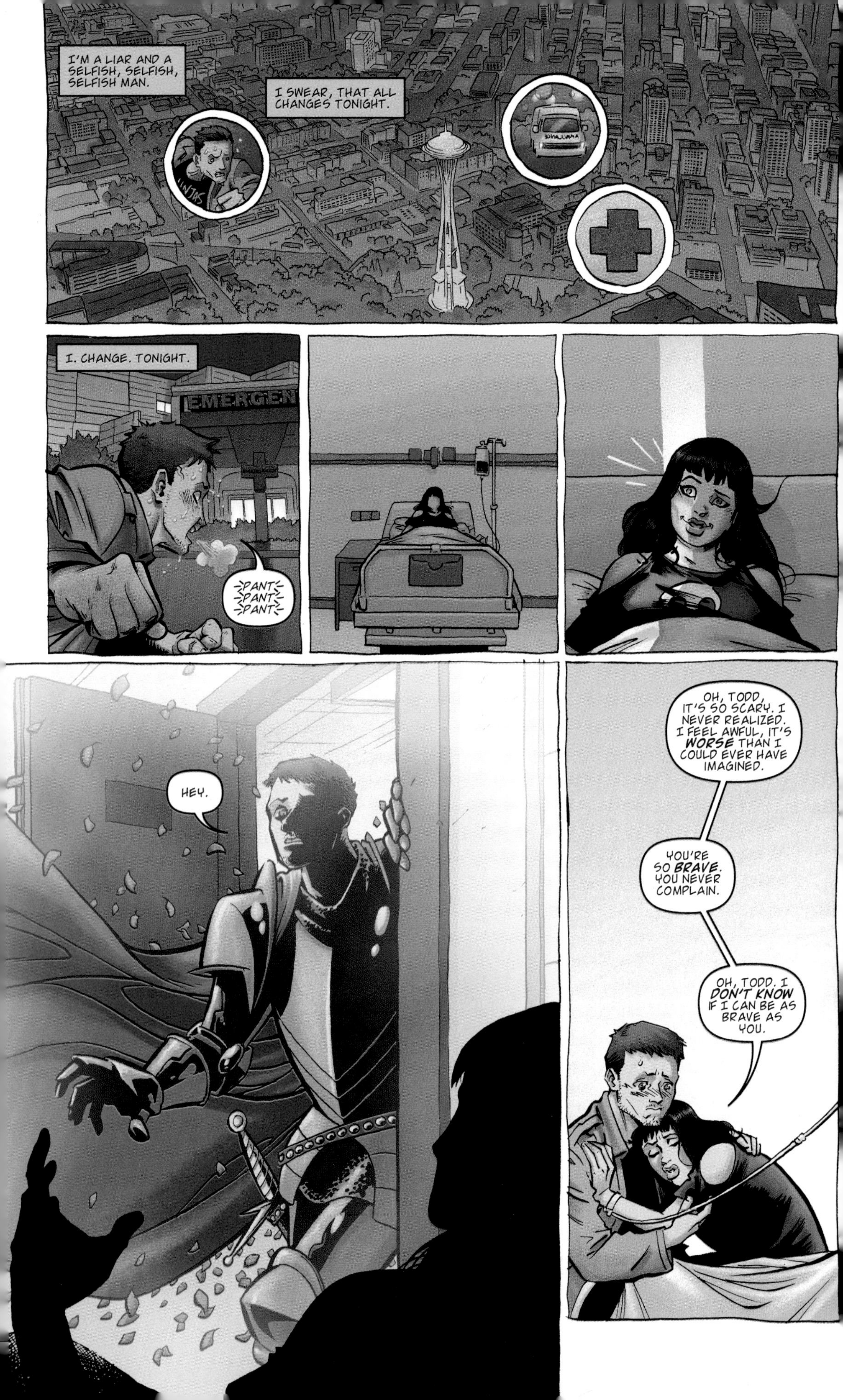
I'M A LIAR AND A SELFISH, SELFISH, SELFISH MAN.
I SWEAR, THAT ALL CHANGES TONIGHT.
AMBULANCE
I. CHANGE. TONIGHT.
EMERGEN
PANT PANT PANT
HEY.
OH, TODD, IT'S SO SCARY. I NEVER REALIZED. I FEEL AWFUL, IT'S WORSE THAN I COULD EVER HAVE IMAGINED.
YOU'RE SO BRAVE. YOU NEVER COMPLAIN.
OH, TODD. I DON'T KNOW IF I CAN BE AS BRAVE AS YOU.

SO I ONLY HAVE THIS TENNER. BUT IT'S POUNDS. POUNDS ARE BETTER THAN DOLLARS.

SO YOU SHOULD WANT IT MORE. CURRENCY. MATH.

I DON'T TAKE POUNDS.

BUT I ONLY HAVE POUNDS, AND I NEED TO GO TO THE HOSPITAL.

THERE IS A MATTER OF A DAMSEL IN DISTRESS.

SIR! COLONEL RIGGINS, SIR.

SERGEANT, REPORT.

PASS ON, DEAR MAN, PASS ON. HERE'S A TENNER FOR YOUR TROUBLE.

IDIOT.

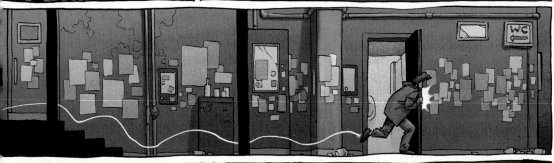

I know him.

TELL ME AGAIN.

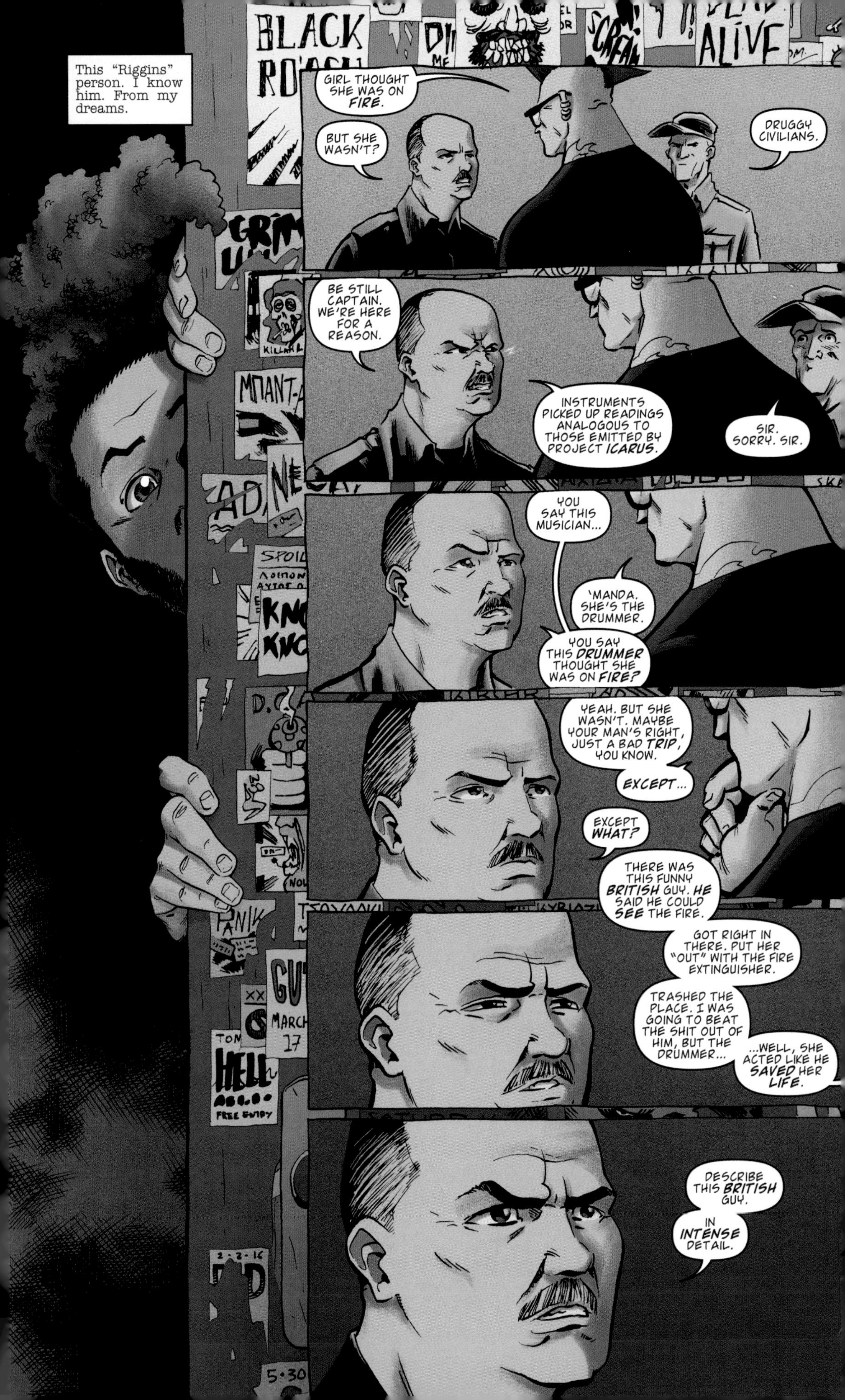
This "Riggins" person. I know him. From my dreams.
GIRL THOUGHT SHE WAS ON FIRE.
BUT SHE WASN'T?
DRUGGY CIVILIANS.
BE STILL CAPTAIN. WE'RE HERE FOR A REASON.
INSTRUMENTS PICKED UP READINGS ANALOGOUS TO THOSE EMITTED BY PROJECT ICARUS.
SIR. SORRY. SIR.
YOU SAY THIS MUSICIAN...
'MANDA. SHE'S THE DRUMMER.
YOU SAY THIS DRUMMER THOUGHT SHE WAS ON FIRE?
YEAH. BUT SHE WASN'T. MAYBE YOUR MAN'S RIGHT, JUST A BAD TRIP, YOU KNOW.
EXCEPT...
EXCEPT WHAT?
THERE WAS THIS FUNNY BRITISH GUY. HE SAID HE COULD SEE THE FIRE.
GOT RIGHT IN THERE. PUT HER "OUT" WITH THE FIRE EXTINGUISHER.
TRASHED THE PLACE. I WAS GOING TO BEAT THE SHIT OUT OF HIM, BUT THE DRUMMER...
...WELL, SHE ACTED LIKE HE SAVED HER LIFE.
DESCRIBE THIS BRITISH GUY.
IN INTENSE DETAIL.
BLACK ROACH
ALIVE
MARCH 17
HELL
FREE ENTRY

THE ROOM BETWEEN.

"HE'S SO SPECIAL."

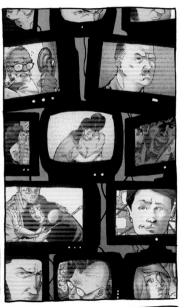

UH... JACKET. IT'S ALL ABOUT THE JACKET.

MILLS SALLY MILLS. TIME TO GET UP.

SVLAD?

WHERE'S LITTLE SVLAD?

HE IS *SAFE*, SALLY MILLS. THANKS TO YOU. SAFE AND ON THE *CORRECT* PATH.

WHAT DO YOU MEAN?

I DIDN'T DO ANYTHING.

INCORRECT.

I'M SORRY.

WAS THAT RUDE?

NEVERTHELESS. INCORRECT. OUR OBSERVATIONS CONFIRM THAT YOU ARE A FIGURE OF THE UTMOST *IMPORTANCE* IN SVLAD CJELLI'S LIFE.

IN ALL HIS *POSSIBLE* LIVES.

I DON'T REALLY UNDERSTAND WHAT'S HAPPENING.

YOU'RE SHOWING ME ALTERNATE HISTORIES?

I DON'T BELIEVE I JUST SAID THAT OUT LOUD. TO A HI-FI SYSTEM.

NOT *ALTERNATIVES.*

ACTUALS. ACTUAL TIME LINES. THE PAST, THE PRESENT, THE FUTURE.

YOU EXPRESSED A WISH TO BETTER KNOW THE MAN DIRK GENTLY.

WE ARE SHOWING YOU HIS *BEGINNINGS.*

BUT THAT WASN'T *MY* DIRK.

ALL HIS BEGINNINGS.

YOU WILL HELP HIM BECOME WHAT HE *MUST* BE.

WHAT MUST HE BE?

CHOOSE ANOTHER SCREEN.

ALSO, I'M NOT A HI-FI.

REG'S BATHROOM.

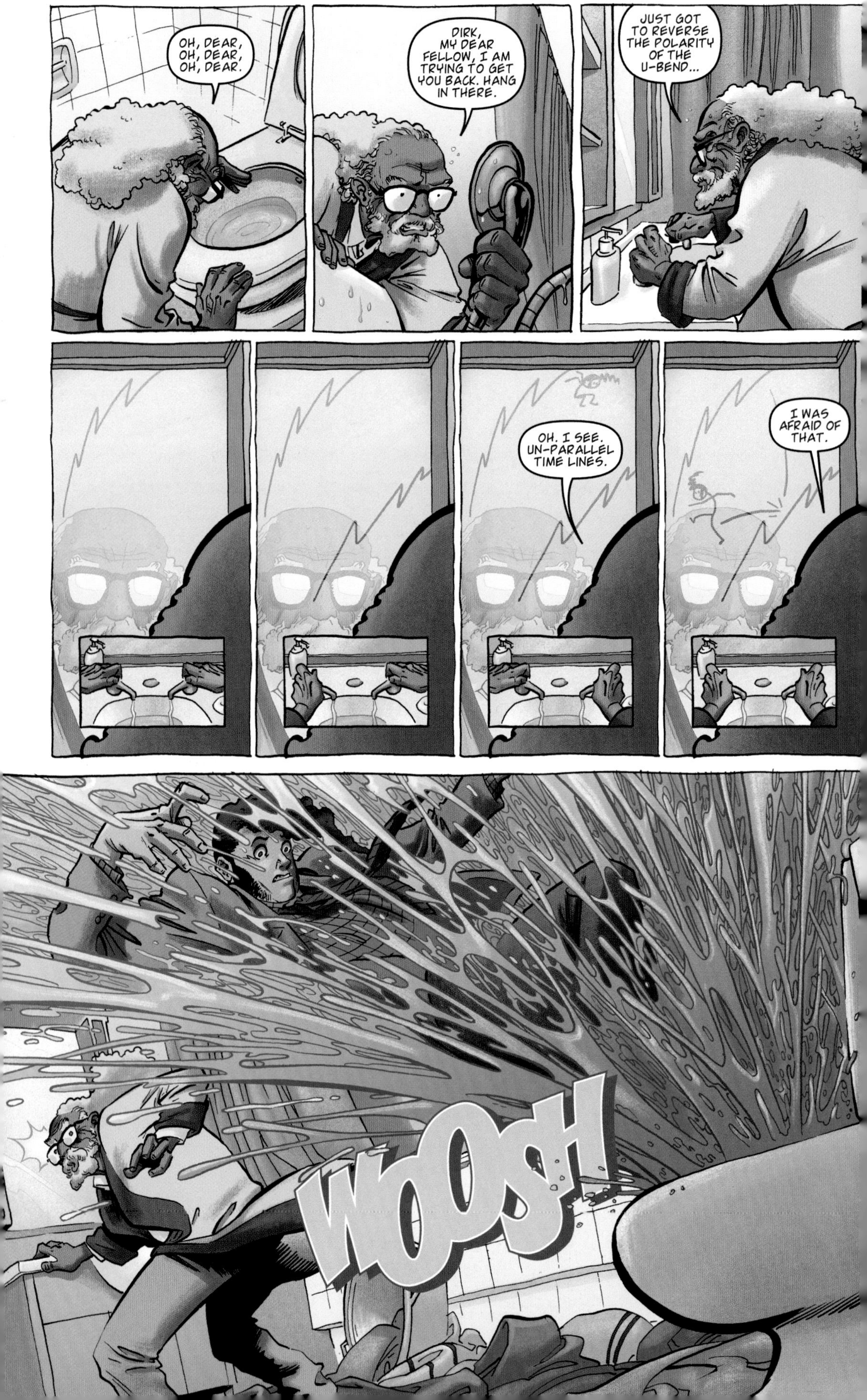

OH, DEAR, OH, DEAR, OH, DEAR.
DIRK, MY DEAR FELLOW, I AM TRYING TO GET YOU BACK. HANG IN THERE.
JUST GOT TO REVERSE THE POLARITY OF THE U-BEND...
OH. I SEE. UN-PARALLEL TIME LINES.
I WAS AFRAID OF THAT.
WOOSH

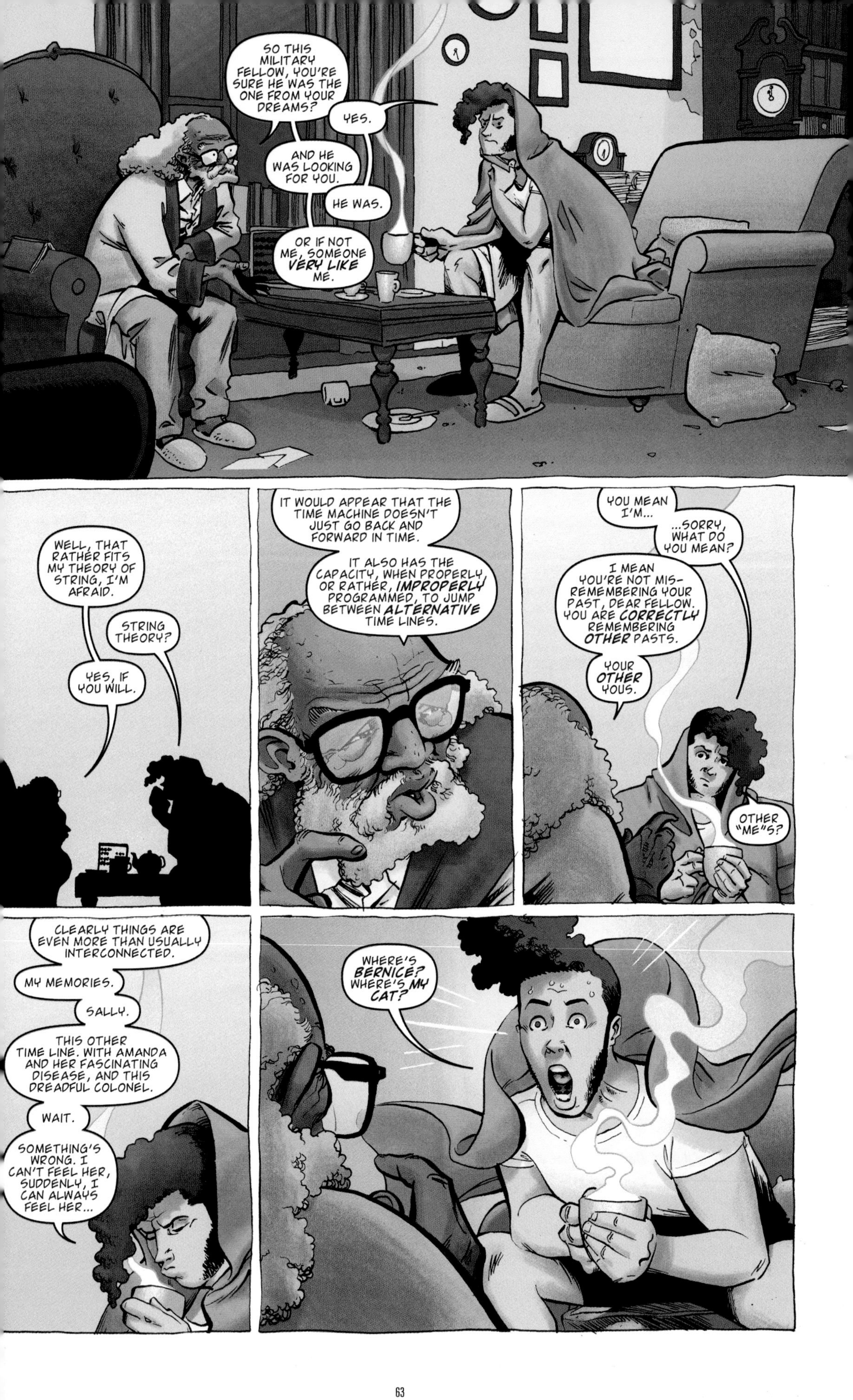
SO THIS MILITARY FELLOW, YOU'RE SURE HE WAS THE ONE FROM YOUR DREAMS?
YES.
AND HE WAS LOOKING FOR YOU.
HE WAS.
OR IF NOT ME, SOMEONE VERY LIKE ME.
WELL, THAT RATHER FITS MY THEORY OF STRING, I'M AFRAID.
STRING THEORY?
YES, IF YOU WILL.
IT WOULD APPEAR THAT THE TIME MACHINE DOESN'T JUST GO BACK AND FORWARD IN TIME.
IT ALSO HAS THE CAPACITY, WHEN PROPERLY OR RATHER, IMPROPERLY PROGRAMMED, TO JUMP BETWEEN ALTERNATIVE TIME LINES.
YOU MEAN I'M...
...SORRY, WHAT DO YOU MEAN?
I MEAN YOU'RE NOT MIS-REMEMBERING YOUR PAST, DEAR FELLOW. YOU ARE CORRECTLY REMEMBERING OTHER PASTS.
YOUR OTHER YOUS.
OTHER "ME"S?
CLEARLY THINGS ARE EVEN MORE THAN USUALLY INTERCONNECTED.
MY MEMORIES.
SALLY.
THIS OTHER TIME LINE. WITH AMANDA AND HER FASCINATING DISEASE, AND THIS DREADFUL COLONEL.
WAIT.
SOMETHING'S WRONG. I CAN'T FEEL HER, SUDDENLY, I CAN ALWAYS FEEL HER...
WHERE'S BERNICE? WHERE'S MY CAT?

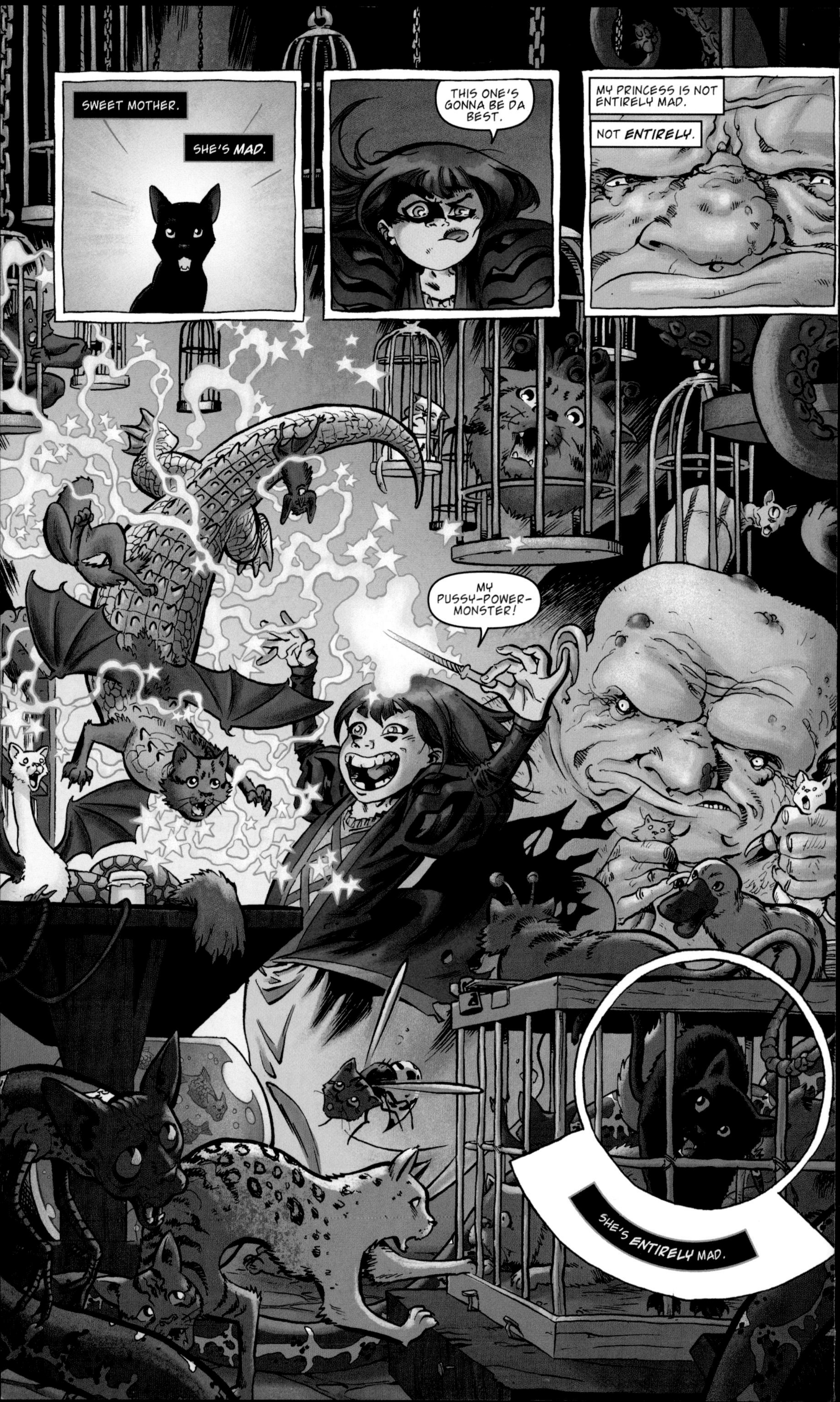
SWEET MOTHER.
SHE'S MAD.
THIS ONE'S GONNA BE DA BEST.
MY PRINCESS IS NOT ENTIRELY MAD.
NOT ENTIRELY.
MY PUSSY-POWER-MONSTER!
SHE'S ENTIRELY MAD.

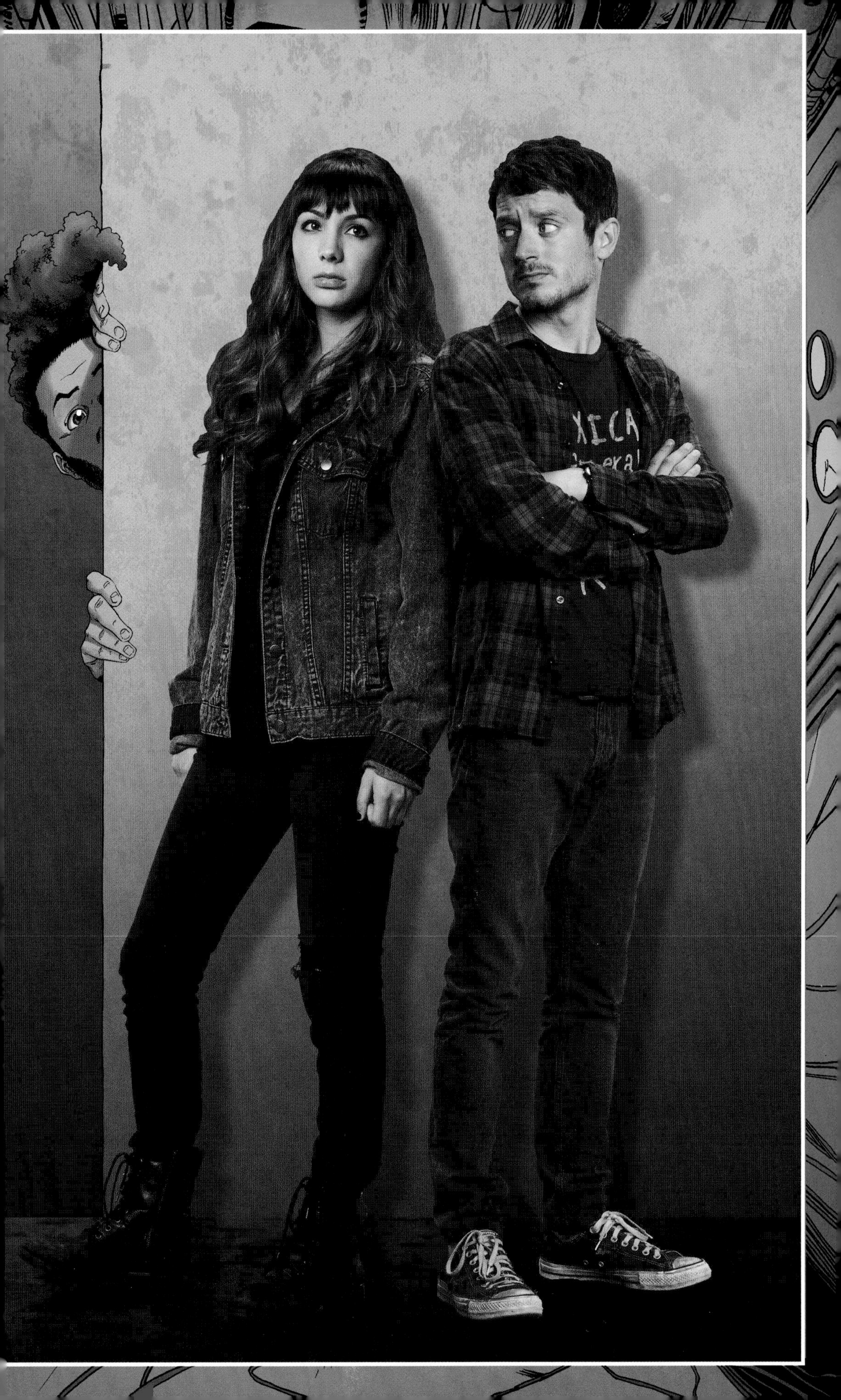

"ALBATROSS"

Written by **Arvind Ethan David** · Art by **Dani Strips**
Colors by **Charlie Kirchoff**

Letters by **Shawn Lee** · Edits by **Denton J. Tipton** · Publisher **Ted Adams** · Executive Producer **Max Landis**

SQUARK!

STUPID BIRD.

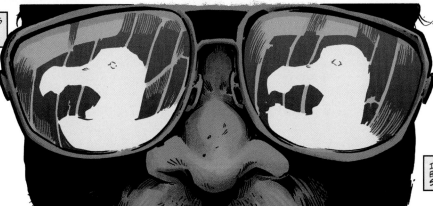

MY NAME IS GORDON RIMMER.

I USED TO BE A ROCK STAR.

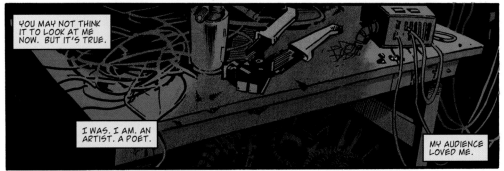

YOU MAY NOT THINK IT TO LOOK AT ME NOW. BUT IT'S TRUE.

I WAS. I AM. AN ARTIST. A POET.

MY AUDIENCE LOVED ME.

NOW THEY'VE GOT ME HERE IN THIS "FACILITY," WHERE MY ONLY ART IS DESTRUCTION, AND MY ONLY AUDIENCE ARE DUMB ANIMALS.

HEH. MAYBE NO CHANGE THERE.

RAINEY SAYS I'M MORE "USEFUL" HERE.

I'LL SHOW THAT BITCH USEFUL.

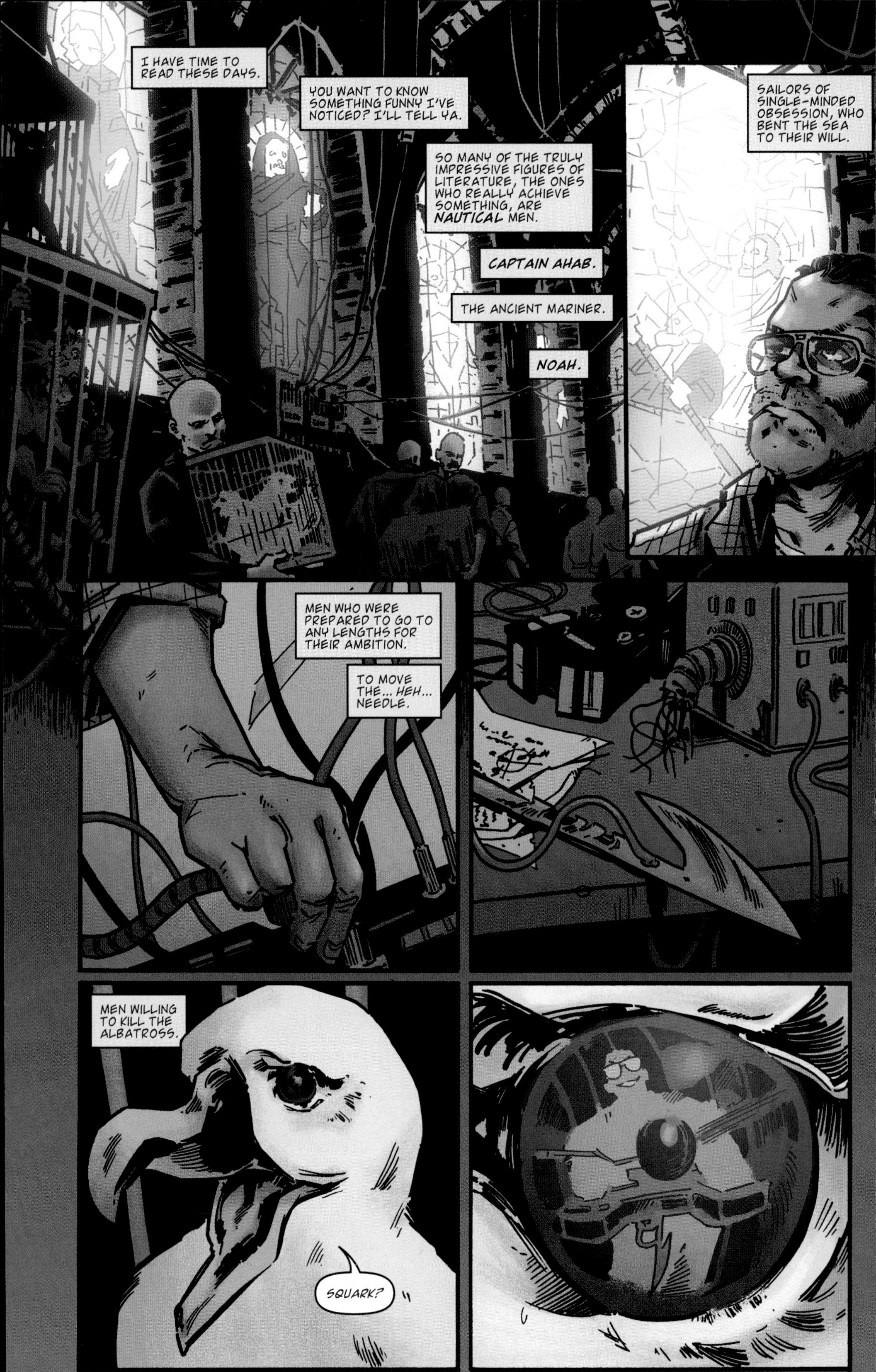

I HAVE TIME TO READ THESE DAYS.
YOU WANT TO KNOW SOMETHING FUNNY I'VE NOTICED? I'LL TELL YA.
SO MANY OF THE TRULY IMPRESSIVE FIGURES OF LITERATURE, THE ONES WHO REALLY ACHIEVE SOMETHING, ARE NAUTICAL MEN.
CAPTAIN AHAB.
THE ANCIENT MARINER.
NOAH.
SAILORS OF SINGLE-MINDED OBSESSION, WHO BENT THE SEA TO THEIR WILL.
MEN WHO WERE PREPARED TO GO TO ANY LENGTHS FOR THEIR AMBITION.
TO MOVE THE... HEH... NEEDLE.
MEN WILLING TO KILL THE ALBATROSS.
SQUARK?

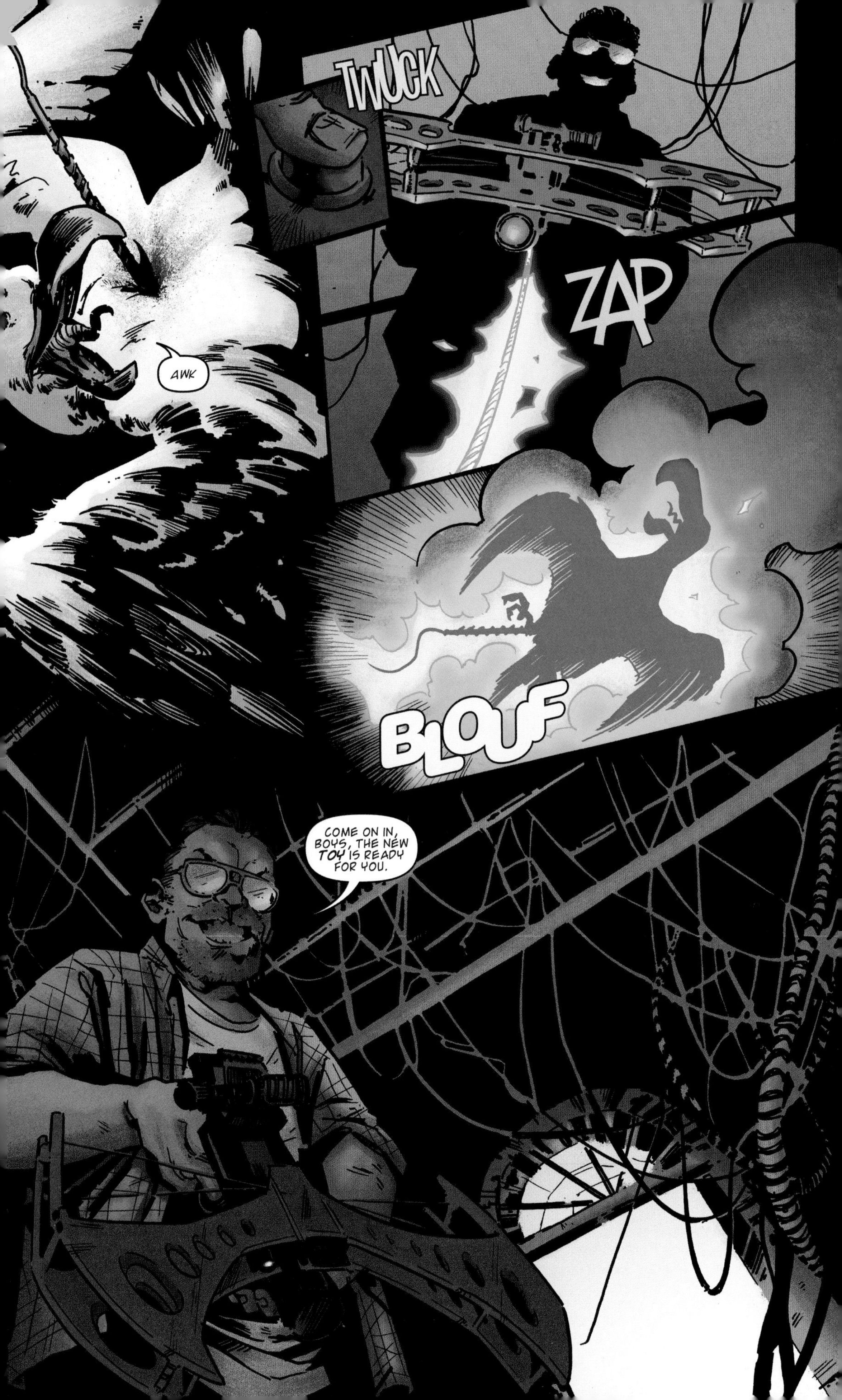
TWUCK
AWK
ZAP
BLOUF
COME ON IN, BOYS, THE NEW TOY IS READY FOR YOU.

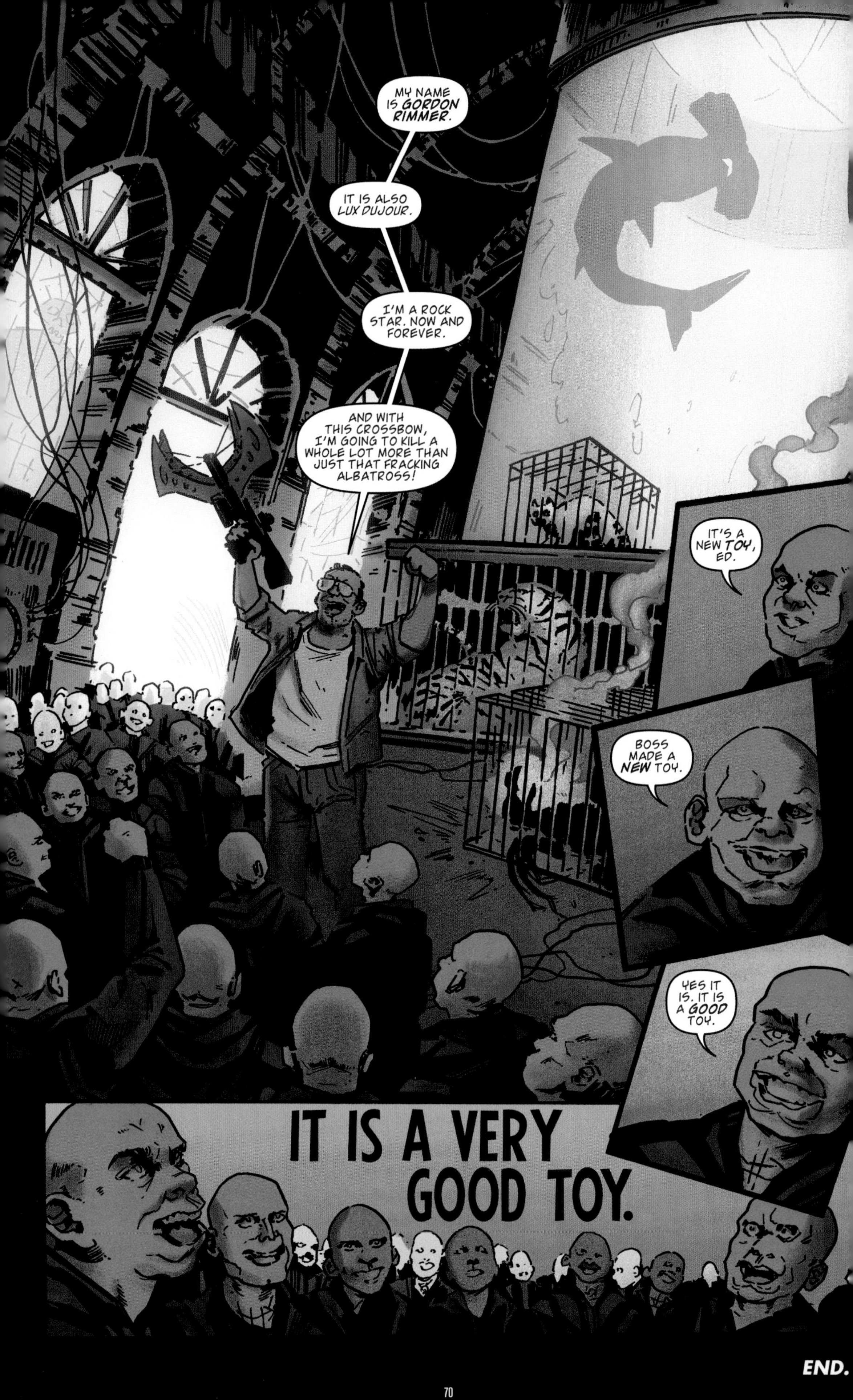

MY NAME IS GORDON RIMMER.
IT IS ALSO LUX DUJOUR.
I'M A ROCK STAR. NOW AND FOREVER.
AND WITH THIS CROSSBOW, I'M GOING TO KILL A WHOLE LOT MORE THAN JUST THAT FRACKING ALBATROSS!
IT'S A NEW TOY, ED.
BOSS MADE A NEW TOY.
YES IT IS. IT IS A GOOD TOY.
IT IS A VERY GOOD TOY.
END.

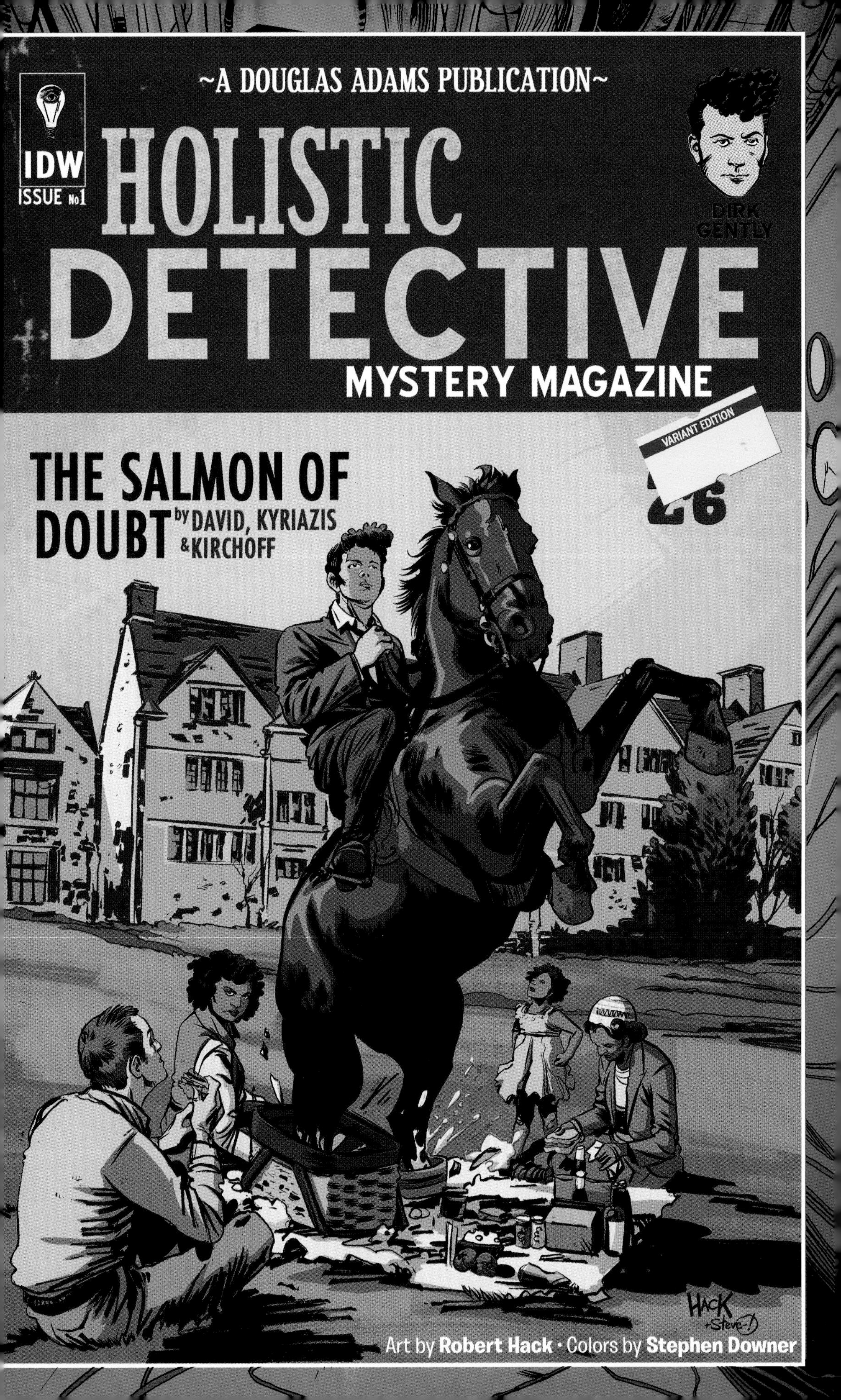

~A DOUGLAS ADAMS PUBLICATION~
IDW
ISSUE No1
HOLISTIC
DETECTIVE
MYSTERY MAGAZINE
DIRK GENTLY
VARIANT EDITION
26
THE SALMON OF DOUBT by DAVID, KYRIAZIS & KIRCHOFF
HACK +Steve-!
Art by Robert Hack · Colors by Stephen Downer

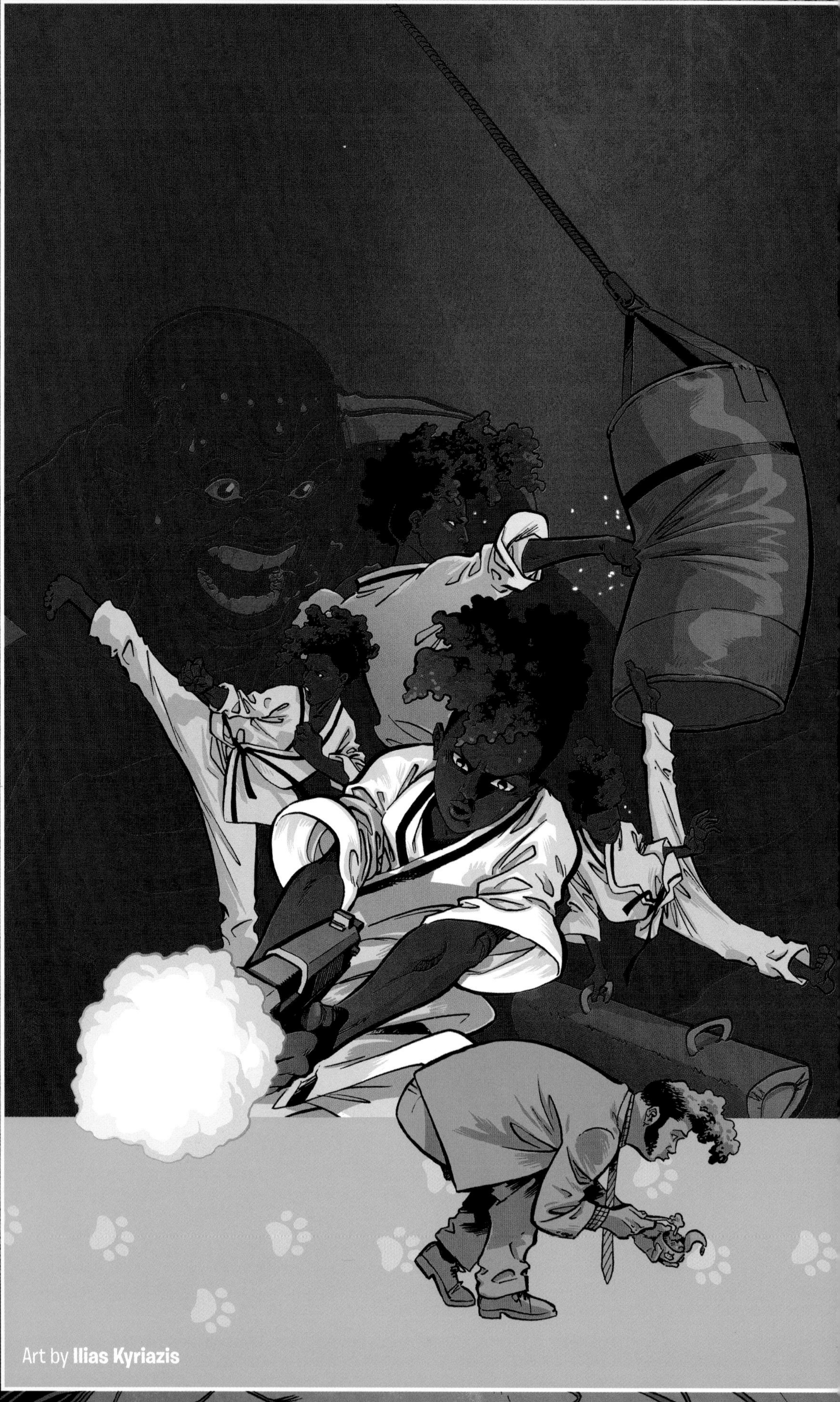

Art by **Ilias Kyriazis**

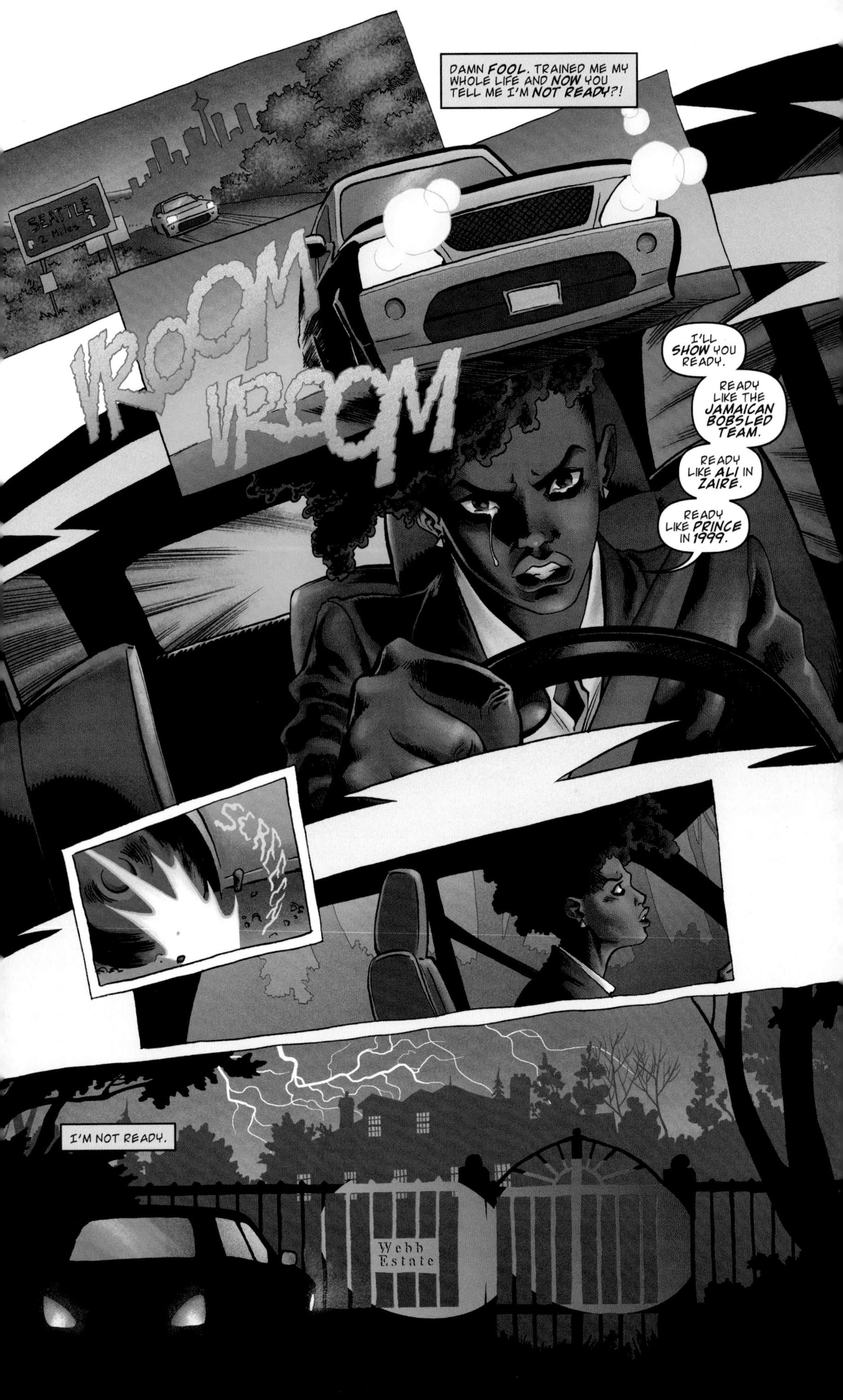
DAMN FOOL. TRAINED ME MY WHOLE LIFE AND NOW YOU TELL ME I'M NOT READY?!
SEATTLE
2 Miles
VROOM VROOM
I'LL SHOW YOU READY.
READY LIKE THE JAMAICAN BOBSLED TEAM.
READY LIKE ALI IN ZAIRE.
READY LIKE PRINCE IN 1999.
SCREECH
I'M NOT READY.
Webb Estate

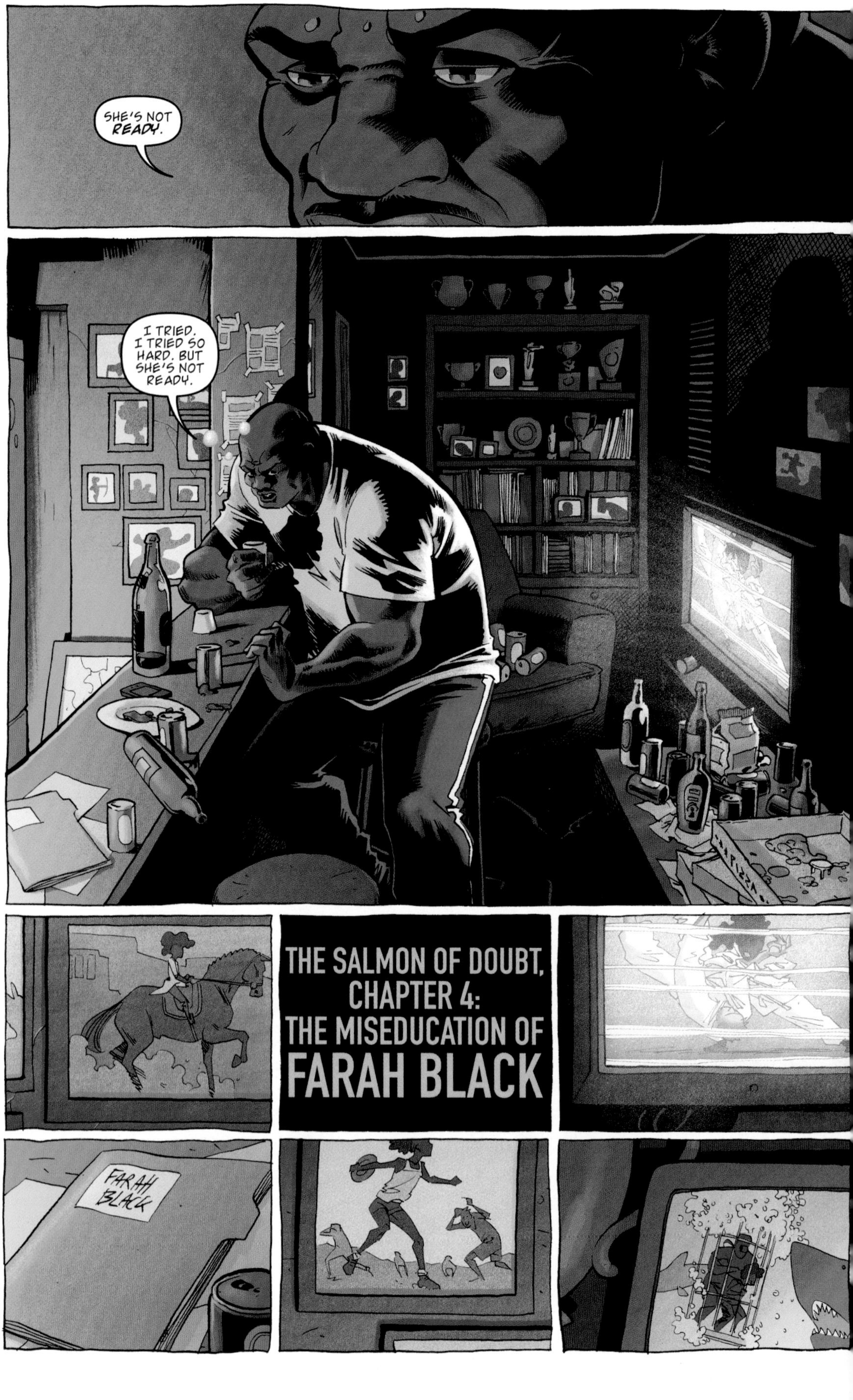
SHE'S NOT READY.
I TRIED. I TRIED SO HARD. BUT SHE'S NOT READY.
THE SALMON OF DOUBT, CHAPTER 4: THE MISEDUCATION OF FARAH BLACK
FARAH BLACK

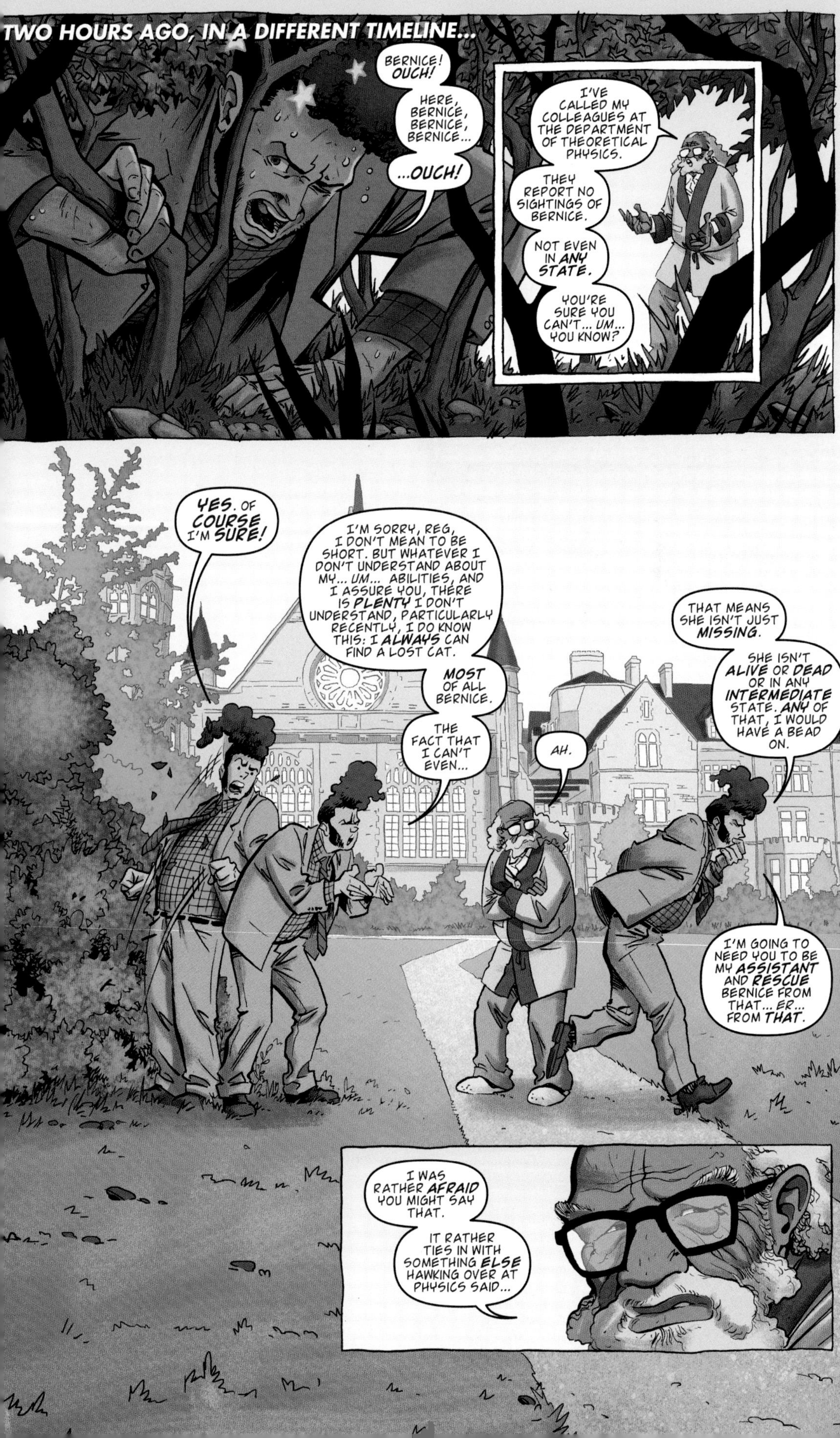

TWO HOURS AGO, IN A DIFFERENT TIMELINE...
BERNICE! OUCH!
HERE, BERNICE, BERNICE, BERNICE...
...OUCH!
I'VE CALLED MY COLLEAGUES AT THE DEPARTMENT OF THEORETICAL PHYSICS.
THEY REPORT NO SIGHTINGS OF BERNICE.
NOT EVEN IN ANY STATE.
YOU'RE SURE YOU CAN'T... UM... YOU KNOW?
YES. OF COURSE I'M SURE!
I'M SORRY, REG, I DON'T MEAN TO BE SHORT. BUT WHATEVER I DON'T UNDERSTAND ABOUT MY... UM... ABILITIES, AND I ASSURE YOU, THERE IS PLENTY I DON'T UNDERSTAND, PARTICULARLY RECENTLY, I DO KNOW THIS: I ALWAYS CAN FIND A LOST CAT.
MOST OF ALL BERNICE.
THE FACT THAT I CAN'T EVEN...
AH.
THAT MEANS SHE ISN'T JUST MISSING.
SHE ISN'T ALIVE OR DEAD OR IN ANY INTERMEDIATE STATE. ANY OF THAT, I WOULD HAVE A BEAD ON.
I'M GOING TO NEED YOU TO BE MY ASSISTANT AND RESCUE BERNICE FROM THAT... ER... FROM THAT.
I WAS RATHER AFRAID YOU MIGHT SAY THAT.
IT RATHER TIES IN WITH SOMETHING ELSE HAWKING OVER AT PHYSICS SAID...

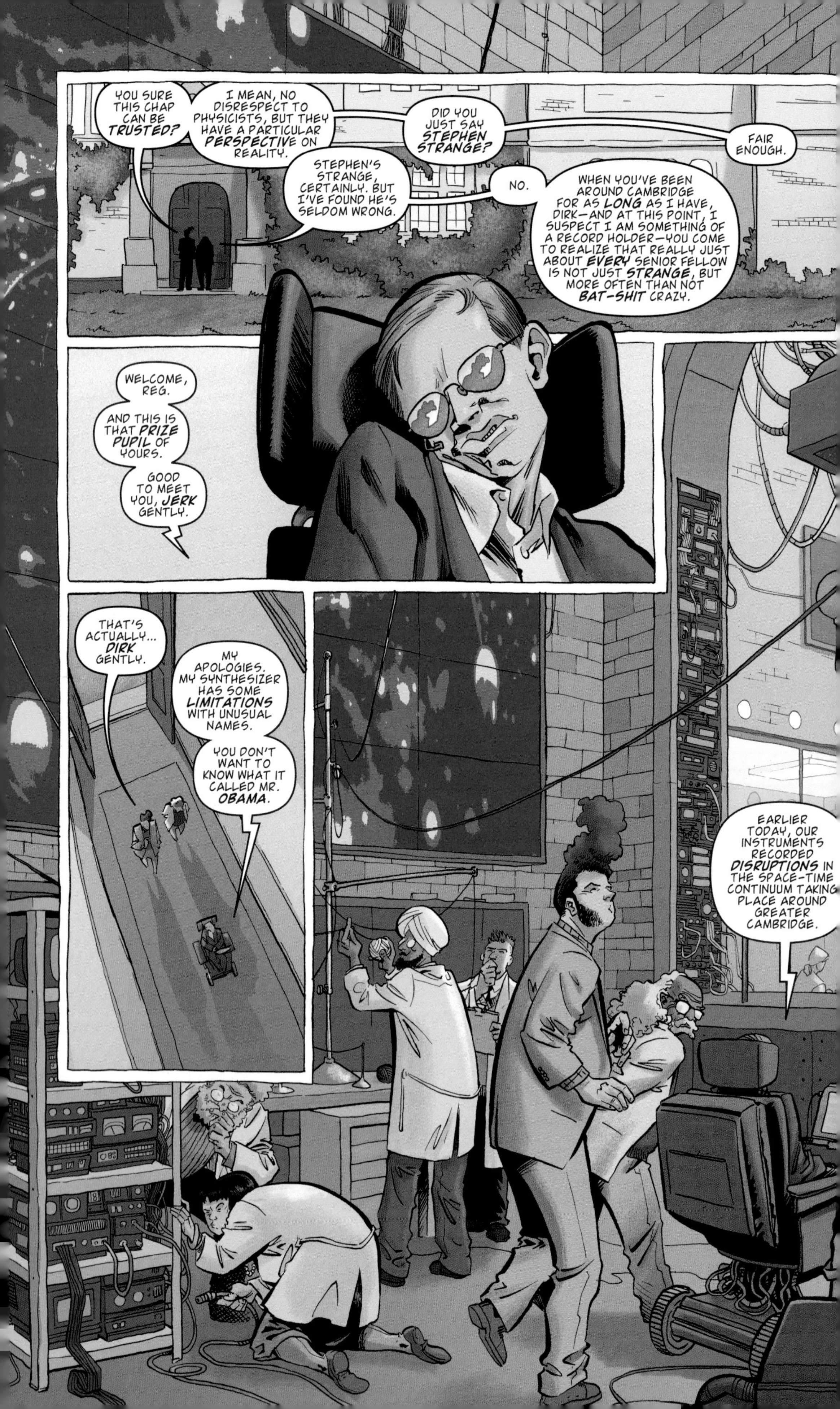

YOU SURE THIS CHAP CAN BE TRUSTED?
I MEAN, NO DISRESPECT TO PHYSICISTS, BUT THEY HAVE A PARTICULAR PERSPECTIVE ON REALITY.
STEPHEN'S STRANGE, CERTAINLY. BUT I'VE FOUND HE'S SELDOM WRONG.
DID YOU JUST SAY STEPHEN STRANGE?
NO.
FAIR ENOUGH.
WHEN YOU'VE BEEN AROUND CAMBRIDGE FOR AS LONG AS I HAVE, DIRK—AND AT THIS POINT, I SUSPECT I AM SOMETHING OF A RECORD HOLDER—YOU COME TO REALIZE THAT REALLY JUST ABOUT EVERY SENIOR FELLOW IS NOT JUST STRANGE, BUT MORE OFTEN THAN NOT BAT-SHIT CRAZY.
WELCOME, REG.
AND THIS IS THAT PRIZE PUPIL OF YOURS.
GOOD TO MEET YOU, JERK GENTLY.
THAT'S ACTUALLY... DIRK GENTLY.
MY APOLOGIES. MY SYNTHESIZER HAS SOME LIMITATIONS WITH UNUSUAL NAMES.
YOU DON'T WANT TO KNOW WHAT IT CALLED MR. OBAMA.
EARLIER TODAY, OUR INSTRUMENTS RECORDED DISRUPTIONS IN THE SPACE-TIME CONTINUUM TAKING PLACE AROUND GREATER CAMBRIDGE.

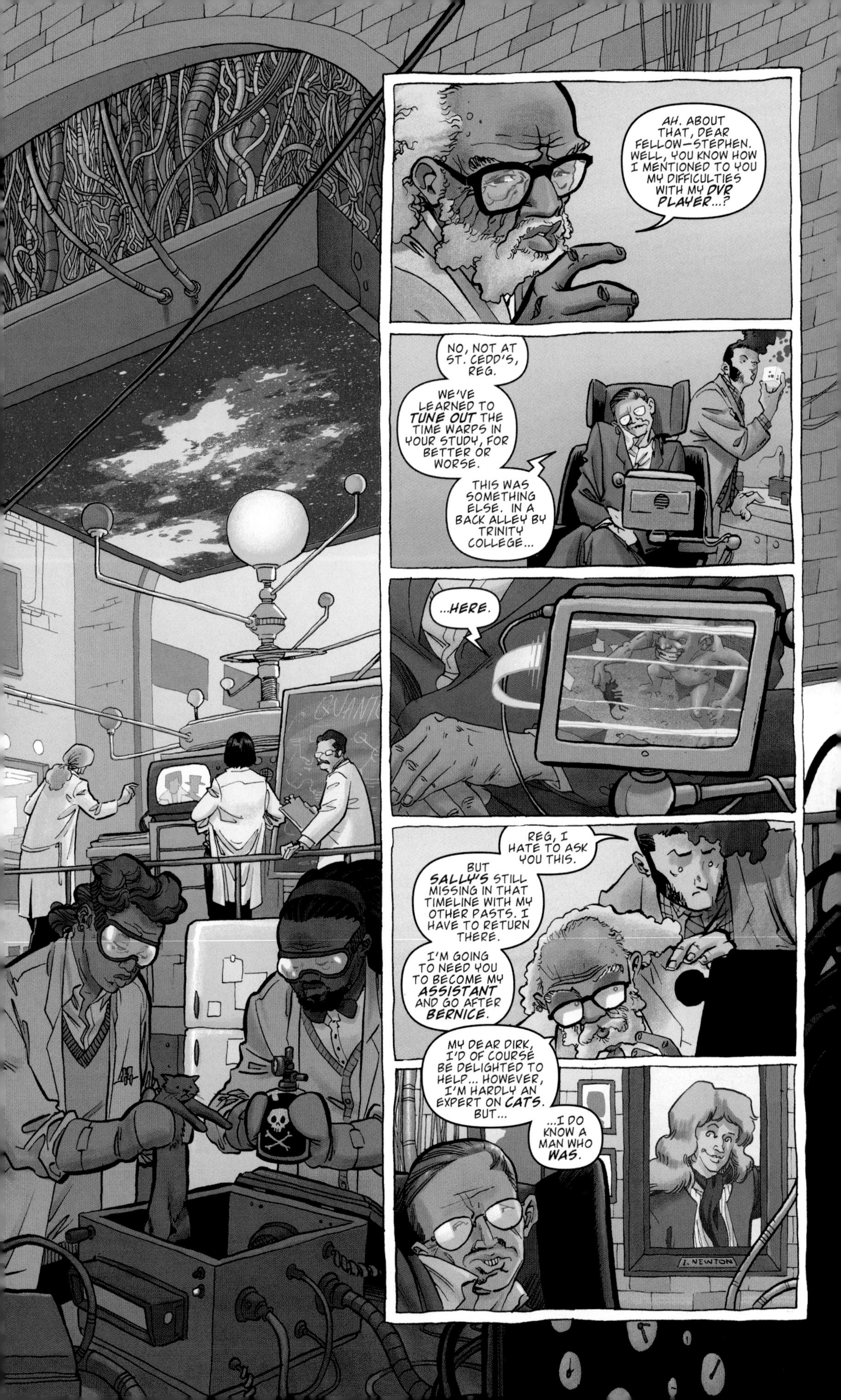

AH. ABOUT THAT, DEAR FELLOW—STEPHEN. WELL, YOU KNOW HOW I MENTIONED TO YOU MY DIFFICULTIES WITH MY *DVR PLAYER*...?
NO, NOT AT ST. CEDD'S, REG.
WE'VE LEARNED TO *TUNE OUT* THE TIME WARPS IN YOUR STUDY, FOR BETTER OR WORSE.
THIS WAS SOMETHING ELSE. IN A BACK ALLEY BY TRINITY COLLEGE...
...*HERE*.
REG, I HATE TO ASK YOU THIS.
BUT *SALLY'S* STILL MISSING IN THAT TIMELINE WITH MY OTHER PASTS. I HAVE TO RETURN THERE.
I'M GOING TO NEED YOU TO BECOME MY *ASSISTANT* AND GO AFTER *BERNICE*.
MY DEAR DIRK, I'D OF COURSE BE DELIGHTED TO HELP... HOWEVER, I'M HARDLY AN EXPERT ON *CATS*. BUT...
...I DO KNOW A MAN WHO *WAS*.
I. NEWTON

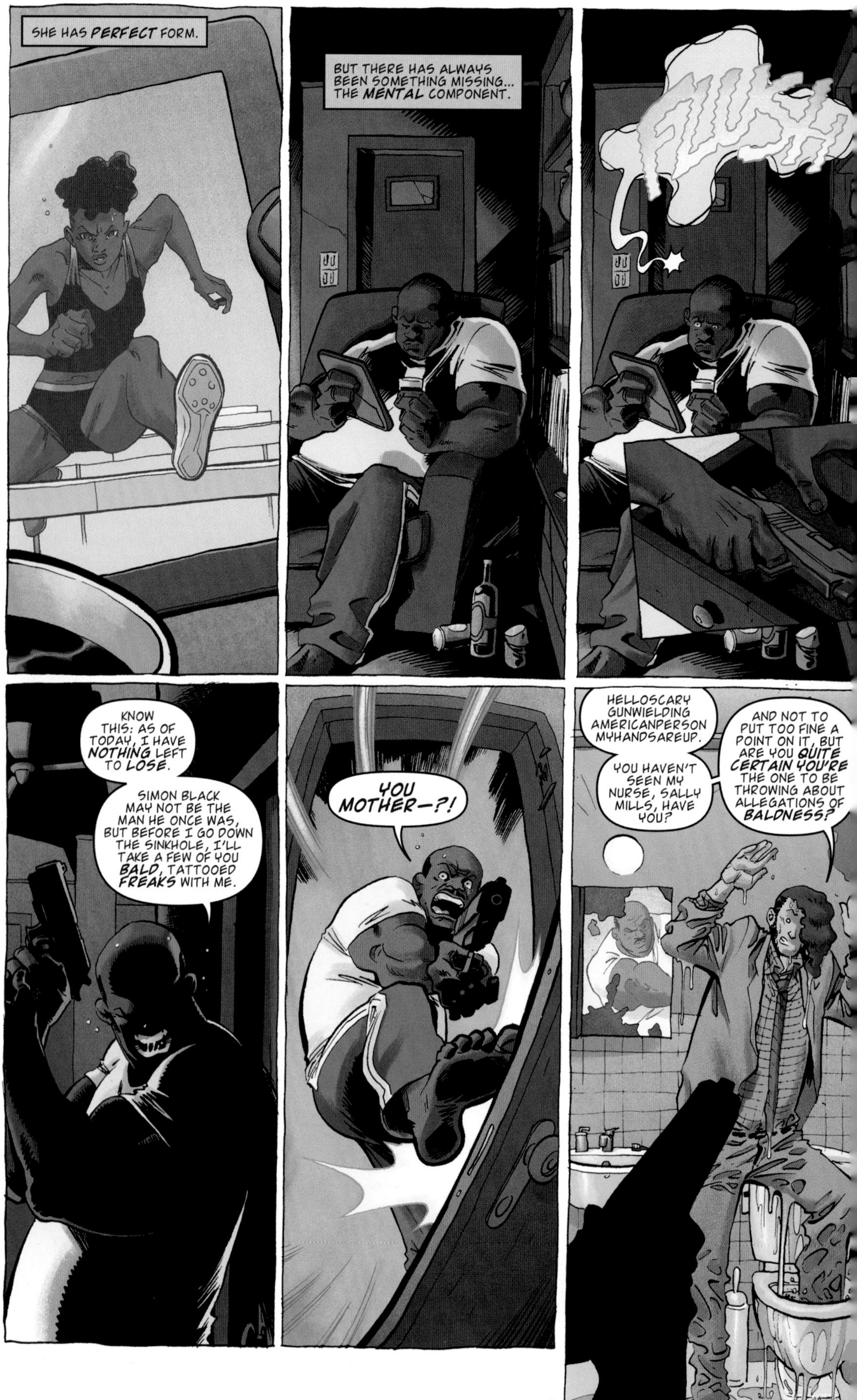

SHE HAS PERFECT FORM.
BUT THERE HAS ALWAYS BEEN SOMETHING MISSING... THE MENTAL COMPONENT.
FLUSH!
KNOW THIS: AS OF TODAY, I HAVE NOTHING LEFT TO LOSE.
SIMON BLACK MAY NOT BE THE MAN HE ONCE WAS, BUT BEFORE I GO DOWN THE SINKHOLE, I'LL TAKE A FEW OF YOU BALD, TATTOOED FREAKS WITH ME.
YOU MOTHER—?!
HELLOSCARY GUNWIELDING AMERICANPERSON MYHANDSAREUP.
YOU HAVEN'T SEEN MY NURSE, SALLY MILLS, HAVE YOU?
AND NOT TO PUT TOO FINE A POINT ON IT, BUT ARE YOU QUITE CERTAIN YOU'RE THE ONE TO BE THROWING ABOUT ALLEGATIONS OF BALDNESS?

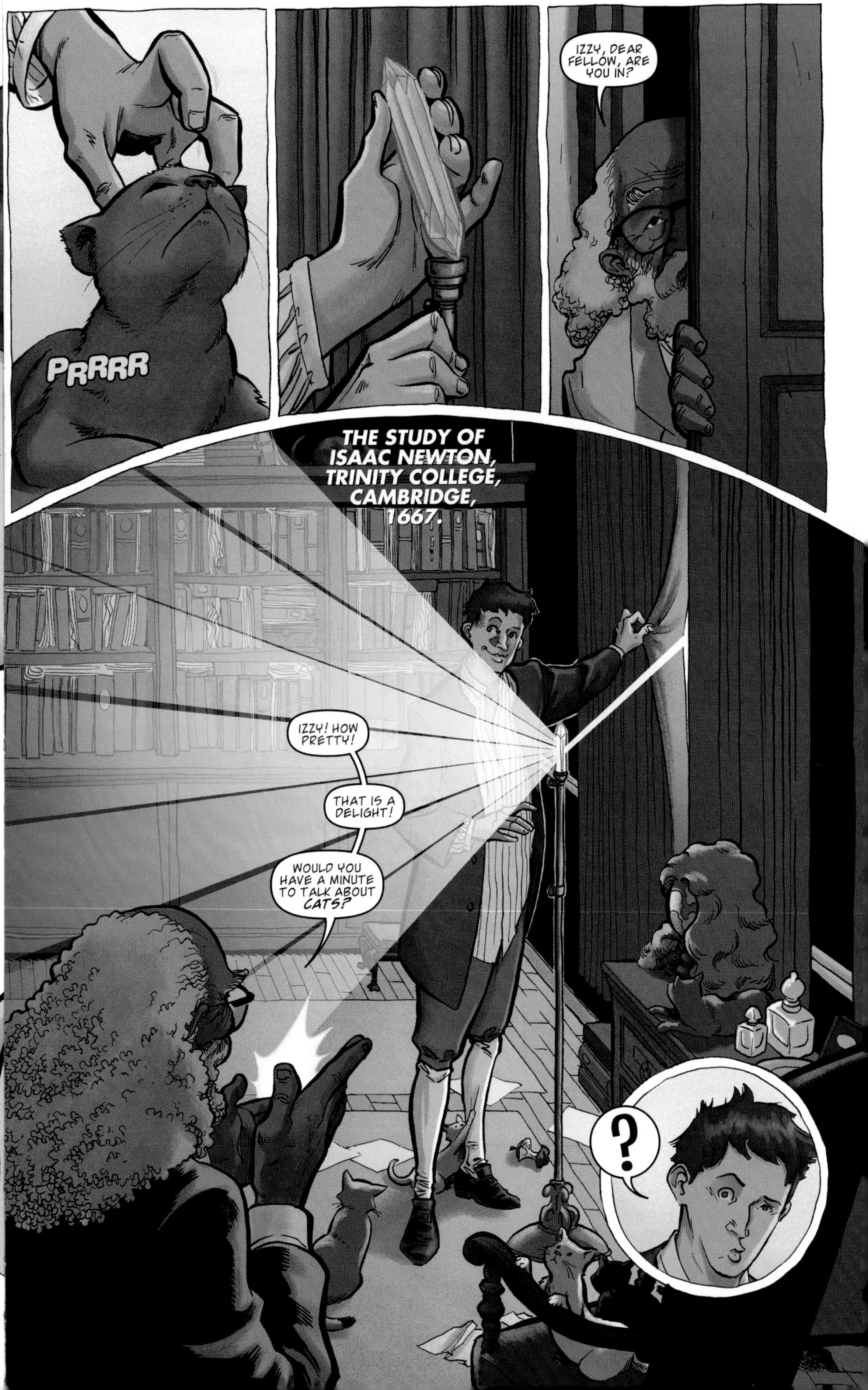
PRRRR
IZZY, DEAR FELLOW, ARE YOU IN?
THE STUDY OF ISAAC NEWTON, TRINITY COLLEGE, CAMBRIDGE, 1667.
IZZY! HOW PRETTY!
THAT IS A DELIGHT!
WOULD YOU HAVE A MINUTE TO TALK ABOUT CATS?
?

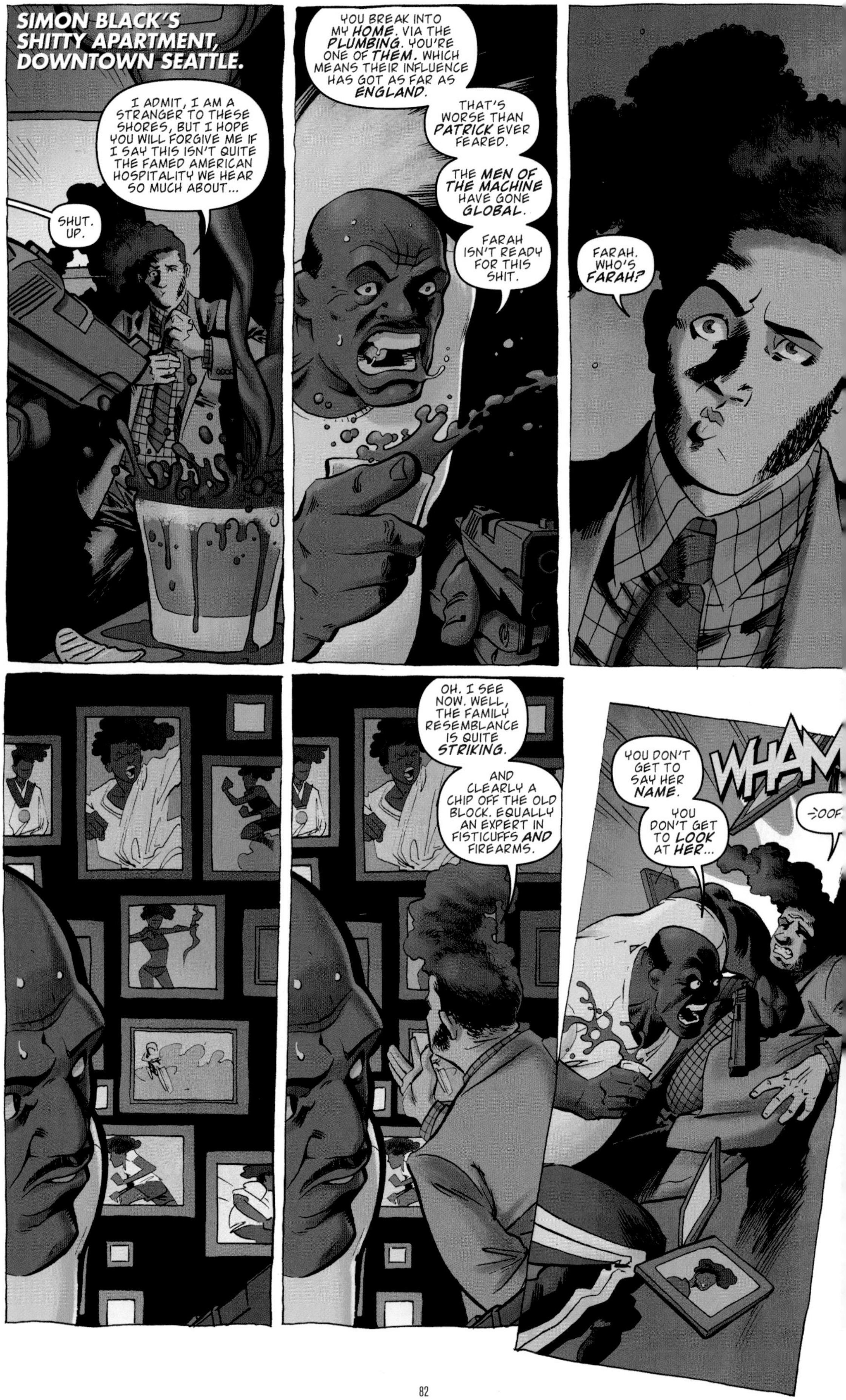
SIMON BLACK'S SHITTY APARTMENT, DOWNTOWN SEATTLE.
I ADMIT, I AM A STRANGER TO THESE SHORES, BUT I HOPE YOU WILL FORGIVE ME IF I SAY THIS ISN'T QUITE THE FAMED AMERICAN HOSPITALITY WE HEAR SO MUCH ABOUT...
SHUT. UP.
YOU BREAK INTO MY HOME. VIA THE PLUMBING. YOU'RE ONE OF THEM. WHICH MEANS THEIR INFLUENCE HAS GOT AS FAR AS ENGLAND.
THAT'S WORSE THAN PATRICK EVER FEARED.
THE MEN OF THE MACHINE HAVE GONE GLOBAL.
FARAH ISN'T READY FOR THIS SHIT.
FARAH. WHO'S FARAH?
OH. I SEE NOW. WELL, THE FAMILY RESEMBLANCE IS QUITE STRIKING.
AND CLEARLY A CHIP OFF THE OLD BLOCK. EQUALLY AN EXPERT IN FISTICUFFS AND FIREARMS.
YOU DON'T GET TO SAY HER NAME.
YOU DON'T GET TO LOOK AT HER...
WHAM
OOF

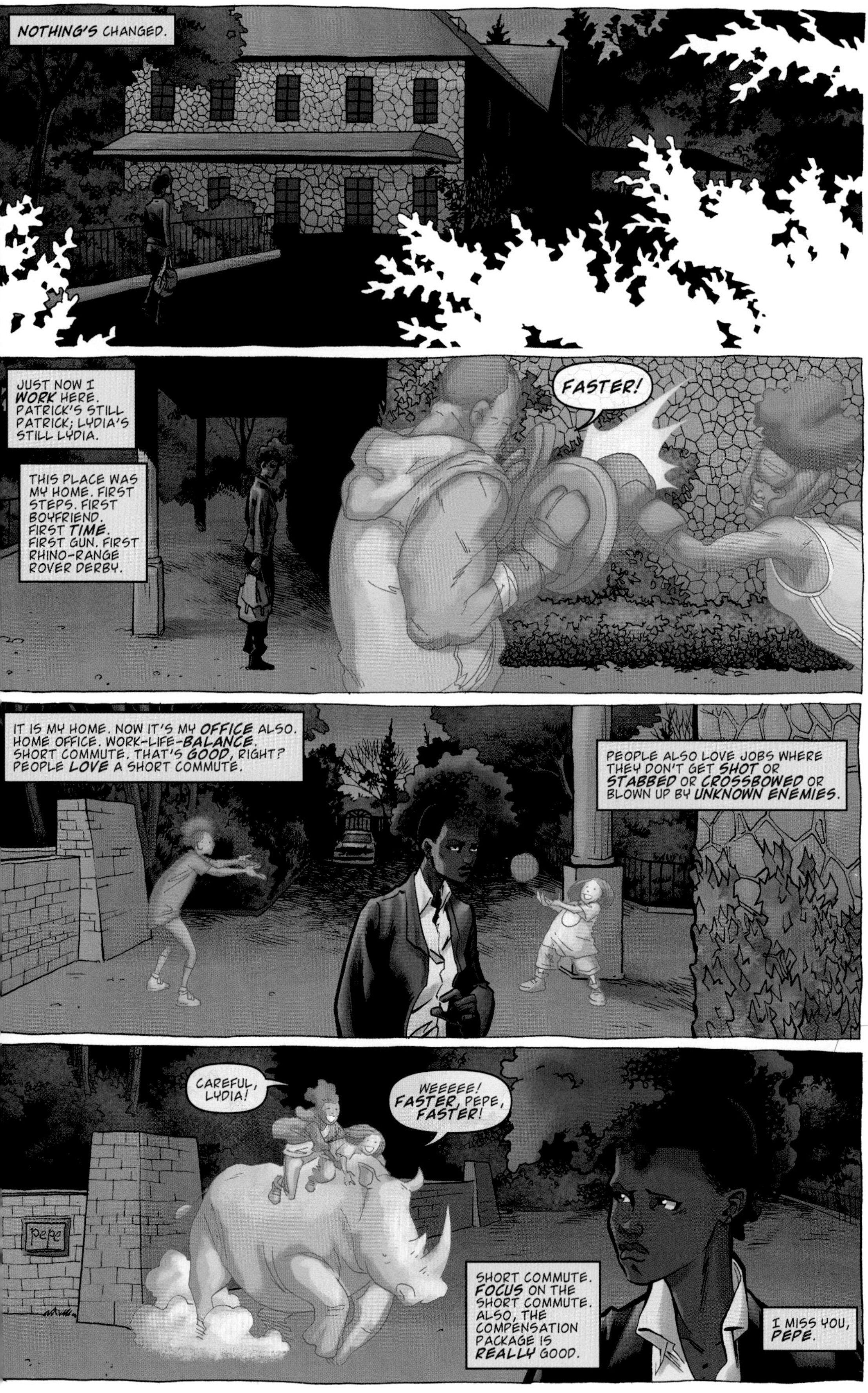
NOTHING'S CHANGED.
JUST NOW I WORK HERE. PATRICK'S STILL PATRICK; LYDIA'S STILL LYDIA.
THIS PLACE WAS MY HOME. FIRST STEPS. FIRST BOYFRIEND. FIRST TIME. FIRST GUN. FIRST RHINO-RANGE ROVER DERBY.
FASTER!
IT IS MY HOME. NOW IT'S MY OFFICE ALSO. HOME OFFICE. WORK-LIFE-BALANCE. SHORT COMMUTE. THAT'S GOOD, RIGHT? PEOPLE LOVE A SHORT COMMUTE.
PEOPLE ALSO LOVE JOBS WHERE THEY DON'T GET SHOT OR STABBED OR CROSSBOWED OR BLOWN UP BY UNKNOWN ENEMIES.
CAREFUL, LYDIA!
WEEEEE! FASTER, PEPE, FASTER!
pepe
SHORT COMMUTE. FOCUS ON THE SHORT COMMUTE. ALSO, THE COMPENSATION PACKAGE IS REALLY GOOD.
I MISS YOU, PEPE.

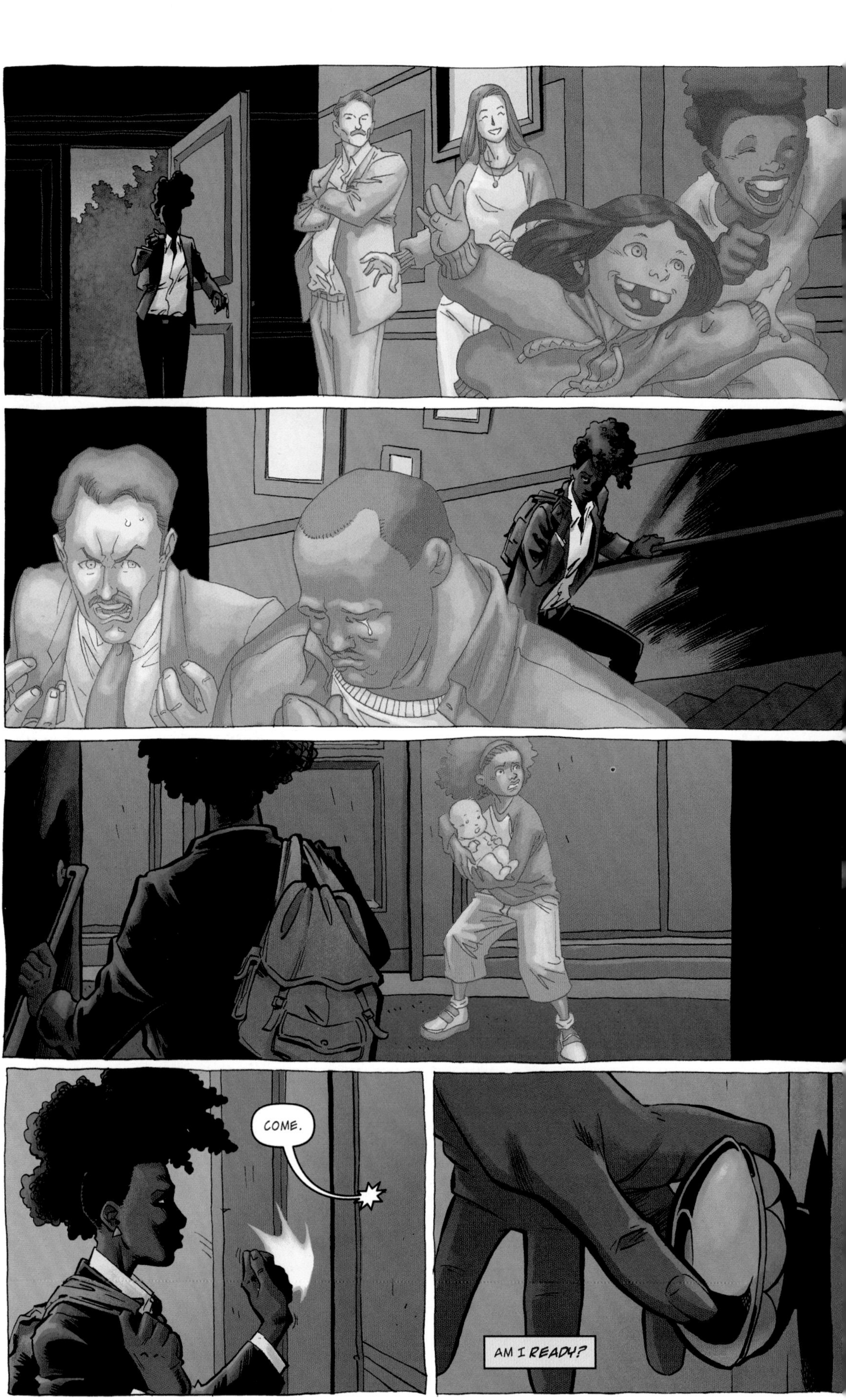
COME.
AM I READY?

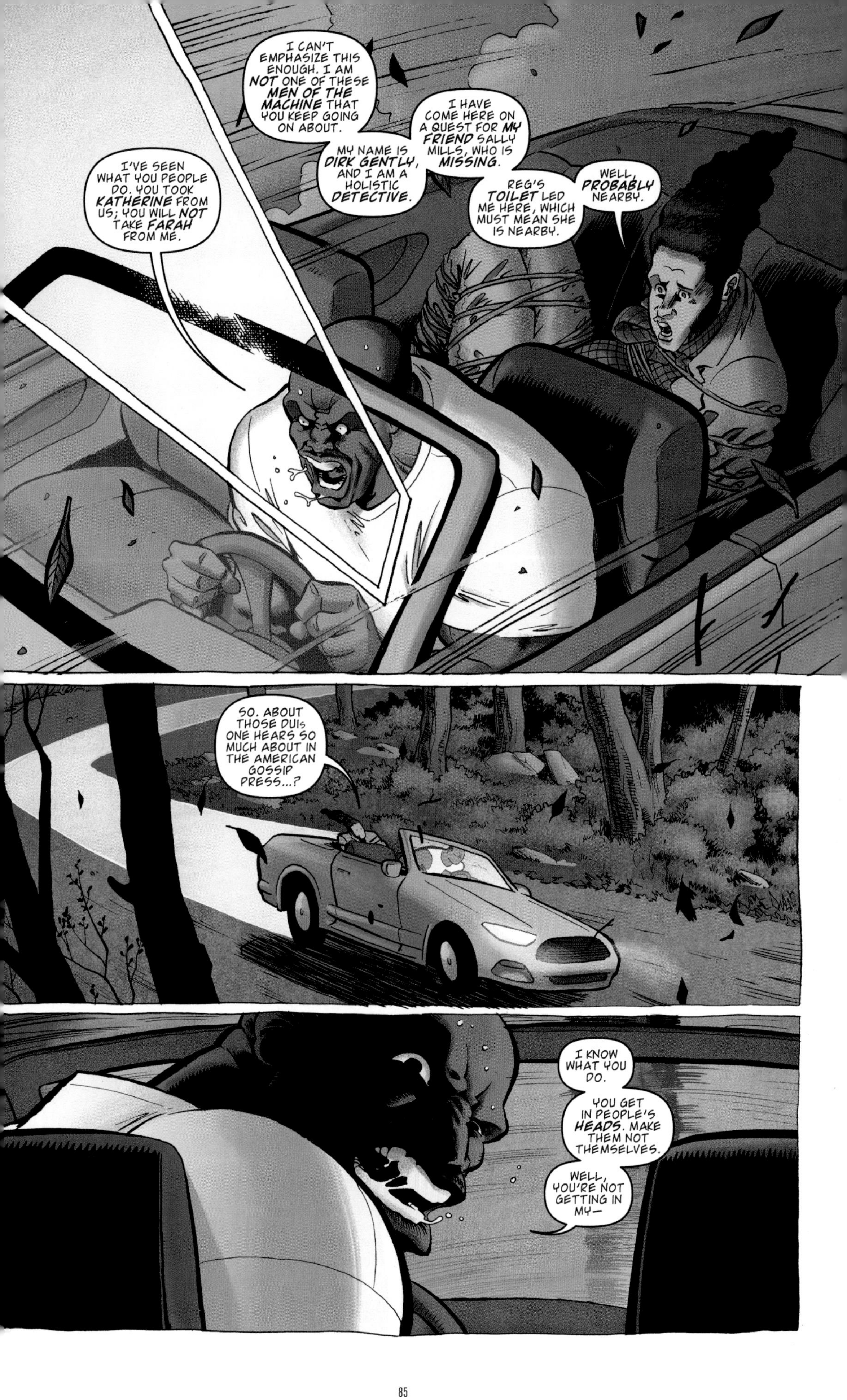
I CAN'T EMPHASIZE THIS ENOUGH. I AM NOT ONE OF THESE MEN OF THE MACHINE THAT YOU KEEP GOING ON ABOUT.
MY NAME IS DIRK GENTLY, AND I AM A HOLISTIC DETECTIVE.
I HAVE COME HERE ON A QUEST FOR MY FRIEND SALLY MILLS, WHO IS MISSING.
REG'S TOILET LED ME HERE, WHICH MUST MEAN SHE IS NEARBY.
WELL, PROBABLY NEARBY.
I'VE SEEN WHAT YOU PEOPLE DO. YOU TOOK KATHERINE FROM US; YOU WILL NOT TAKE FARAH FROM ME.
SO. ABOUT THOSE DUIs ONE HEARS SO MUCH ABOUT IN THE AMERICAN GOSSIP PRESS...?
I KNOW WHAT YOU DO.
YOU GET IN PEOPLE'S HEADS. MAKE THEM NOT THEMSELVES.
WELL, YOU'RE NOT GETTING IN MY—

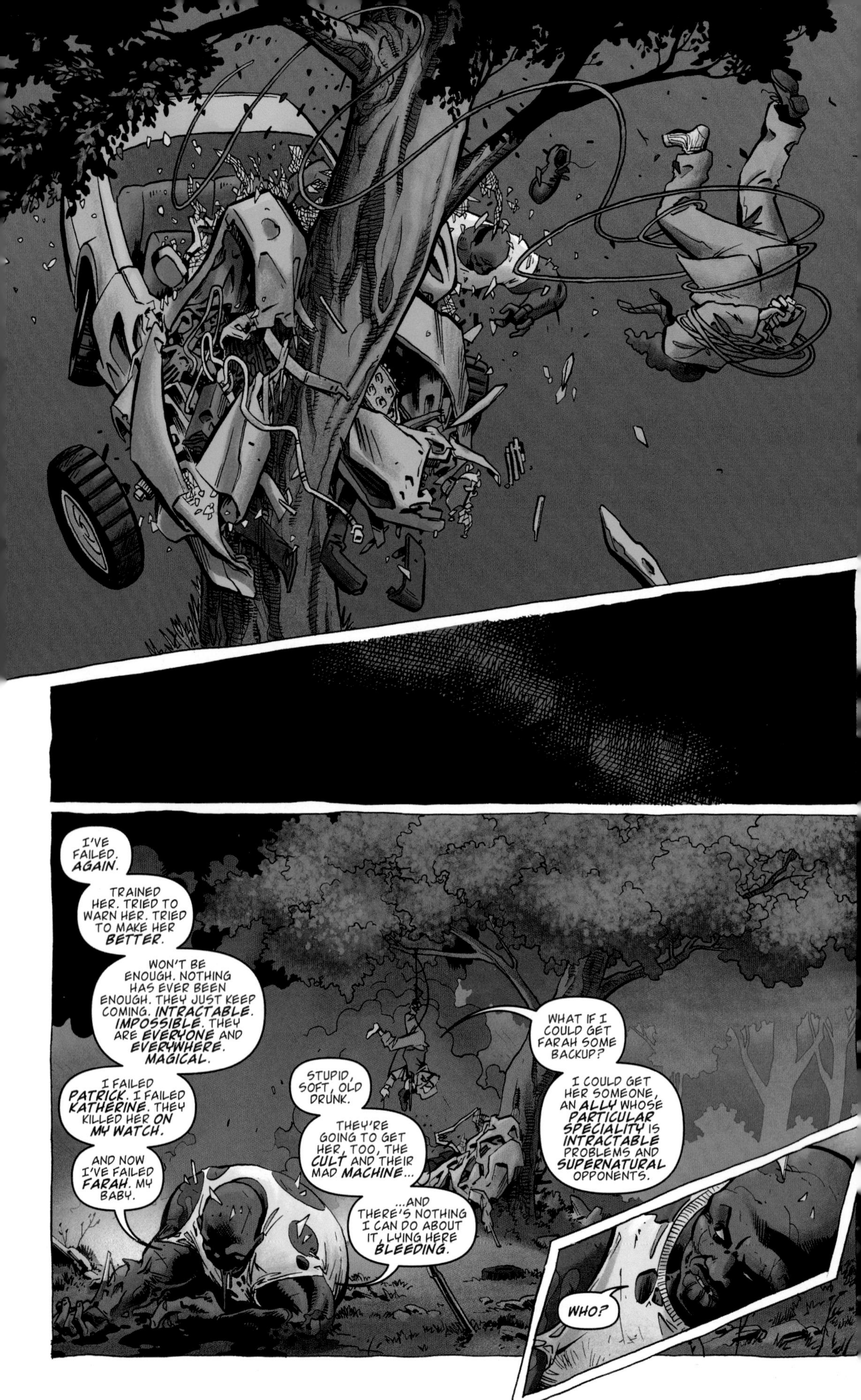

I'VE FAILED. AGAIN.
TRAINED HER. TRIED TO WARN HER. TRIED TO MAKE HER BETTER.
WON'T BE ENOUGH. NOTHING HAS EVER BEEN ENOUGH. THEY JUST KEEP COMING. INTRACTABLE. IMPOSSIBLE. THEY ARE EVERYONE AND EVERYWHERE. MAGICAL.
I FAILED PATRICK. I FAILED KATHERINE. THEY KILLED HER ON MY WATCH.
AND NOW I'VE FAILED FARAH. MY BABY.
STUPID, SOFT, OLD DRUNK.
THEY'RE GOING TO GET HER, TOO, THE CULT AND THEIR MAD MACHINE...
...AND THERE'S NOTHING I CAN DO ABOUT IT, LYING HERE BLEEDING.
WHAT IF I COULD GET FARAH SOME BACKUP?
I COULD GET HER SOMEONE, AN ALLY WHOSE PARTICULAR SPECIALITY IS INTRACTABLE PROBLEMS AND SUPERNATURAL OPPONENTS.
WHO?

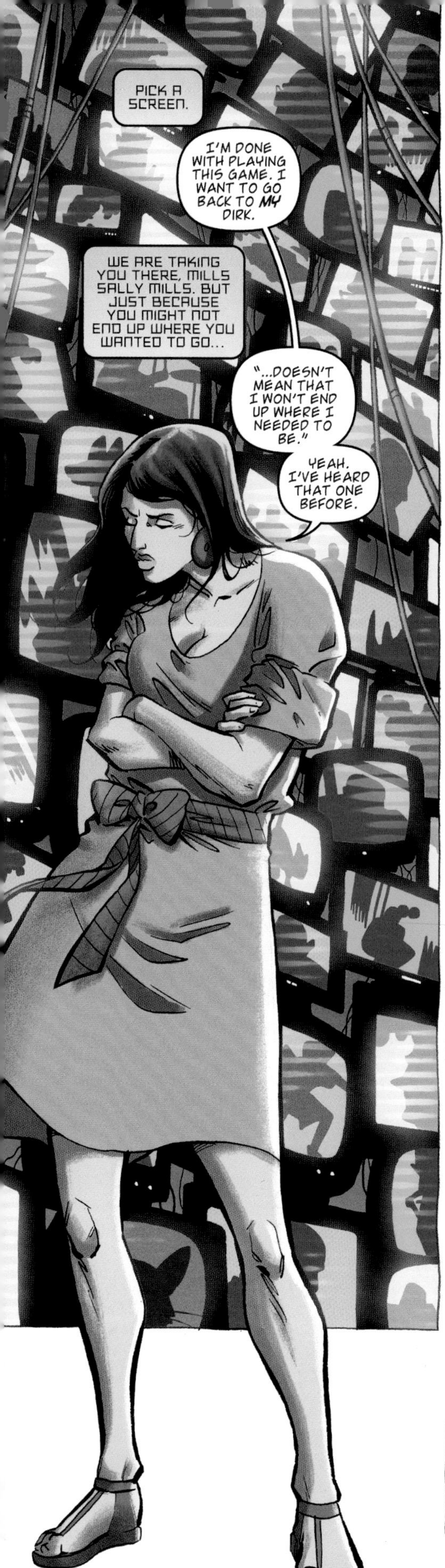
PICK A SCREEN.
I'M DONE WITH PLAYING THIS GAME. I WANT TO GO BACK TO MY DIRK.
WE ARE TAKING YOU THERE, MILLS SALLY MILLS. BUT JUST BECAUSE YOU MIGHT NOT END UP WHERE YOU WANTED TO GO...
"...DOESN'T MEAN THAT I WON'T END UP WHERE I NEEDED TO BE."
YEAH. I'VE HEARD THAT ONE BEFORE.

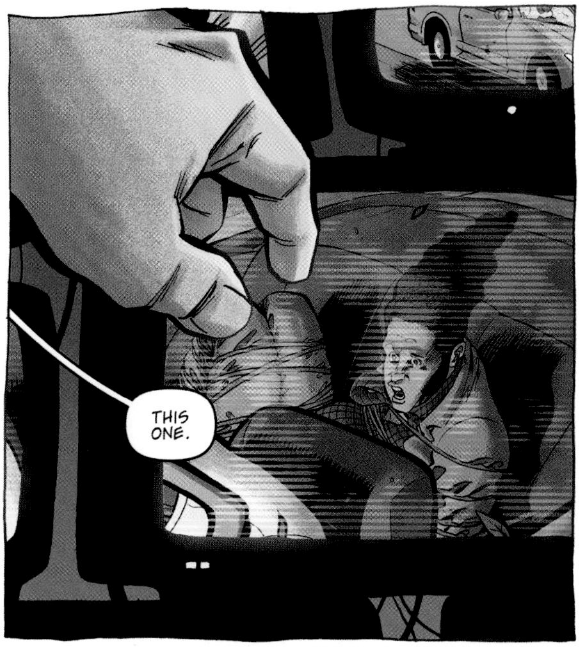
THIS ONE.

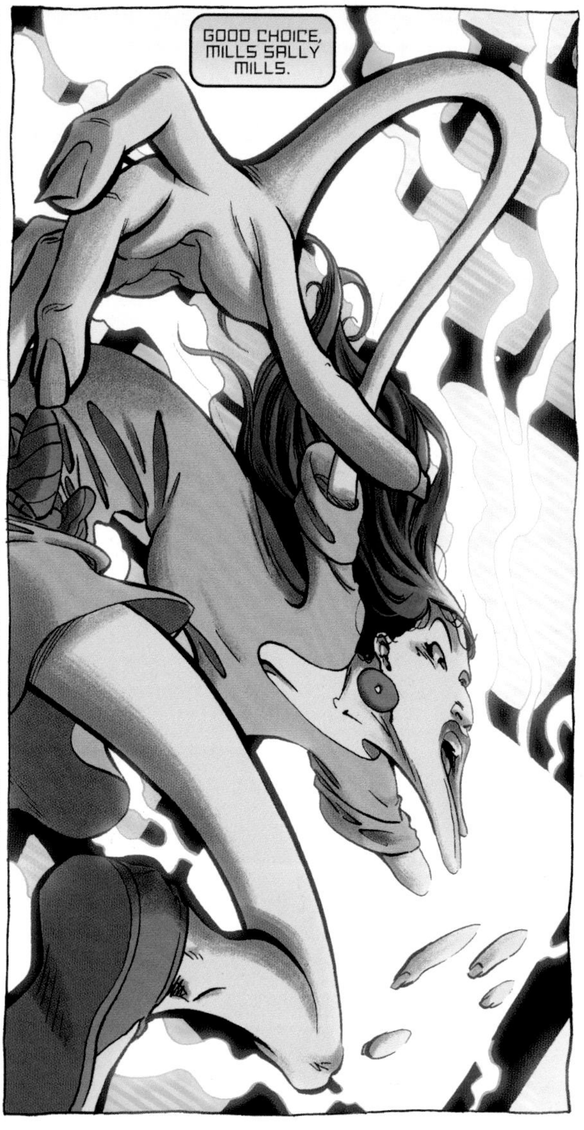
GOOD CHOICE, MILLS SALLY MILLS.

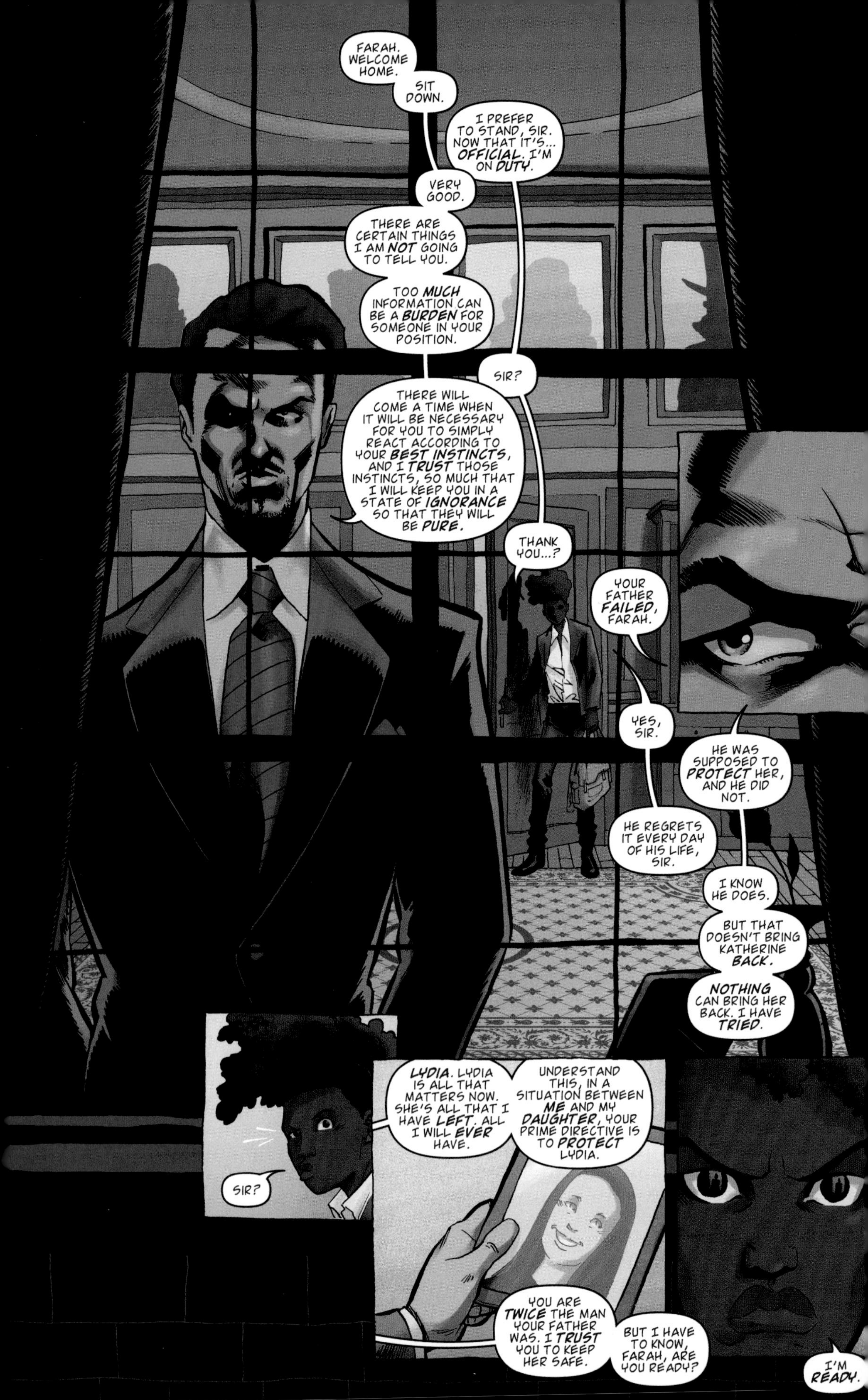
FARAH. WELCOME HOME.
SIT DOWN.
I PREFER TO STAND, SIR. NOW THAT IT'S... OFFICIAL, I'M ON DUTY.
VERY GOOD.
THERE ARE CERTAIN THINGS I AM NOT GOING TO TELL YOU.
TOO MUCH INFORMATION CAN BE A BURDEN FOR SOMEONE IN YOUR POSITION.
SIR?
THERE WILL COME A TIME WHEN IT WILL BE NECESSARY FOR YOU TO SIMPLY REACT ACCORDING TO YOUR BEST INSTINCTS, AND I TRUST THOSE INSTINCTS, SO MUCH THAT I WILL KEEP YOU IN A STATE OF IGNORANCE SO THAT THEY WILL BE PURE.
THANK YOU...?
YOUR FATHER FAILED, FARAH.
YES, SIR.
HE WAS SUPPOSED TO PROTECT HER, AND HE DID NOT.
HE REGRETS IT EVERY DAY OF HIS LIFE, SIR.
I KNOW HE DOES.
BUT THAT DOESN'T BRING KATHERINE BACK.
NOTHING CAN BRING HER BACK. I HAVE TRIED.
SIR?
LYDIA. LYDIA IS ALL THAT MATTERS NOW. SHE'S ALL THAT I HAVE LEFT. ALL I WILL EVER HAVE.
UNDERSTAND THIS, IN A SITUATION BETWEEN ME AND MY DAUGHTER, YOUR PRIME DIRECTIVE IS TO PROTECT LYDIA.
YOU ARE TWICE THE MAN YOUR FATHER WAS. I TRUST YOU TO KEEP HER SAFE.
BUT I HAVE TO KNOW, FARAH, ARE YOU READY?
I'M READY.

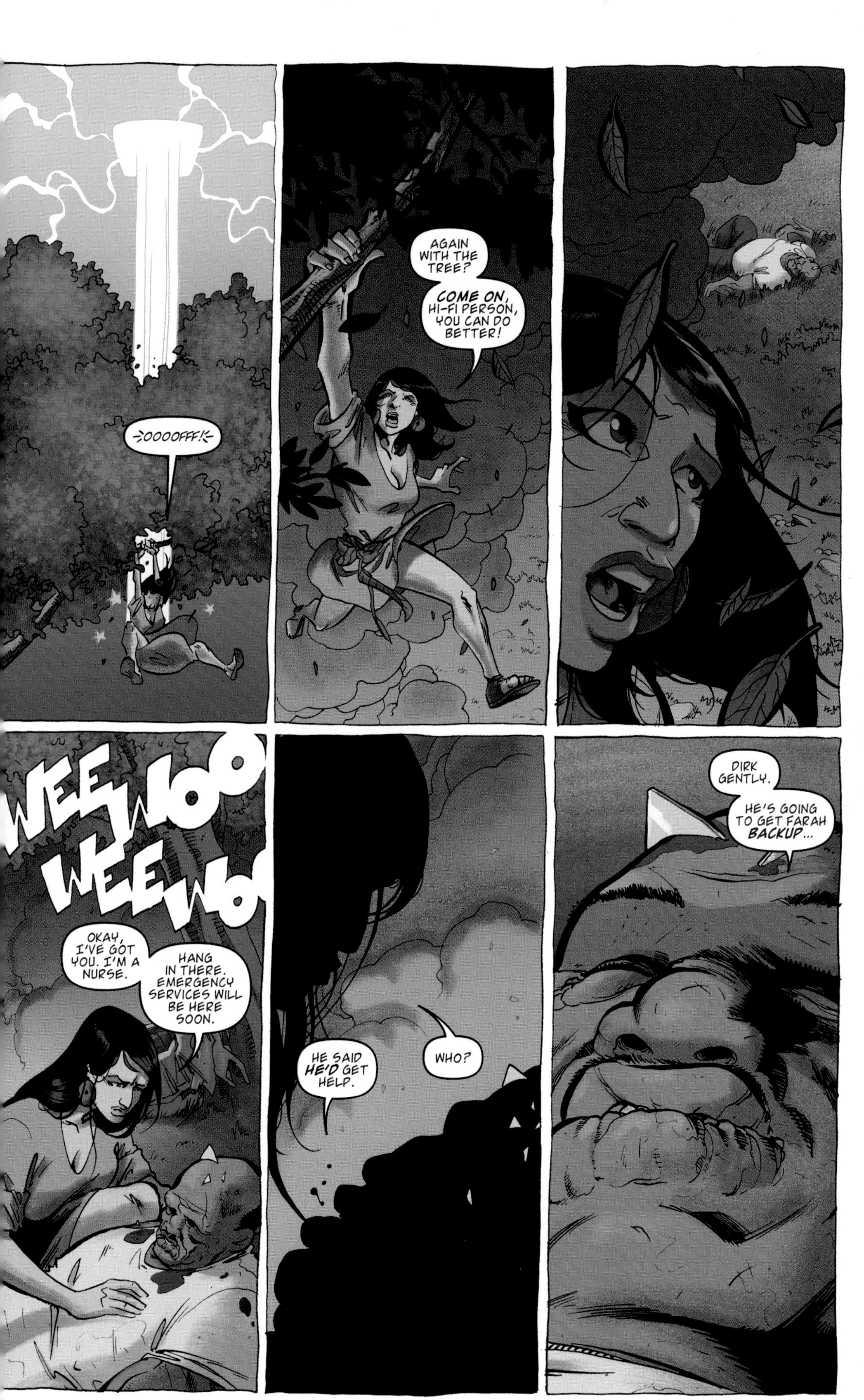

-OOOOFFF!-
AGAIN WITH THE TREE?
COME ON, HI-FI PERSON, YOU CAN DO BETTER!
WEE WOO WEE WOO
OKAY, I'VE GOT YOU. I'M A NURSE.
HANG IN THERE. EMERGENCY SERVICES WILL BE HERE SOON.
HE SAID HE'D GET HELP.
WHO?
DIRK GENTLY.
HE'S GOING TO GET FARAH BACKUP...

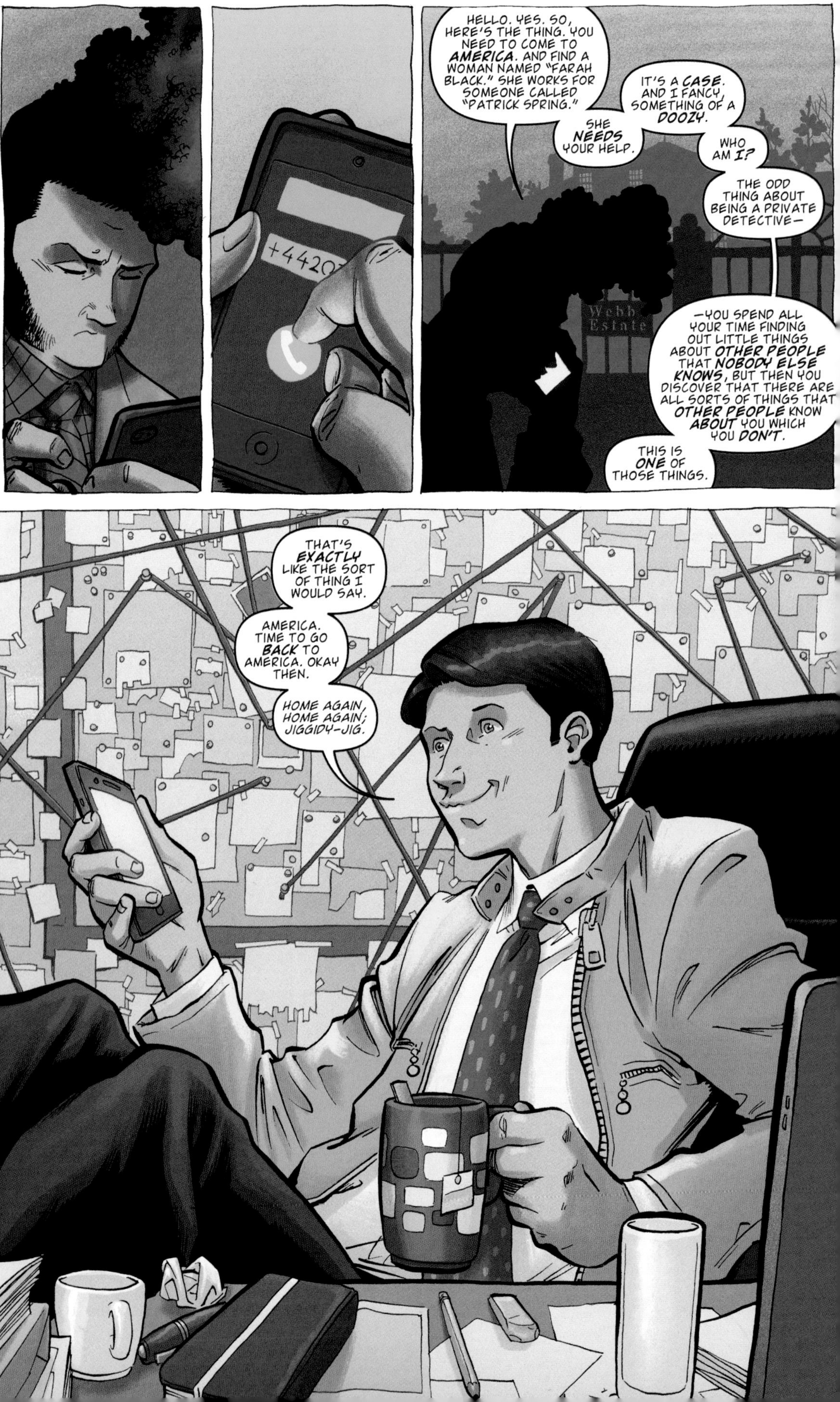
+4420
HELLO. YES. SO, HERE'S THE THING. YOU NEED TO COME TO AMERICA. AND FIND A WOMAN NAMED "FARAH BLACK." SHE WORKS FOR SOMEONE CALLED "PATRICK SPRING."
SHE NEEDS YOUR HELP.
IT'S A CASE. AND I FANCY, SOMETHING OF A DOOZY.
WHO AM I?
THE ODD THING ABOUT BEING A PRIVATE DETECTIVE—
Webb Estate
—YOU SPEND ALL YOUR TIME FINDING OUT LITTLE THINGS ABOUT OTHER PEOPLE THAT NOBODY ELSE KNOWS, BUT THEN YOU DISCOVER THAT THERE ARE ALL SORTS OF THINGS THAT OTHER PEOPLE KNOW ABOUT YOU WHICH YOU DON'T.
THIS IS ONE OF THOSE THINGS.
THAT'S EXACTLY LIKE THE SORT OF THING I WOULD SAY.
AMERICA. TIME TO GO BACK TO AMERICA. OKAY THEN.
HOME AGAIN, HOME AGAIN; JIGGIDY-JIG.

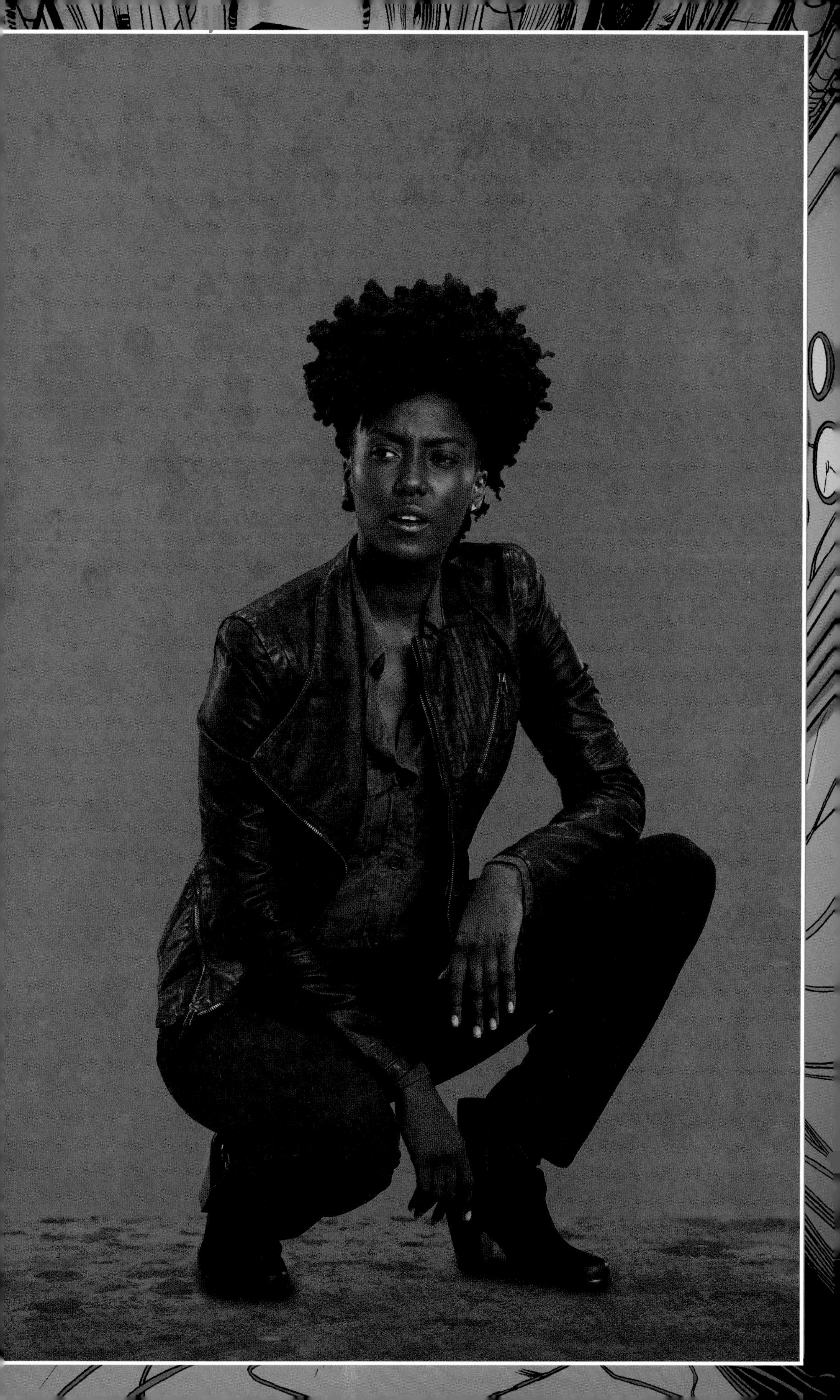

"PATRICK SPRING & THE 7 STAGES"

Written by **Arvind Ethan David** • Art by **Dani Strips**
Colors by **Charlie Kirchoff**

Letters by **Shawn Lee** • Edits by **Denton J. Tipton** • Publisher **Ted Adams** • Executive Producer **Max Landis**

Based on an idea by **Robert Cooper**

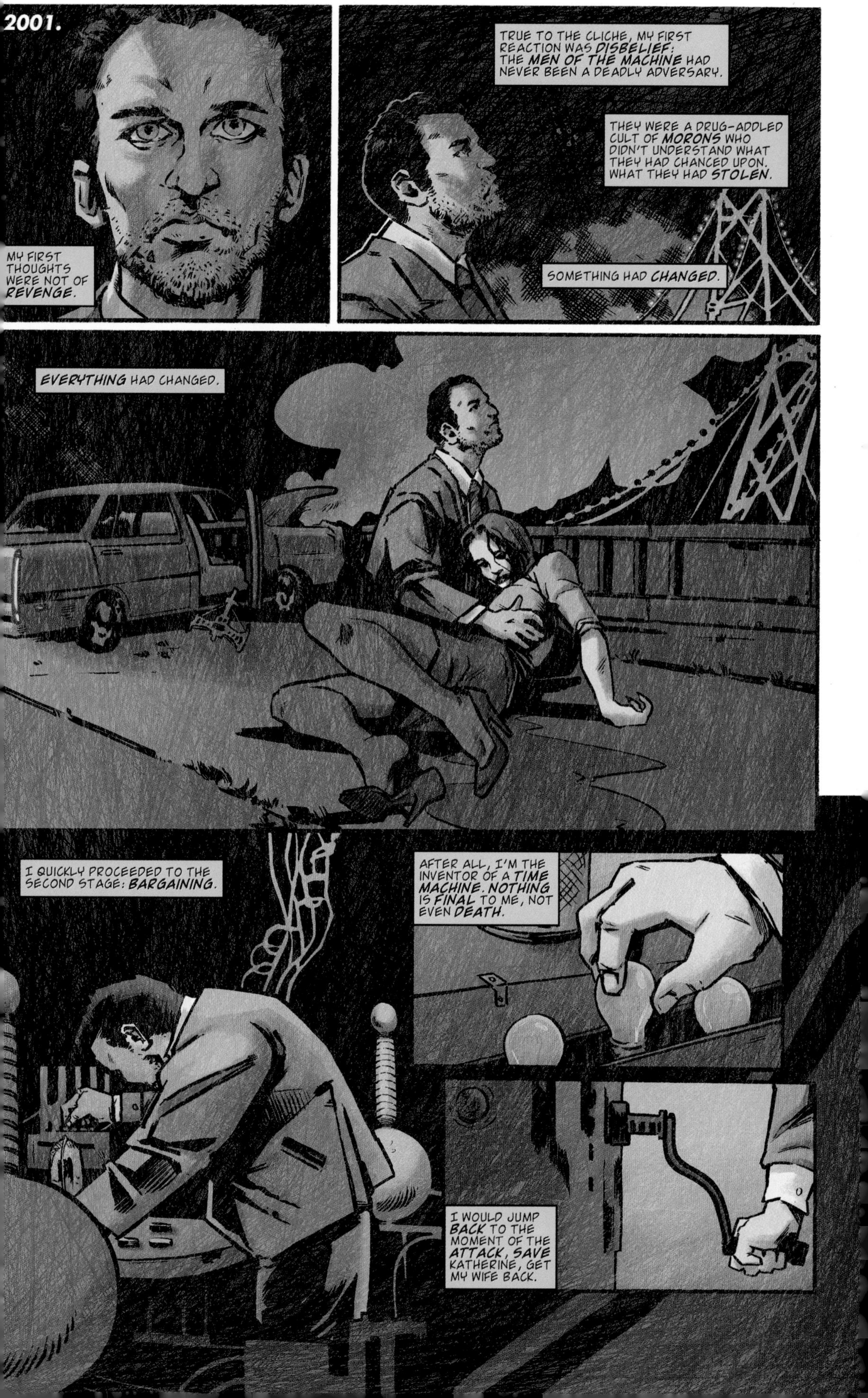
2001.
MY FIRST THOUGHTS WERE NOT OF REVENGE.
TRUE TO THE CLICHE, MY FIRST REACTION WAS DISBELIEF: THE MEN OF THE MACHINE HAD NEVER BEEN A DEADLY ADVERSARY.
THEY WERE A DRUG-ADDLED CULT OF MORONS WHO DIDN'T UNDERSTAND WHAT THEY HAD CHANCED UPON. WHAT THEY HAD STOLEN.
SOMETHING HAD CHANGED.
EVERYTHING HAD CHANGED.
I QUICKLY PROCEEDED TO THE SECOND STAGE: BARGAINING.
AFTER ALL, I'M THE INVENTOR OF A TIME MACHINE. NOTHING IS FINAL TO ME, NOT EVEN DEATH.
I WOULD JUMP BACK TO THE MOMENT OF THE ATTACK, SAVE KATHERINE, GET MY WIFE BACK.

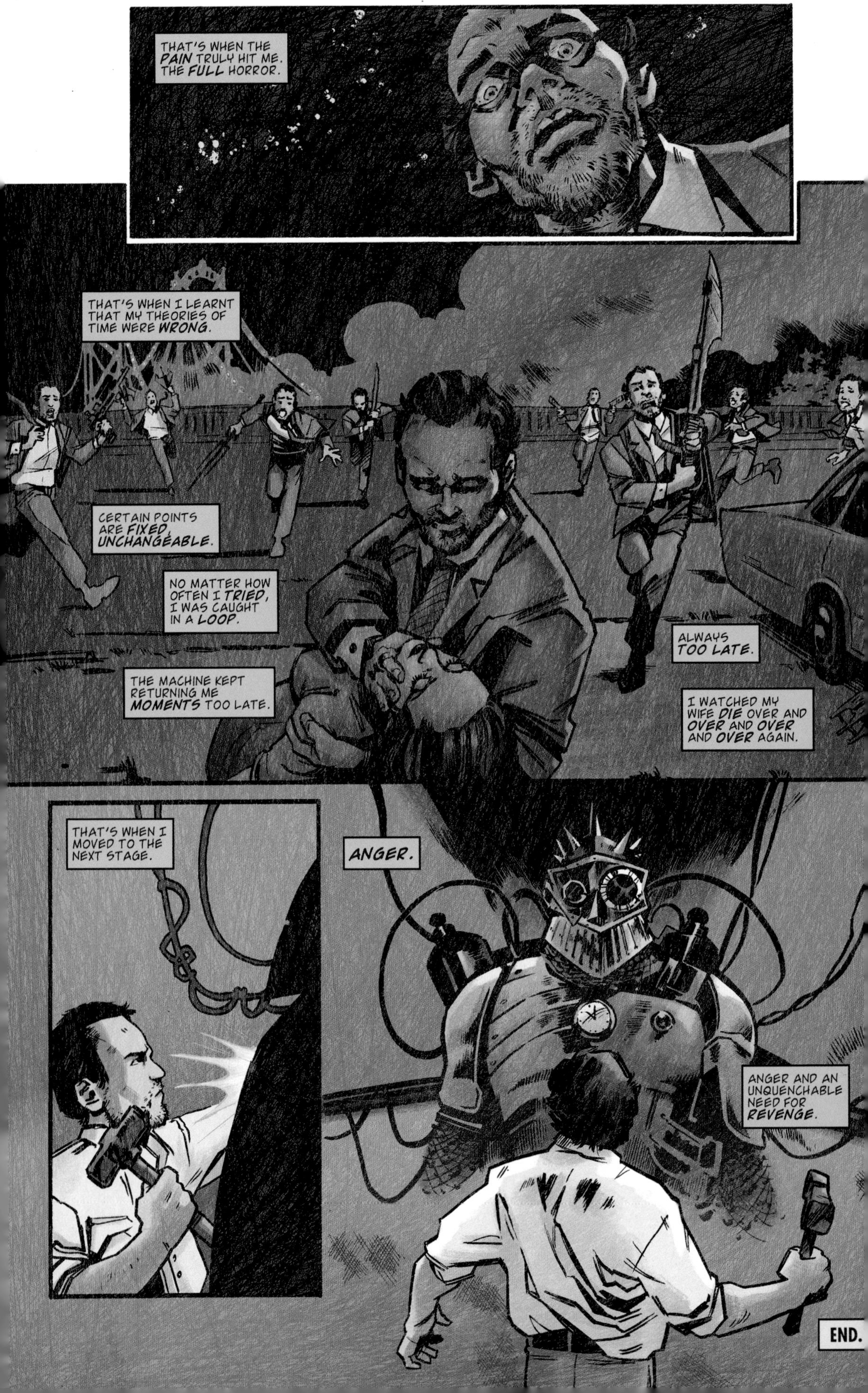
THAT'S WHEN THE PAIN TRULY HIT ME. THE FULL HORROR.
THAT'S WHEN I LEARNT THAT MY THEORIES OF TIME WERE WRONG.
CERTAIN POINTS ARE FIXED, UNCHANGEABLE.
NO MATTER HOW OFTEN I TRIED, I WAS CAUGHT IN A LOOP.
THE MACHINE KEPT RETURNING ME MOMENTS TOO LATE.
ALWAYS TOO LATE.
I WATCHED MY WIFE DIE OVER AND OVER AND OVER AND OVER AGAIN.
THAT'S WHEN I MOVED TO THE NEXT STAGE.
ANGER.
ANGER AND AN UNQUENCHABLE NEED FOR REVENGE.
END.

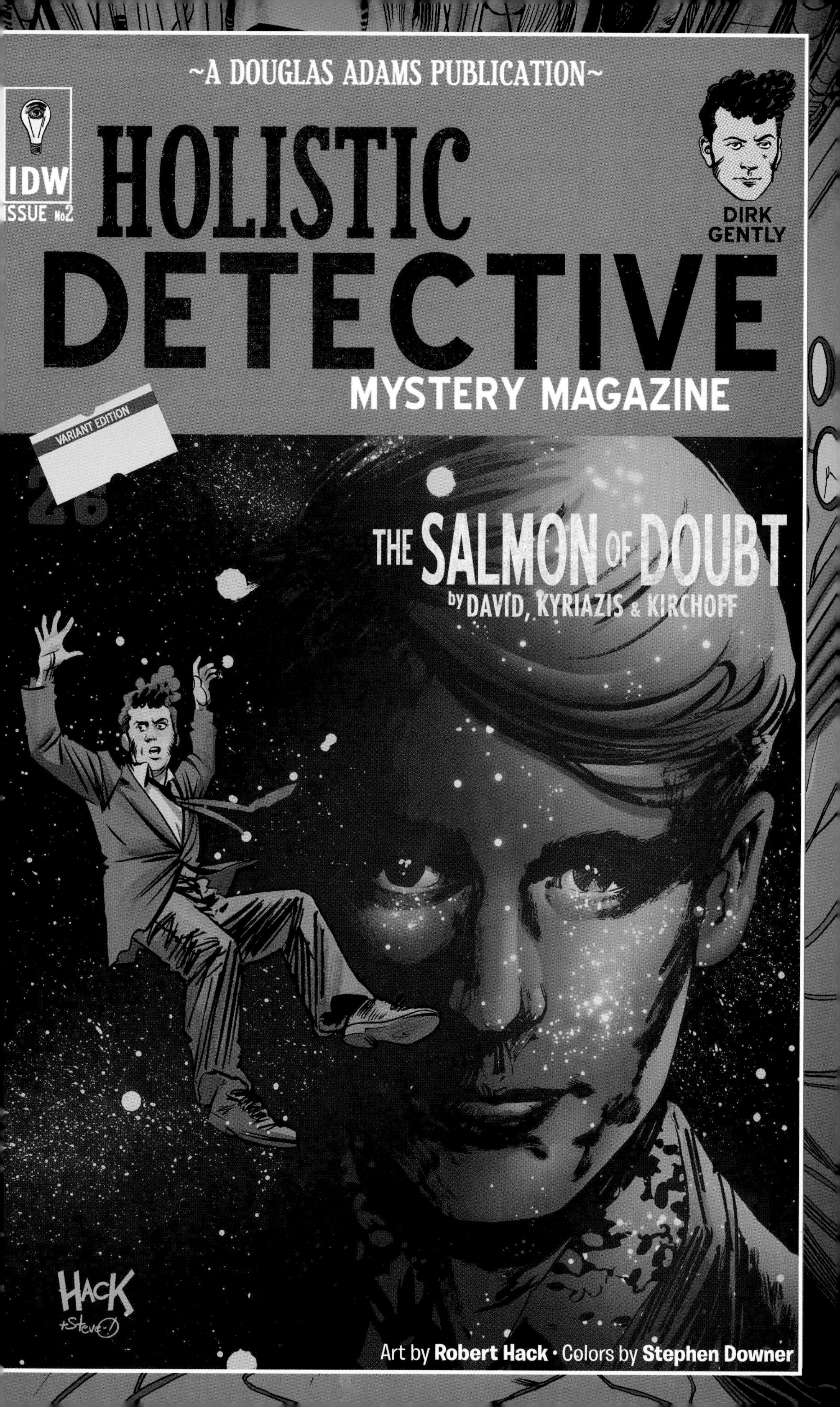
~A DOUGLAS ADAMS PUBLICATION~
IDW
ISSUE No2
HOLISTIC
DETECTIVE
MYSTERY MAGAZINE
DIRK
GENTLY
VARIANT EDITION
THE SALMON OF DOUBT
by DAVID, KYRIAZIS & KIRCHOFF
HACK
+Steve-D
Art by Robert Hack · Colors by Stephen Downer

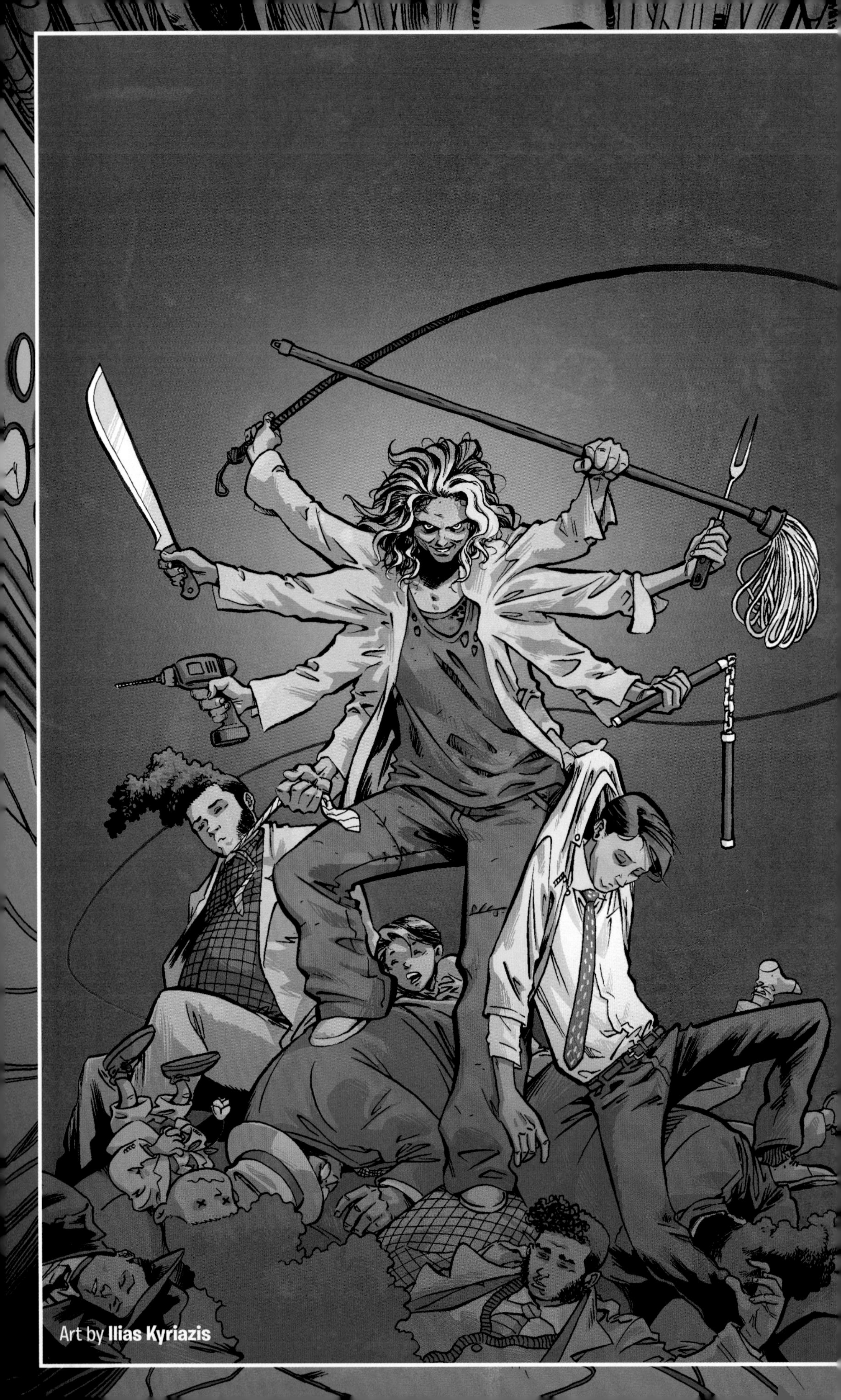

Art by **Ilias Kyriazis**

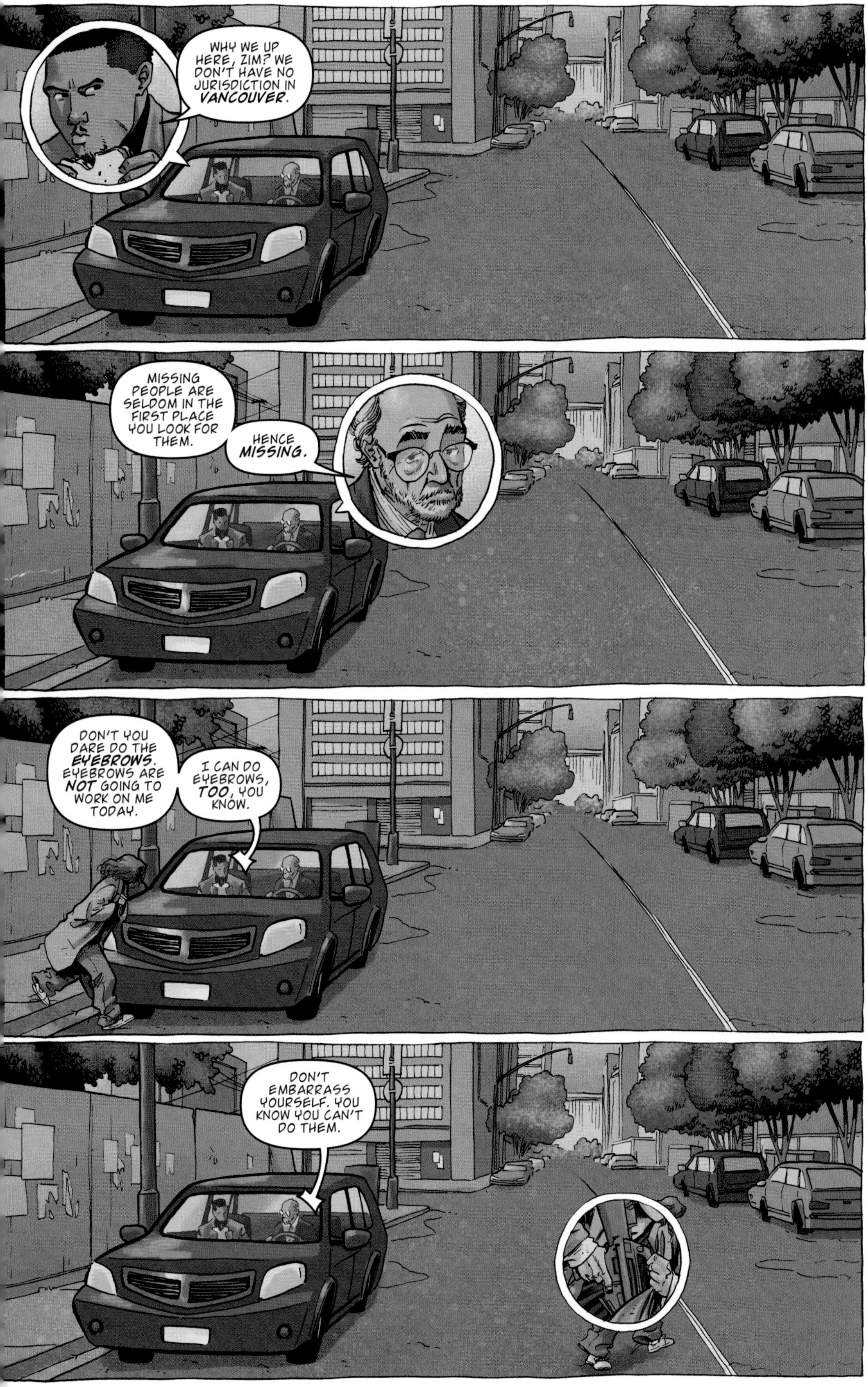
WHY WE UP HERE, ZIM? WE DON'T HAVE NO JURISDICTION IN *VANCOUVER*.
MISSING PEOPLE ARE SELDOM IN THE FIRST PLACE YOU LOOK FOR THEM.
HENCE *MISSING*.
DON'T YOU DARE DO THE *EYEBROWS*. EYEBROWS ARE *NOT* GOING TO WORK ON ME TODAY.
I CAN DO EYEBROWS, *TOO*, YOU KNOW.
DON'T EMBARRASS YOURSELF. YOU KNOW YOU CAN'T DO THEM.

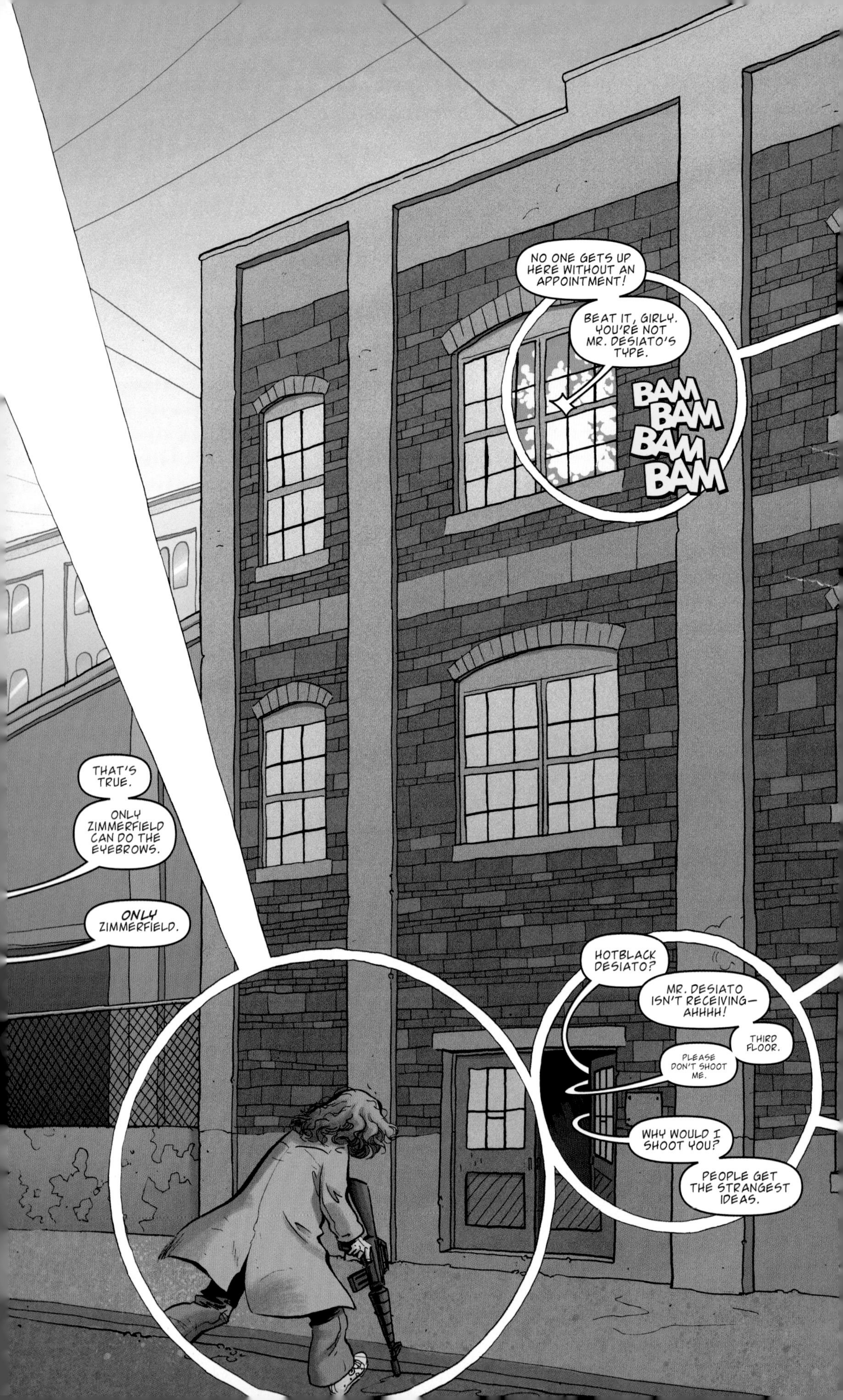

NO ONE GETS UP HERE WITHOUT AN APPOINTMENT!
BEAT IT, GIRLY. YOU'RE NOT MR. DESIATO'S TYPE.
BAM BAM BAM BAM
THAT'S TRUE.
ONLY ZIMMERFIELD CAN DO THE EYEBROWS.
ONLY ZIMMERFIELD.
HOTBLACK DESIATO?
MR. DESIATO ISN'T RECEIVING— AHHHH!
THIRD FLOOR.
PLEASE DON'T SHOOT ME.
WHY WOULD I SHOOT YOU?
PEOPLE GET THE STRANGEST IDEAS.

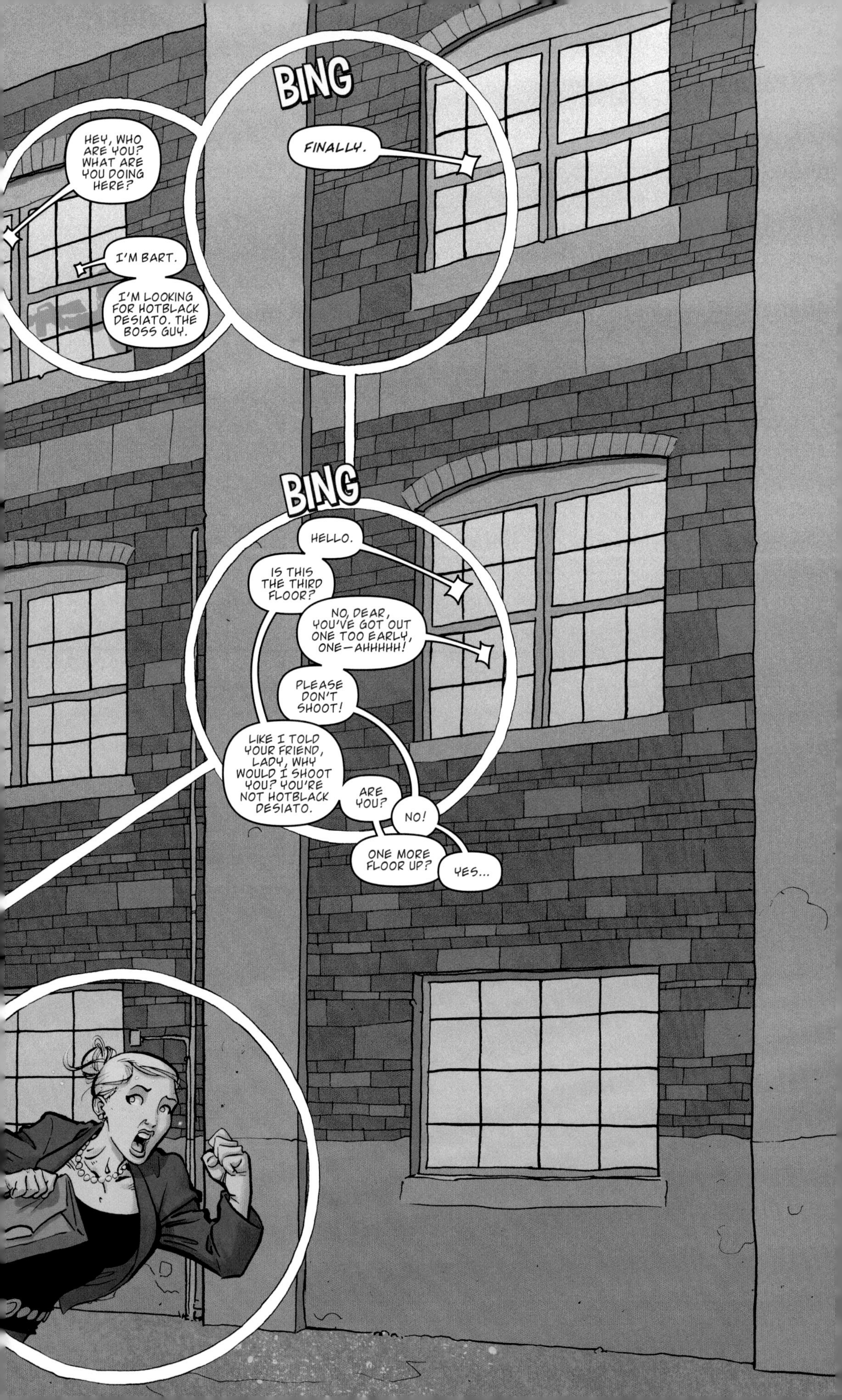
HEY, WHO ARE YOU? WHAT ARE YOU DOING HERE?
I'M BART.
I'M LOOKING FOR HOTBLACK DESIATO. THE BOSS GUY.
BING
FINALLY.
BING
HELLO.
IS THIS THE THIRD FLOOR?
NO, DEAR, YOU'VE GOT OUT ONE TOO EARLY, ONE—AHHHHH!
PLEASE DON'T SHOOT!
LIKE I TOLD YOUR FRIEND, LADY, WHY WOULD I SHOOT YOU? YOU'RE NOT HOTBLACK DESIATO.
ARE YOU?
NO!
ONE MORE FLOOR UP?
YES...

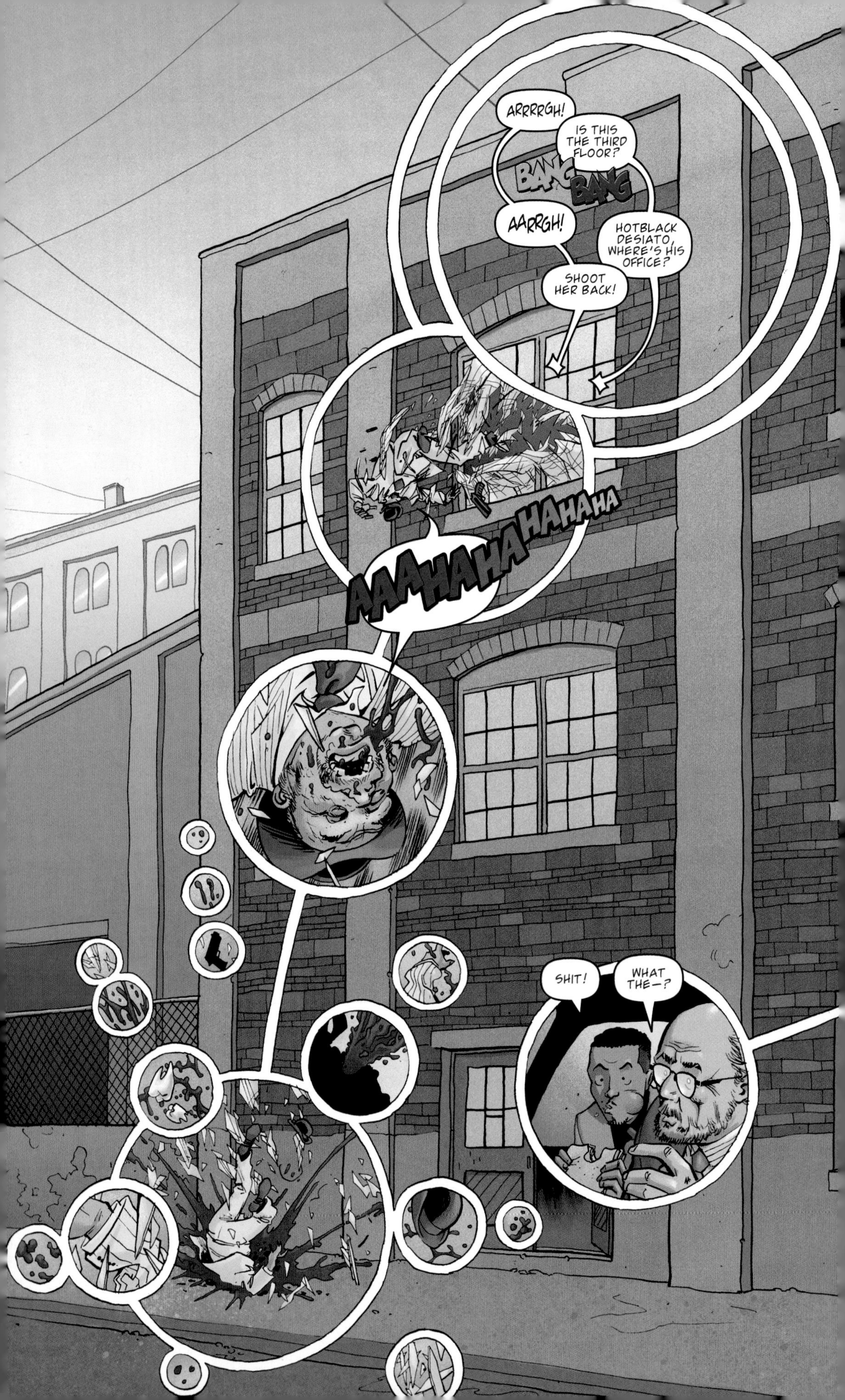
ARRRRGH!
IS THIS THE THIRD FLOOR?
BANG
BANG
AARRGH!
HOTBLACK DESIATO, WHERE'S HIS OFFICE?
SHOOT HER BACK!
AAAHAHAHAHAHA
SHIT!
WHAT THE—?

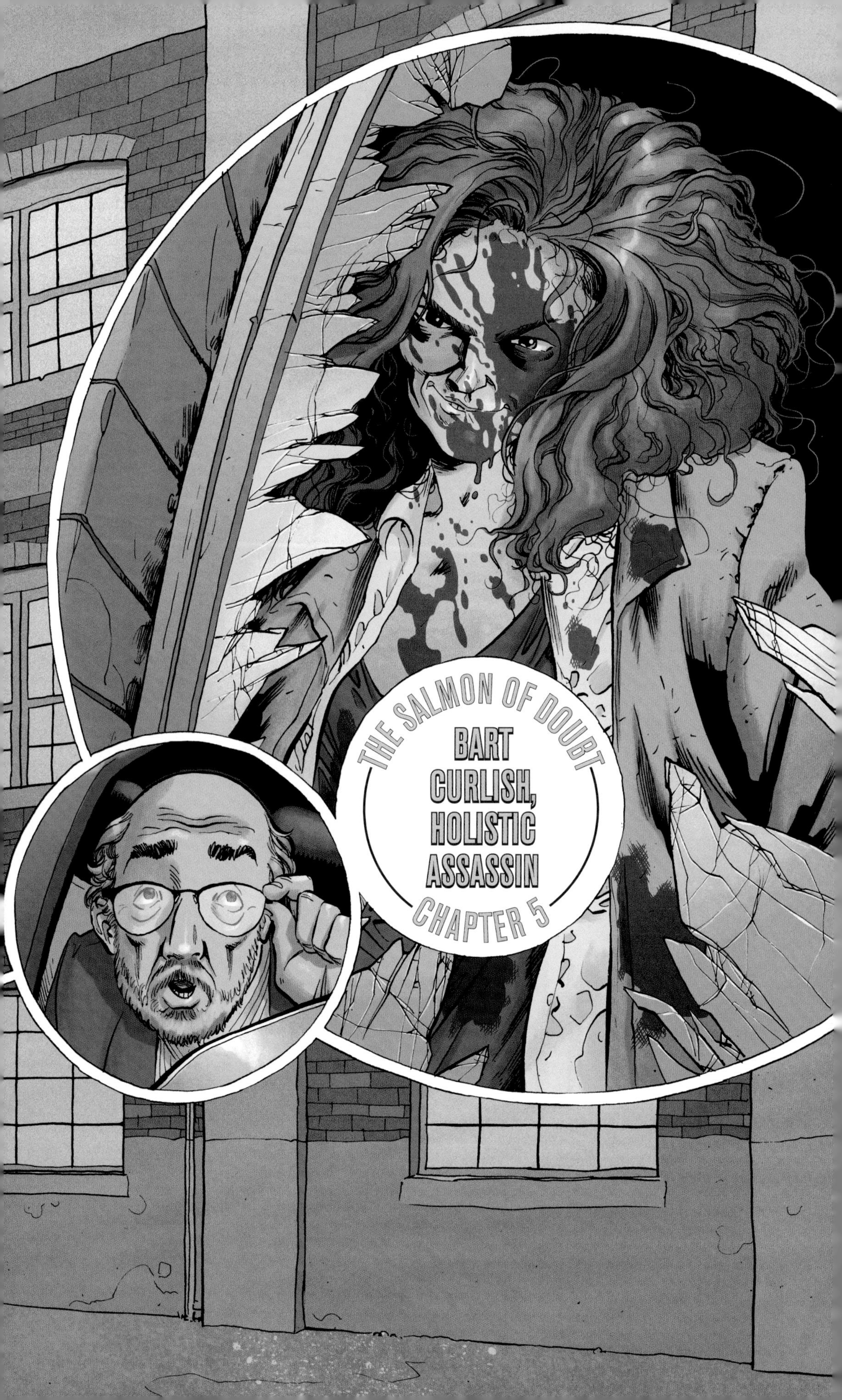
THE SALMON OF DOUBT
BART CURLISH, HOLISTIC ASSASSIN
CHAPTER 5

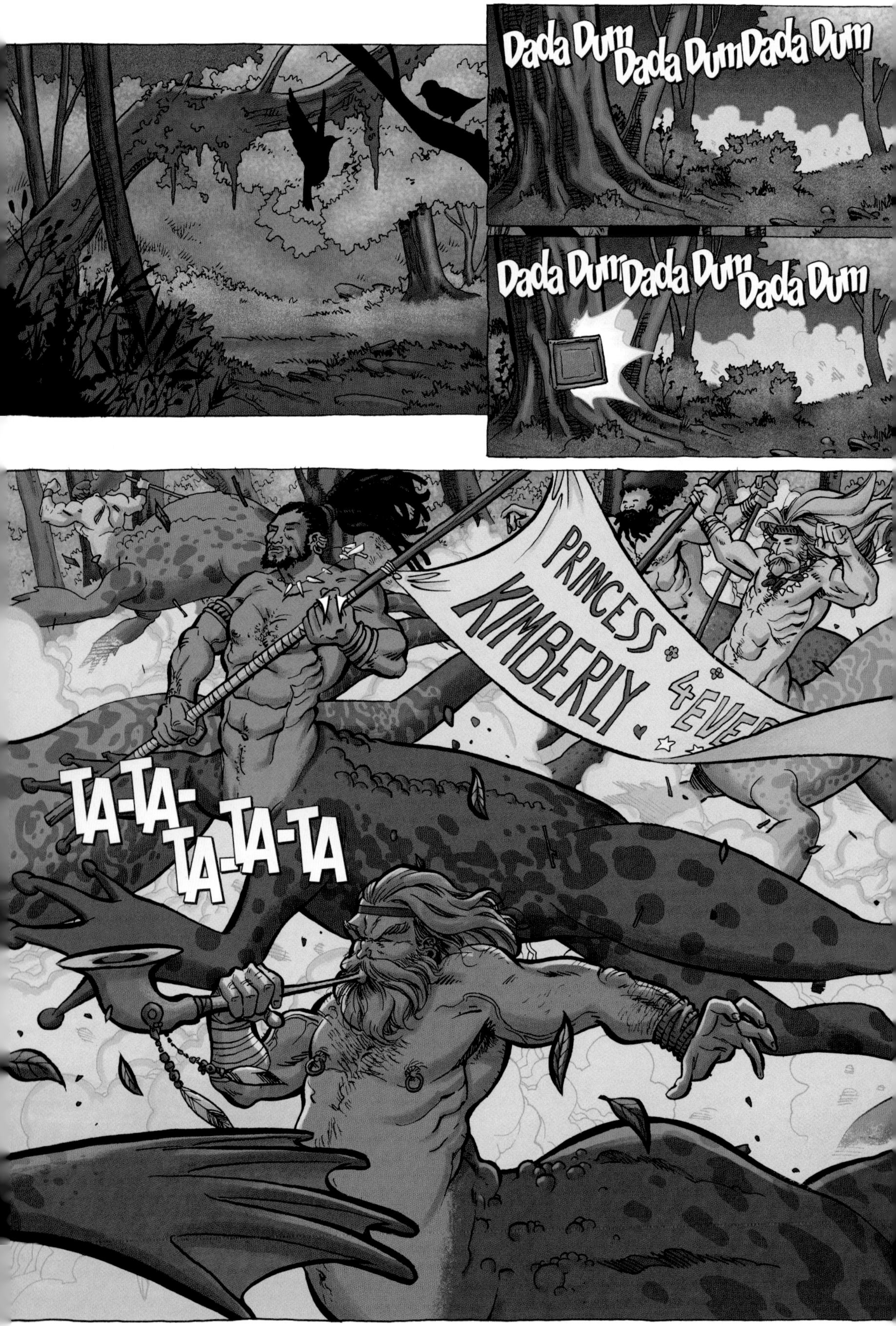

Dada Dum Dada Dum Dada Dum
Dada Dum Dada Dum Dada Dum
PRINCESS KIMBERLY 4EVER
TA-TA-TA-TA-TA

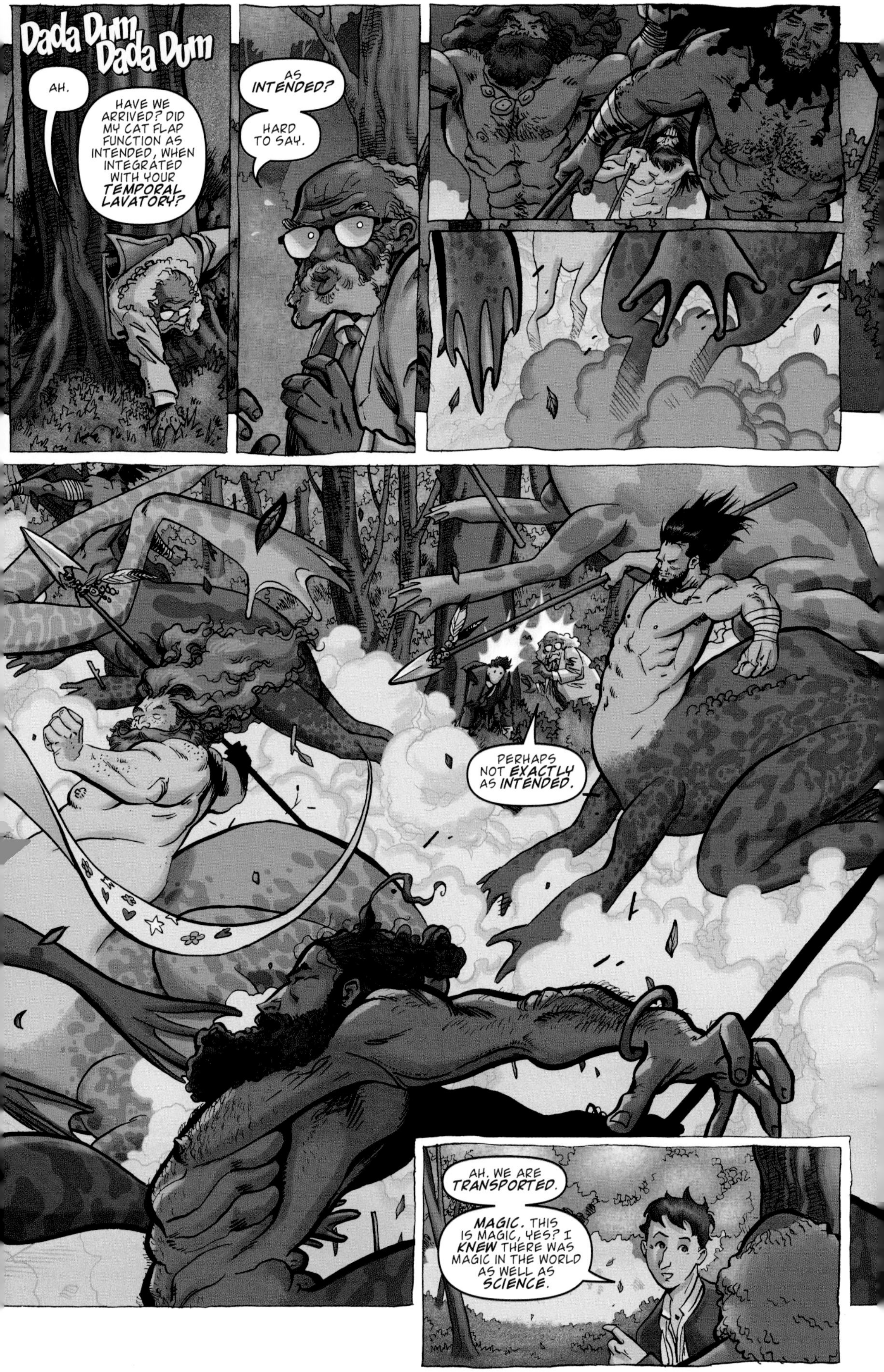
Dada Dum Dada Dum
AH.
HAVE WE ARRIVED? DID MY CAT FLAP FUNCTION AS INTENDED, WHEN INTEGRATED WITH YOUR TEMPORAL LAVATORY?
AS INTENDED?
HARD TO SAY.
PERHAPS NOT EXACTLY AS INTENDED.
AH. WE ARE TRANSPORTED.
MAGIC. THIS IS MAGIC, YES? I KNEW THERE WAS MAGIC IN THE WORLD AS WELL AS SCIENCE.

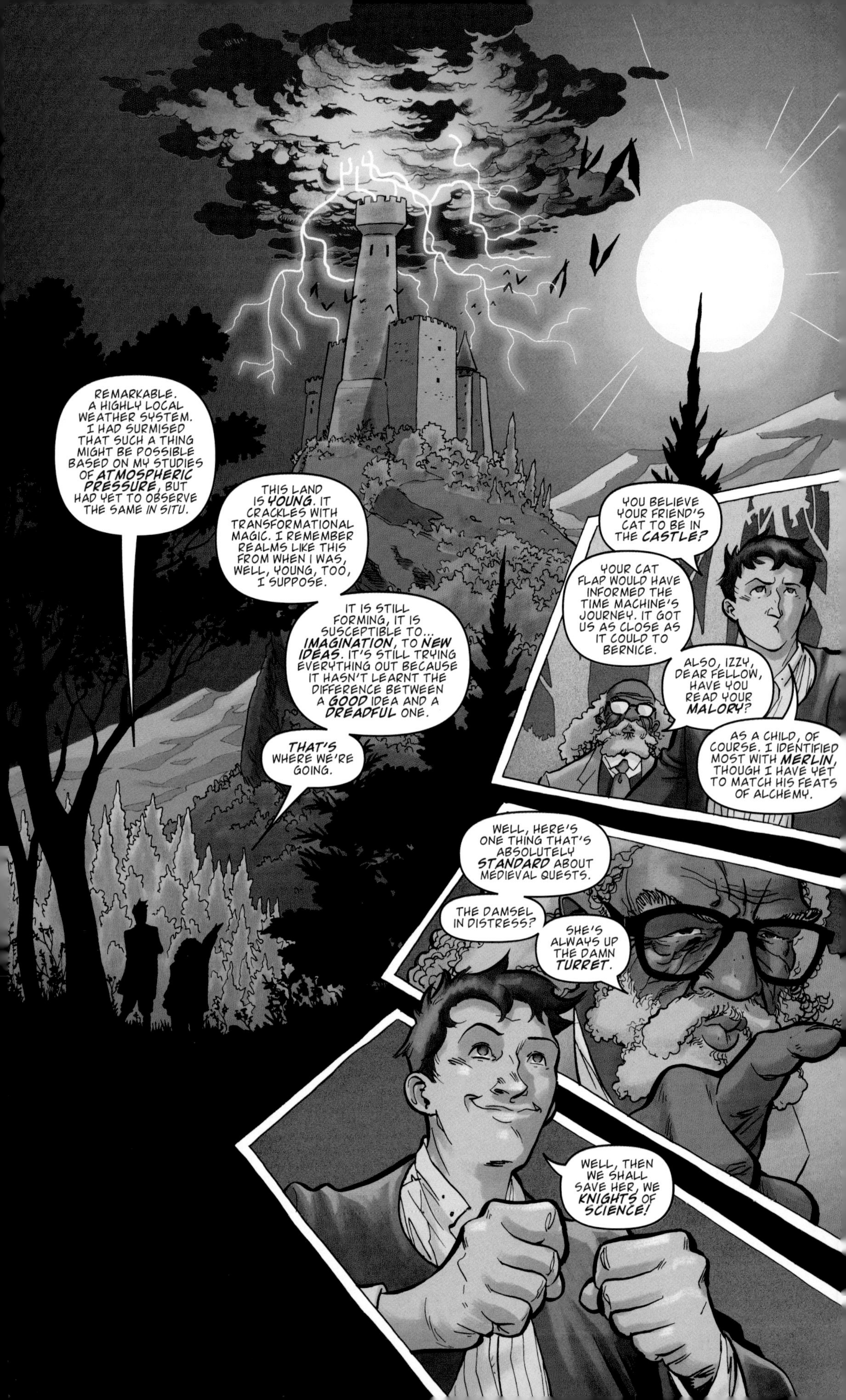
REMARKABLE. A HIGHLY LOCAL WEATHER SYSTEM. I HAD SURMISED THAT SUCH A THING MIGHT BE POSSIBLE BASED ON MY STUDIES OF ATMOSPHERIC PRESSURE, BUT HAD YET TO OBSERVE THE SAME IN SITU.
THIS LAND IS YOUNG. IT CRACKLES WITH TRANSFORMATIONAL MAGIC. I REMEMBER REALMS LIKE THIS FROM WHEN I WAS, WELL, YOUNG, TOO, I SUPPOSE.
IT IS STILL FORMING, IT IS SUSCEPTIBLE TO... IMAGINATION, TO NEW IDEAS. IT'S STILL TRYING EVERYTHING OUT BECAUSE IT HASN'T LEARNT THE DIFFERENCE BETWEEN A GOOD IDEA AND A DREADFUL ONE.
THAT'S WHERE WE'RE GOING.
YOU BELIEVE YOUR FRIEND'S CAT TO BE IN THE CASTLE?
YOUR CAT FLAP WOULD HAVE INFORMED THE TIME MACHINE'S JOURNEY. IT GOT US AS CLOSE AS IT COULD TO BERNICE.
ALSO, IZZY, DEAR FELLOW, HAVE YOU READ YOUR MALORY?
AS A CHILD, OF COURSE. I IDENTIFIED MOST WITH MERLIN, THOUGH I HAVE YET TO MATCH HIS FEATS OF ALCHEMY.
WELL, HERE'S ONE THING THAT'S ABSOLUTELY STANDARD ABOUT MEDIEVAL QUESTS.
THE DAMSEL IN DISTRESS?
SHE'S ALWAYS UP THE DAMN TURRET.
WELL, THEN WE SHALL SAVE HER, WE KNIGHTS OF SCIENCE!

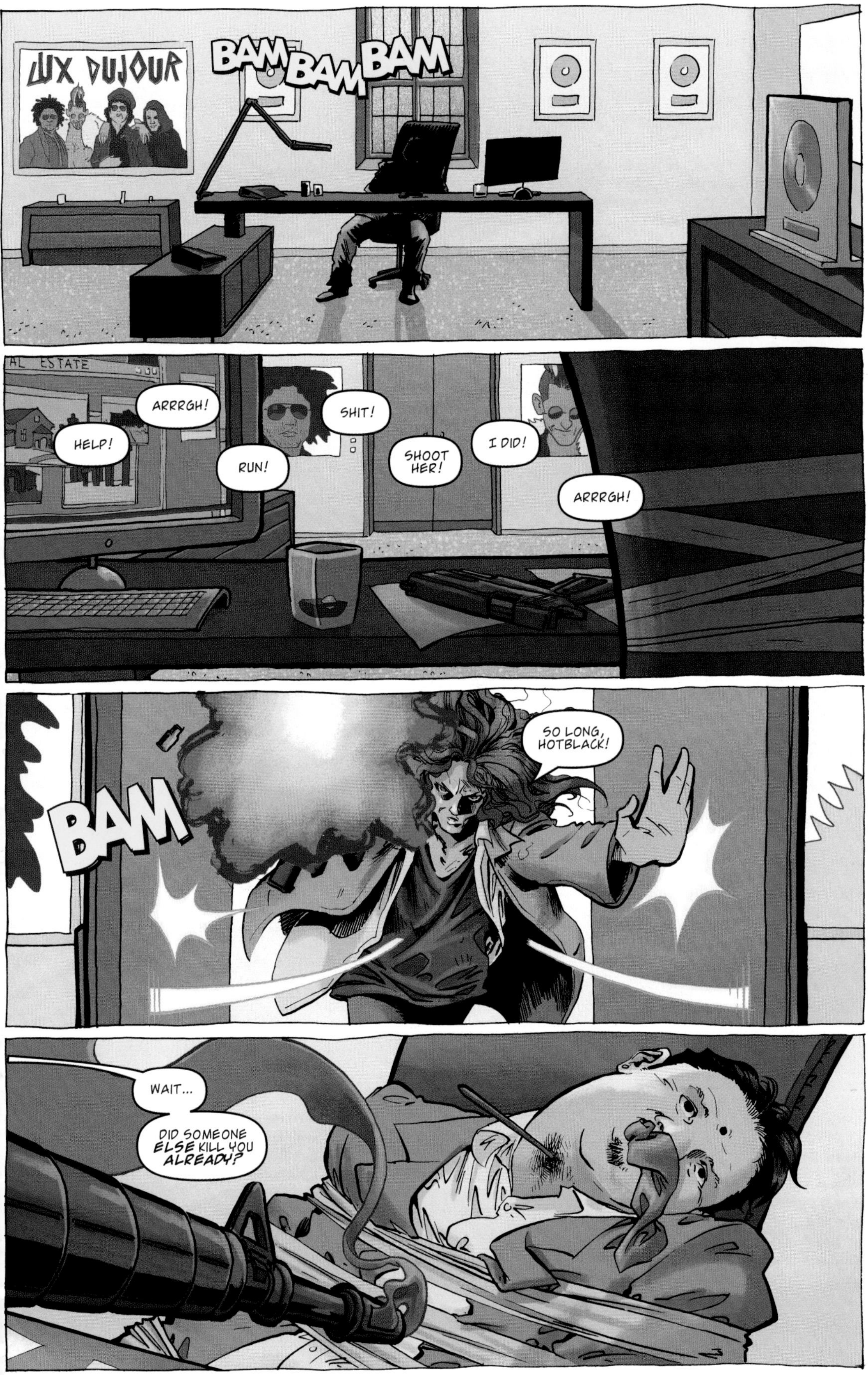
LUX DUJOUR
BAM BAM BAM
AL ESTATE
HELP!
ARRRGH!
RUN!
SHIT!
SHOOT HER!
I DID!
ARRRGH!
BAM
SO LONG, HOTBLACK!
WAIT...
DID SOMEONE ELSE KILL YOU ALREADY?

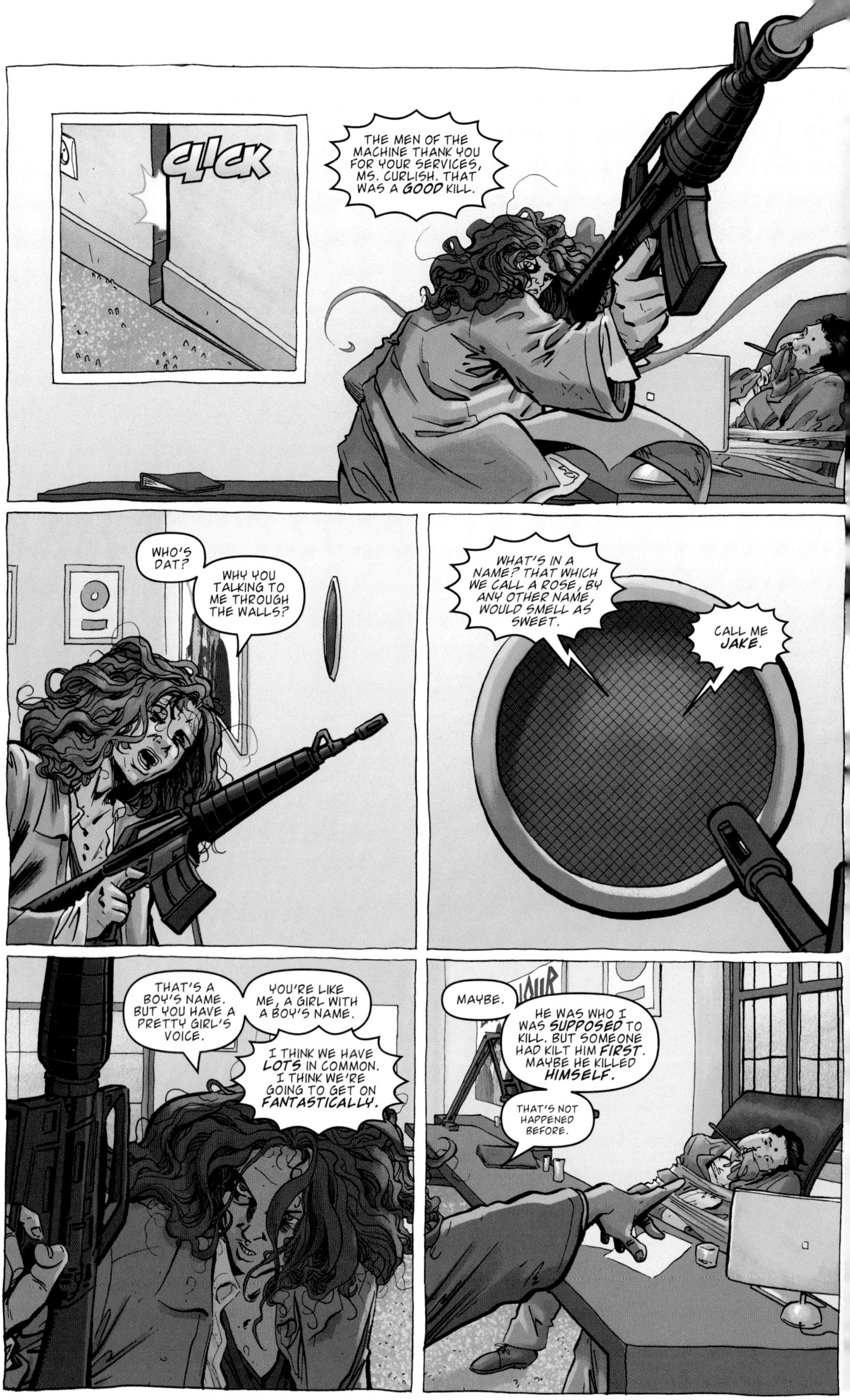
CLICK
THE MEN OF THE MACHINE THANK YOU FOR YOUR SERVICES, MS. CURLISH. THAT WAS A GOOD KILL.
WHO'S DAT?
WHY YOU TALKING TO ME THROUGH THE WALLS?
WHAT'S IN A NAME? THAT WHICH WE CALL A ROSE, BY ANY OTHER NAME, WOULD SMELL AS SWEET.
CALL ME JAKE.
THAT'S A BOY'S NAME. BUT YOU HAVE A PRETTY GIRL'S VOICE.
YOU'RE LIKE ME, A GIRL WITH A BOY'S NAME.
I THINK WE HAVE LOTS IN COMMON. I THINK WE'RE GOING TO GET ON FANTASTICALLY.
MAYBE.
HE WAS WHO I WAS SUPPOSED TO KILL. BUT SOMEONE HAD KILT HIM FIRST. MAYBE HE KILLED HIMSELF.
THAT'S NOT HAPPENED BEFORE.

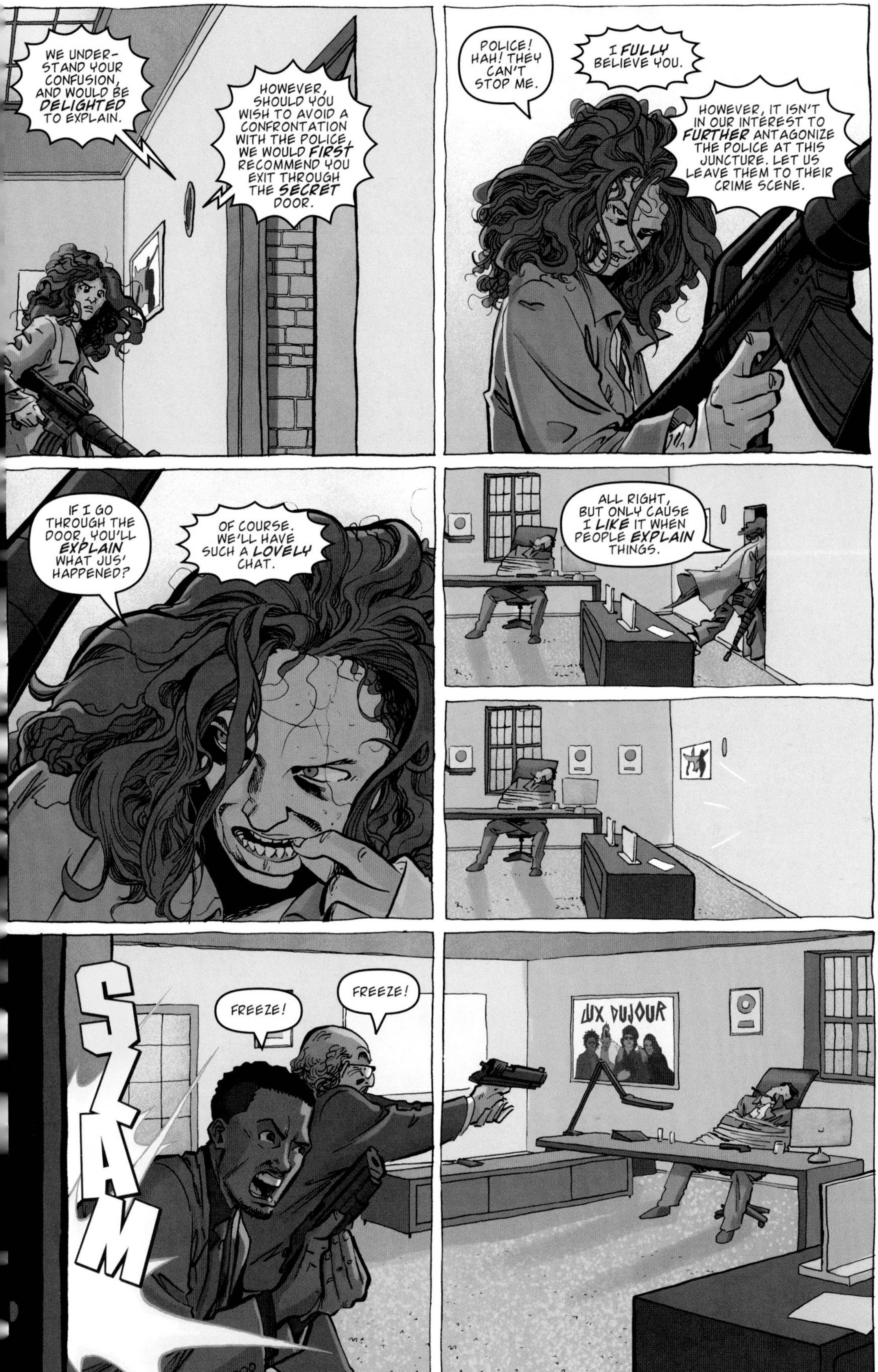
WE UNDER-STAND YOUR CONFUSION, AND WOULD BE DELIGHTED TO EXPLAIN.
HOWEVER, SHOULD YOU WISH TO AVOID A CONFRONTATION WITH THE POLICE, WE WOULD FIRST RECOMMEND YOU EXIT THROUGH THE SECRET DOOR.
POLICE! HAH! THEY CAN'T STOP ME.
I FULLY BELIEVE YOU.
HOWEVER, IT ISN'T IN OUR INTEREST TO FURTHER ANTAGONIZE THE POLICE AT THIS JUNCTURE. LET US LEAVE THEM TO THEIR CRIME SCENE.
IF I GO THROUGH THE DOOR, YOU'LL EXPLAIN WHAT JUS' HAPPENED?
OF COURSE. WE'LL HAVE SUCH A LOVELY CHAT.
ALL RIGHT, BUT ONLY CAUSE I LIKE IT WHEN PEOPLE EXPLAIN THINGS.
SLAM
FREEZE!
FREEZE!
LUX DUJOUR

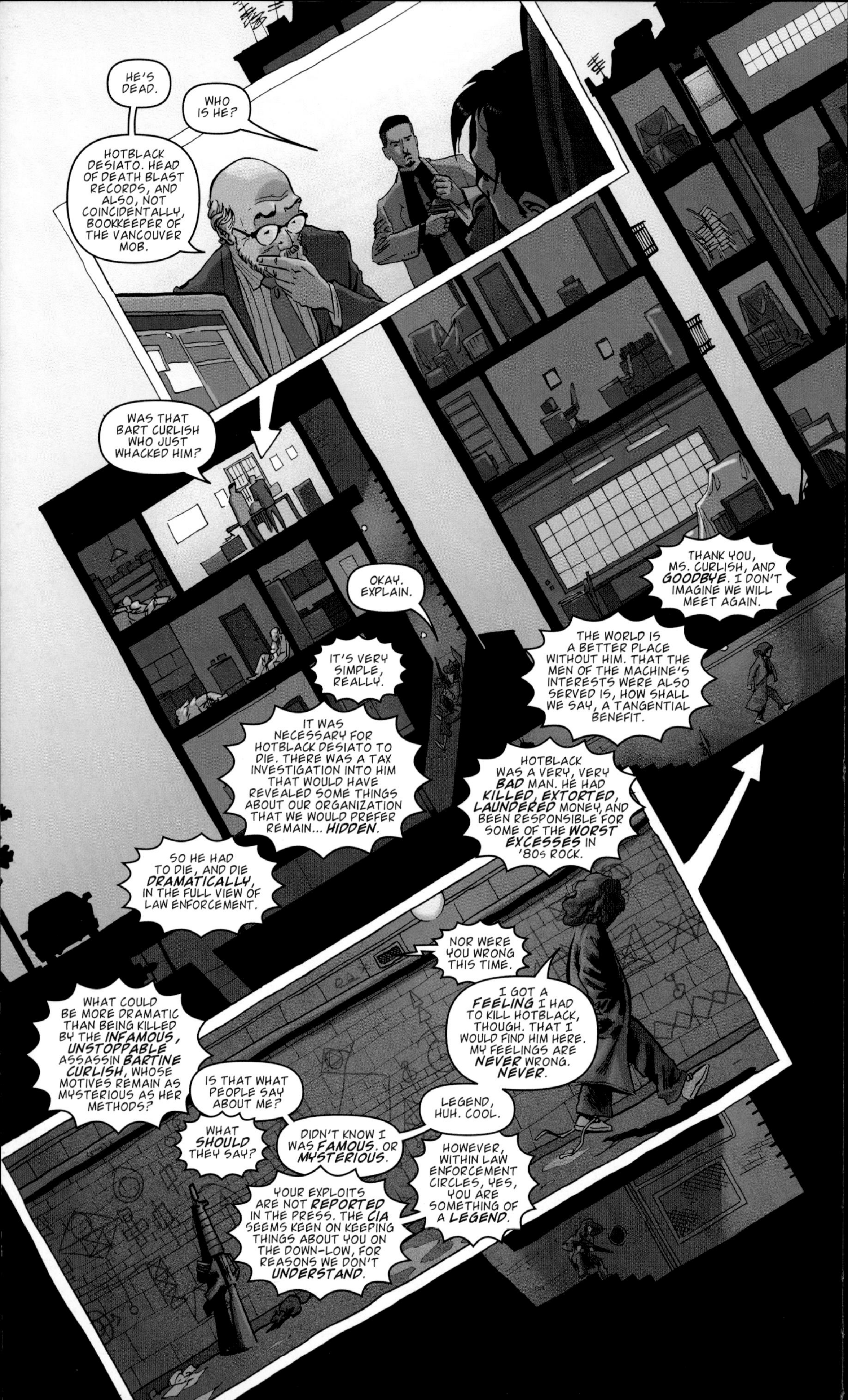
HE'S DEAD.
WHO IS HE?
HOTBLACK DESIATO. HEAD OF DEATH BLAST RECORDS, AND ALSO, NOT COINCIDENTALLY, BOOKKEEPER OF THE VANCOUVER MOB.
WAS THAT BART CURLISH WHO JUST WHACKED HIM?
OKAY. EXPLAIN.
IT'S VERY SIMPLE, REALLY.
IT WAS NECESSARY FOR HOTBLACK DESIATO TO DIE. THERE WAS A TAX INVESTIGATION INTO HIM THAT WOULD HAVE REVEALED SOME THINGS ABOUT OUR ORGANIZATION THAT WE WOULD PREFER REMAIN... HIDDEN.
SO HE HAD TO DIE, AND DIE DRAMATICALLY, IN THE FULL VIEW OF LAW ENFORCEMENT.
THANK YOU, MS. CURLISH, AND GOODBYE. I DON'T IMAGINE WE WILL MEET AGAIN.
THE WORLD IS A BETTER PLACE WITHOUT HIM. THAT THE MEN OF THE MACHINE'S INTERESTS WERE ALSO SERVED IS, HOW SHALL WE SAY, A TANGENTIAL BENEFIT.
HOTBLACK WAS A VERY, VERY BAD MAN. HE HAD KILLED, EXTORTED, LAUNDERED MONEY, AND BEEN RESPONSIBLE FOR SOME OF THE WORST EXCESSES IN '80s ROCK.
NOR WERE YOU WRONG THIS TIME.
I GOT A FEELING I HAD TO KILL HOTBLACK, THOUGH. THAT I WOULD FIND HIM HERE. MY FEELINGS ARE NEVER WRONG. NEVER.
WHAT COULD BE MORE DRAMATIC THAN BEING KILLED BY THE INFAMOUS, UNSTOPPABLE ASSASSIN BARTINE CURLISH, WHOSE MOTIVES REMAIN AS MYSTERIOUS AS HER METHODS?
IS THAT WHAT PEOPLE SAY ABOUT ME?
WHAT SHOULD THEY SAY?
DIDN'T KNOW I WAS FAMOUS. OR MYSTERIOUS.
LEGEND, HUH. COOL.
HOWEVER, WITHIN LAW ENFORCEMENT CIRCLES, YES, YOU ARE SOMETHING OF A LEGEND.
YOUR EXPLOITS ARE NOT REPORTED IN THE PRESS. THE CIA SEEMS KEEN ON KEEPING THINGS ABOUT YOU ON THE DOWN-LOW, FOR REASONS WE DON'T UNDERSTAND.

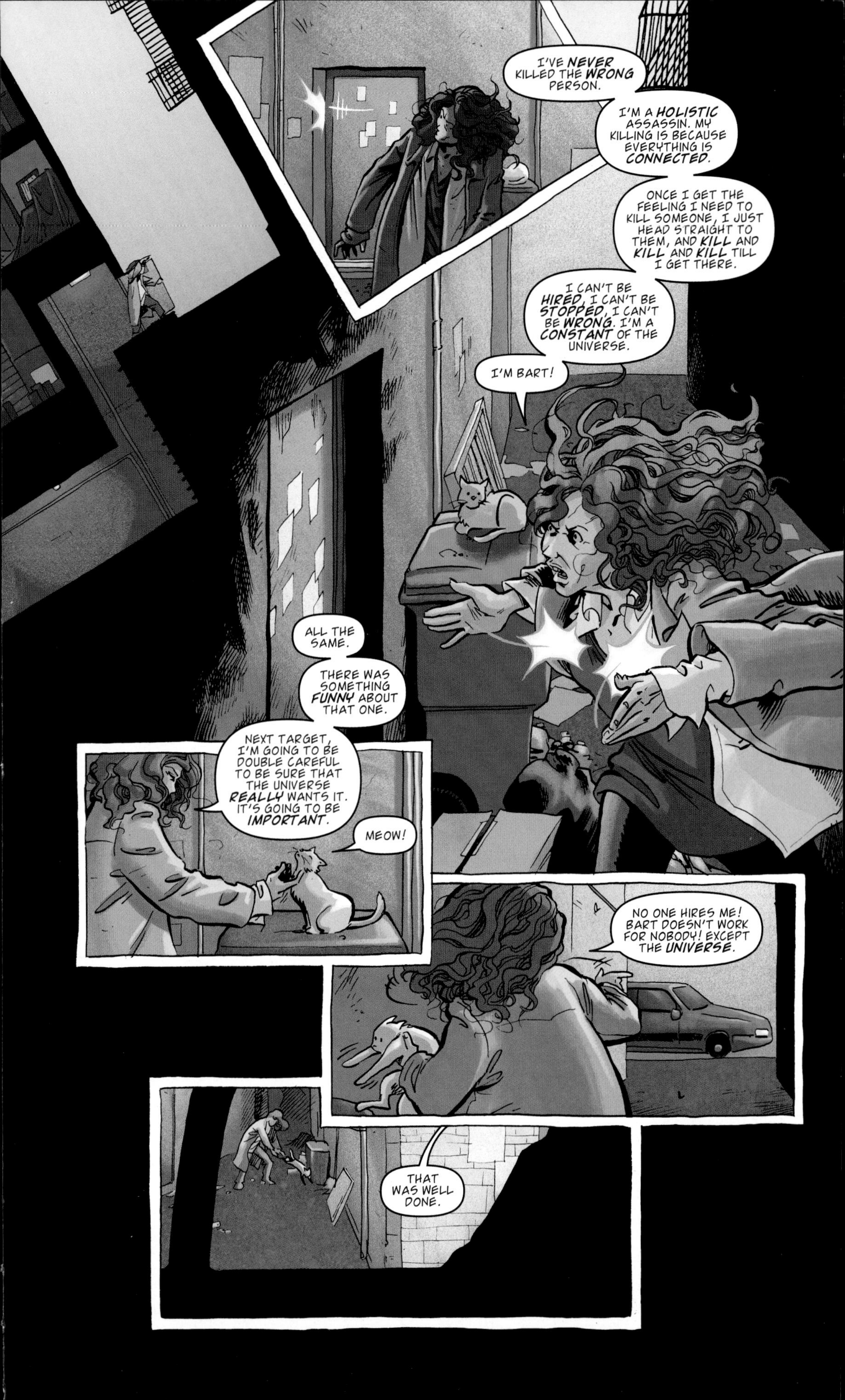

I'VE NEVER KILLED THE WRONG PERSON.
I'M A HOLISTIC ASSASSIN. MY KILLING IS BECAUSE EVERYTHING IS CONNECTED.
ONCE I GET THE FEELING I NEED TO KILL SOMEONE, I JUST HEAD STRAIGHT TO THEM, AND KILL AND KILL AND KILL TILL I GET THERE.
I CAN'T BE HIRED, I CAN'T BE STOPPED, I CAN'T BE WRONG. I'M A CONSTANT OF THE UNIVERSE.
I'M BART!
ALL THE SAME.
THERE WAS SOMETHING FUNNY ABOUT THAT ONE.
NEXT TARGET, I'M GOING TO BE DOUBLE CAREFUL TO BE SURE THAT THE UNIVERSE REALLY WANTS IT. IT'S GOING TO BE IMPORTANT.
MEOW!
NO ONE HIRES ME! BART DOESN'T WORK FOR NOBODY! EXCEPT THE UNIVERSE.
THAT WAS WELL DONE.

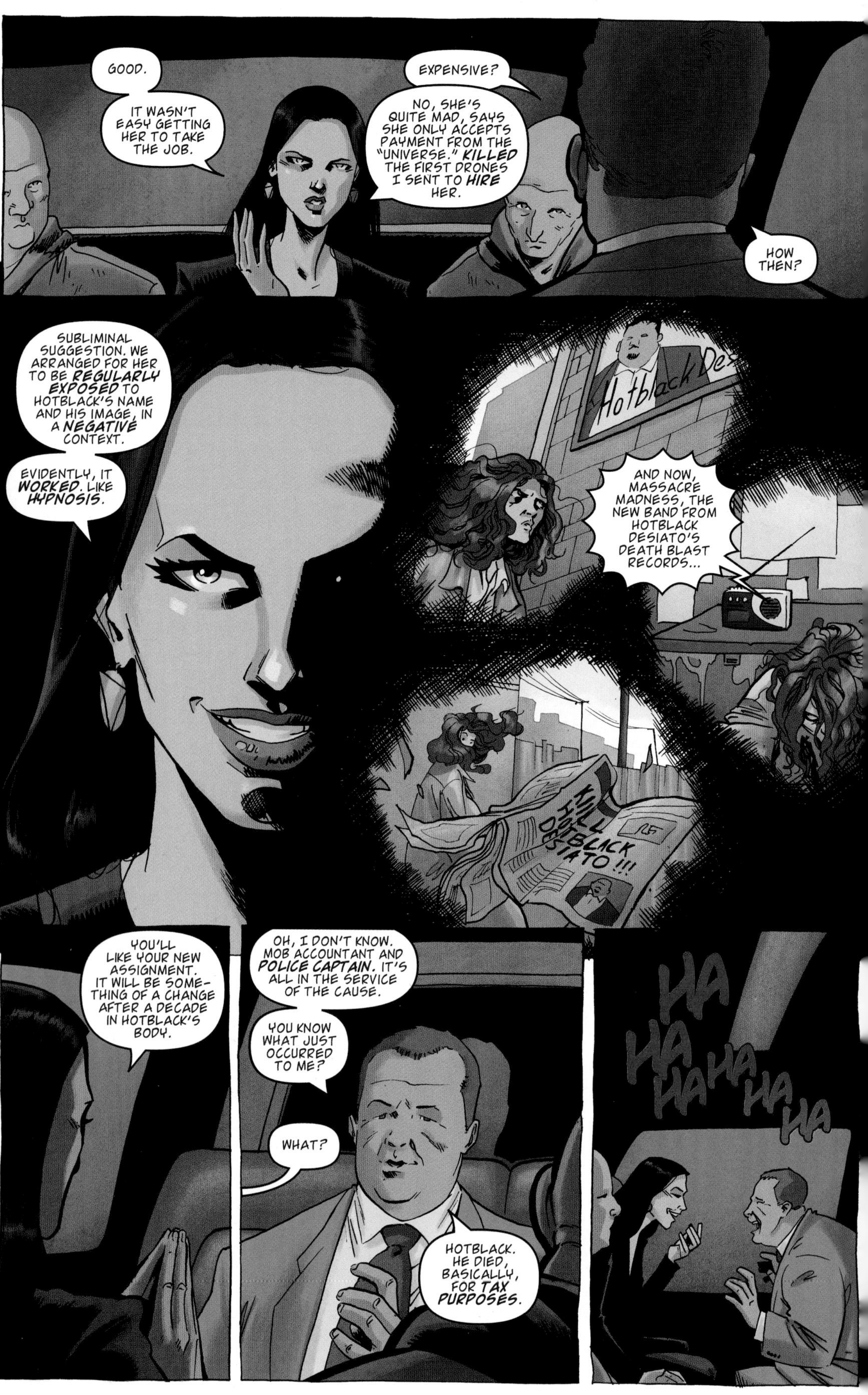
GOOD.
IT WASN'T EASY GETTING HER TO TAKE THE JOB.
EXPENSIVE?
NO, SHE'S QUITE MAD, SAYS SHE ONLY ACCEPTS PAYMENT FROM THE "UNIVERSE." KILLED THE FIRST DRONES I SENT TO HIRE HER.
HOW THEN?
SUBLIMINAL SUGGESTION. WE ARRANGED FOR HER TO BE REGULARLY EXPOSED TO HOTBLACK'S NAME AND HIS IMAGE, IN A NEGATIVE CONTEXT.
EVIDENTLY, IT WORKED. LIKE HYPNOSIS.
Hotblack De
AND NOW, MASSACRE MADNESS, THE NEW BAND FROM HOTBLACK DESIATO'S DEATH BLAST RECORDS...
KILL HOTBLACK DESIATO!!!
YOU'LL LIKE YOUR NEW ASSIGNMENT. IT WILL BE SOMETHING OF A CHANGE AFTER A DECADE IN HOTBLACK'S BODY.
OH, I DON'T KNOW. MOB ACCOUNTANT AND POLICE CAPTAIN. IT'S ALL IN THE SERVICE OF THE CAUSE.
YOU KNOW WHAT JUST OCCURRED TO ME?
WHAT?
HOTBLACK. HE DIED, BASICALLY, FOR TAX PURPOSES.
HA HA HA HA HA HA HA

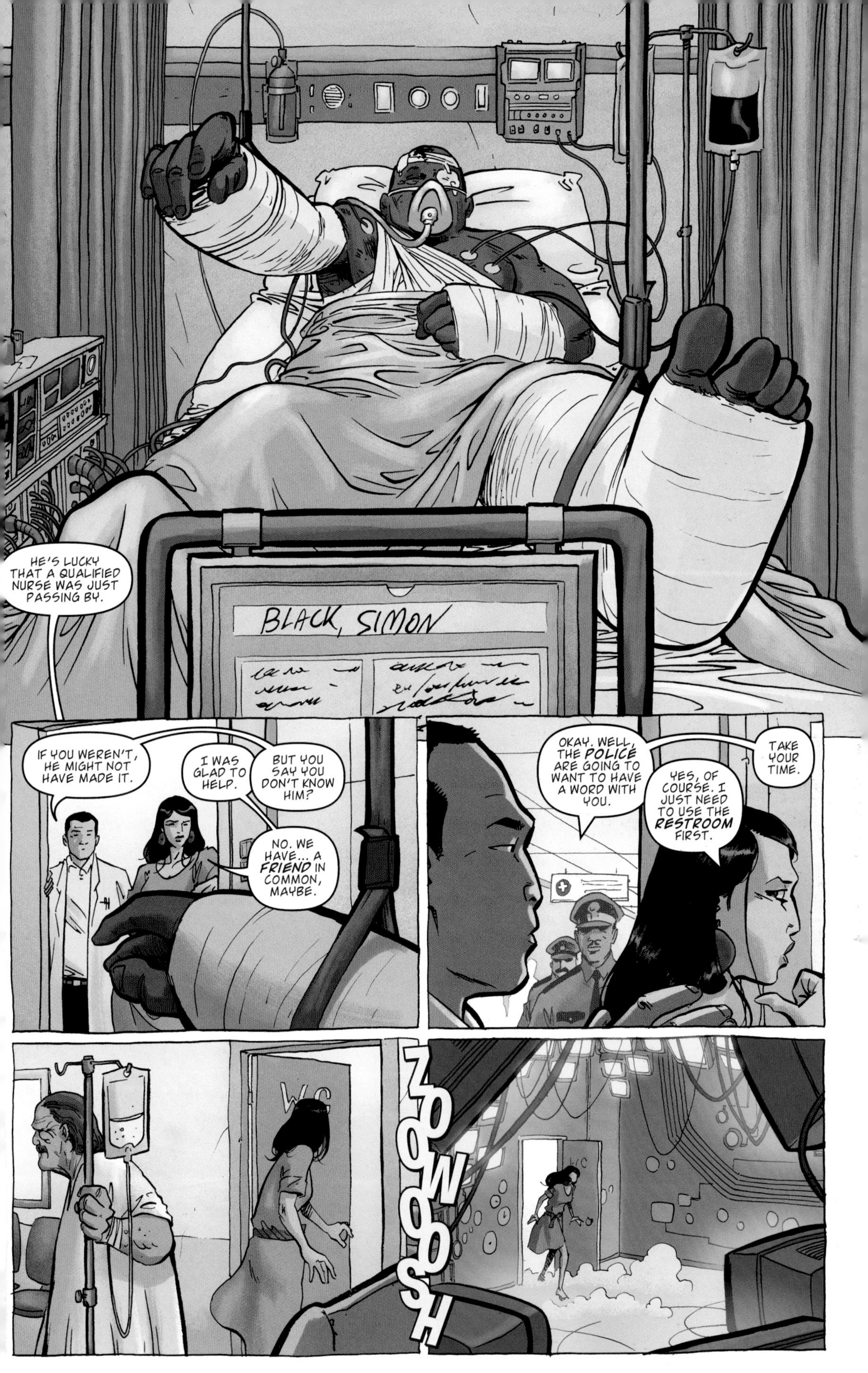
HE'S LUCKY THAT A QUALIFIED NURSE WAS JUST PASSING BY.
BLACK, SIMON
IF YOU WEREN'T, HE MIGHT NOT HAVE MADE IT.
I WAS GLAD TO HELP.
BUT YOU SAY YOU DON'T KNOW HIM?
NO. WE HAVE... A FRIEND IN COMMON, MAYBE.
OKAY. WELL, THE POLICE ARE GOING TO WANT TO HAVE A WORD WITH YOU.
TAKE YOUR TIME.
YES, OF COURSE. I JUST NEED TO USE THE RESTROOM FIRST.
WC
ZOOOOSH
WC

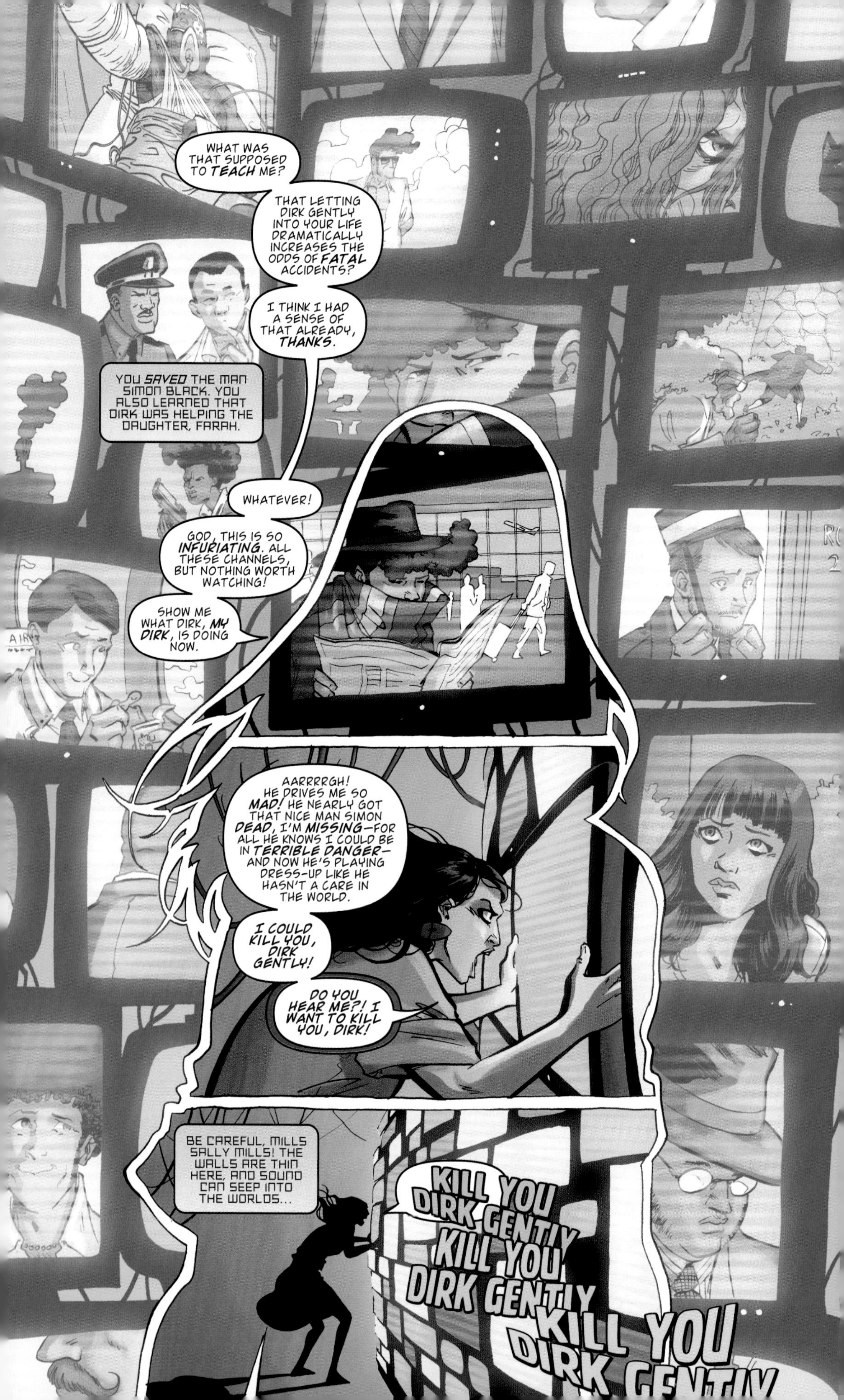
WHAT WAS THAT SUPPOSED TO TEACH ME?
THAT LETTING DIRK GENTLY INTO YOUR LIFE DRAMATICALLY INCREASES THE ODDS OF FATAL ACCIDENTS?
I THINK I HAD A SENSE OF THAT ALREADY, THANKS.
YOU SAVED THE MAN SIMON BLACK. YOU ALSO LEARNED THAT DIRK WAS HELPING THE DAUGHTER, FARAH.
WHATEVER!
GOD, THIS IS SO INFURIATING. ALL THESE CHANNELS, BUT NOTHING WORTH WATCHING!
SHOW ME WHAT DIRK, MY DIRK, IS DOING NOW.
AARRRRGH! HE DRIVES ME SO MAD! HE NEARLY GOT THAT NICE MAN SIMON DEAD, I'M MISSING—FOR ALL HE KNOWS I COULD BE IN TERRIBLE DANGER—AND NOW HE'S PLAYING DRESS-UP LIKE HE HASN'T A CARE IN THE WORLD.
I COULD KILL YOU, DIRK GENTLY!
DO YOU HEAR ME?! I WANT TO KILL YOU, DIRK!
BE CAREFUL, MILLS SALLY MILLS! THE WALLS ARE THIN HERE, AND SOUND CAN SEEP INTO THE WORLDS...
KILL YOU DIRK GENTLY
KILL YOU DIRK GENTLY
KILL YOU DIRK GENTLY

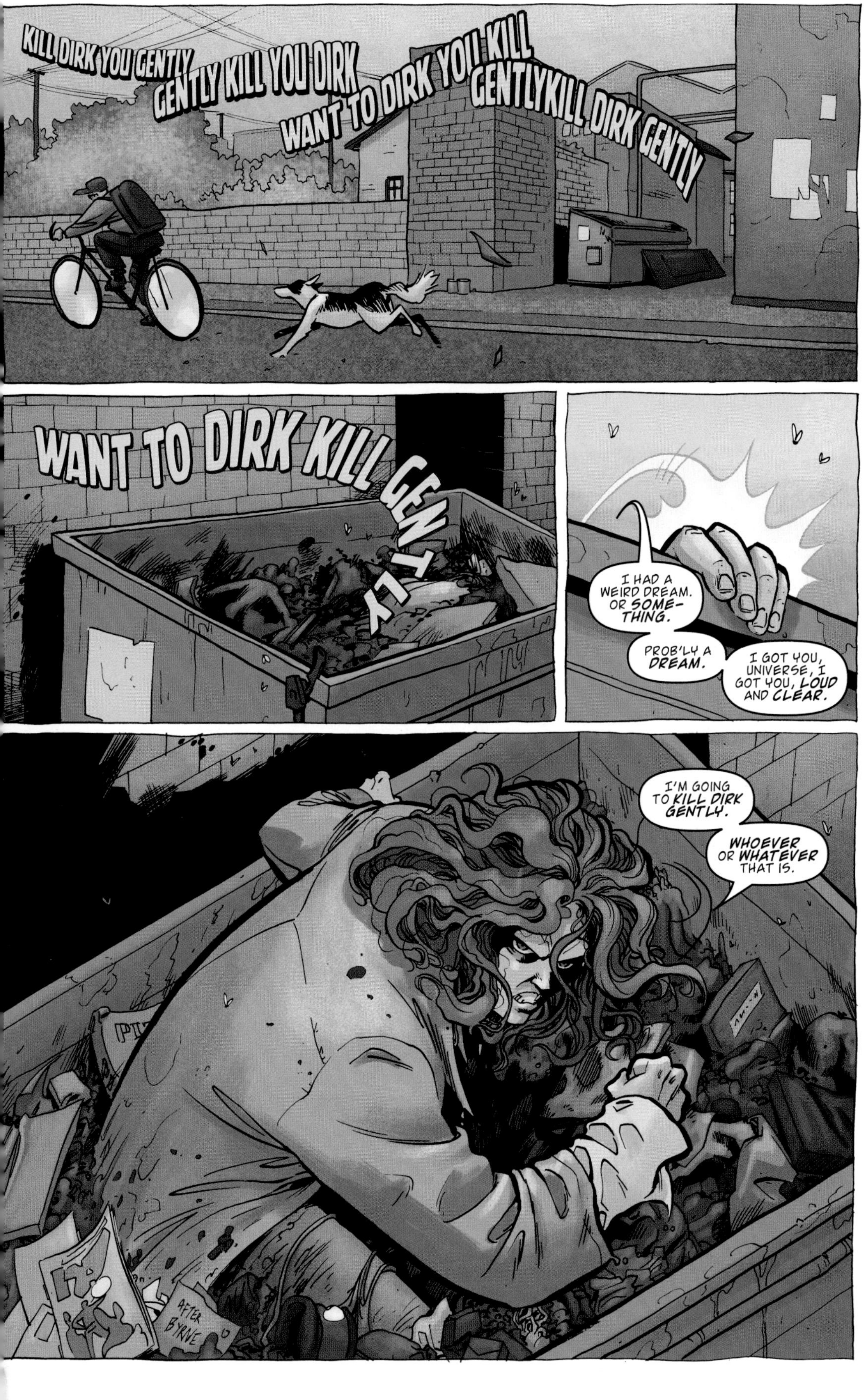
KILL DIRK YOU GENTLY
GENTLY KILL YOU DIRK
WANT TO DIRK YOU KILL
GENTLYKILL DIRK GENTLY
WANT TO DIRK KILL GENTLY
I HAD A WEIRD DREAM. OR SOMETHING.
PROB'LY A DREAM.
I GOT YOU, UNIVERSE, I GOT YOU, LOUD AND CLEAR.
I'M GOING TO KILL DIRK GENTLY.
WHOEVER OR WHATEVER THAT IS.
AFTER BYRNE

ARRIVALS
16:53

		ARRIVING
OSLO	NORWEGIAN AIR 666	1442
LONDON	BRITISH AIRWAYS 901	1625 LANDED
ATHENS	OLYMPIC AIR 556	1700
	AIR FRANCE 990	1720
	NORWEGIAN AIR 666	1442
	BRITISH AIRWAYS 901	1625

BRIAN LEONARD

DIRK GENTLY

OH, HELLO, THAT'S *ME*, ISN'T IT?

WHAT A SNAZZY *HAT* YOU HAVE.

DOES MR. SPRING CHOOSE ALL YOUR HATS HIMSELF? IS IT *GOOD* WORKING FOR A *BILLIONAIRE?* SO FAR, I QUITE LIKE IT. DO YOU KNOW, IN FIRST CLASS, THEY GIVE YOU THE CUTEST *PAJAMAS?*

I'VE TAKEN *THREE* SETS. WOULD YOU LIKE ONE?

MS. BLACK SAID I WAS TO TAKE YOU DIRECTLY TO THE PERIMAN GRAND, SIR. A ROOM HAS BEEN PREPARED FOR YOU.

WELL. HE'S... *THINNER* THAN I IMAGINED.

AIR CAFE

To be Continued...

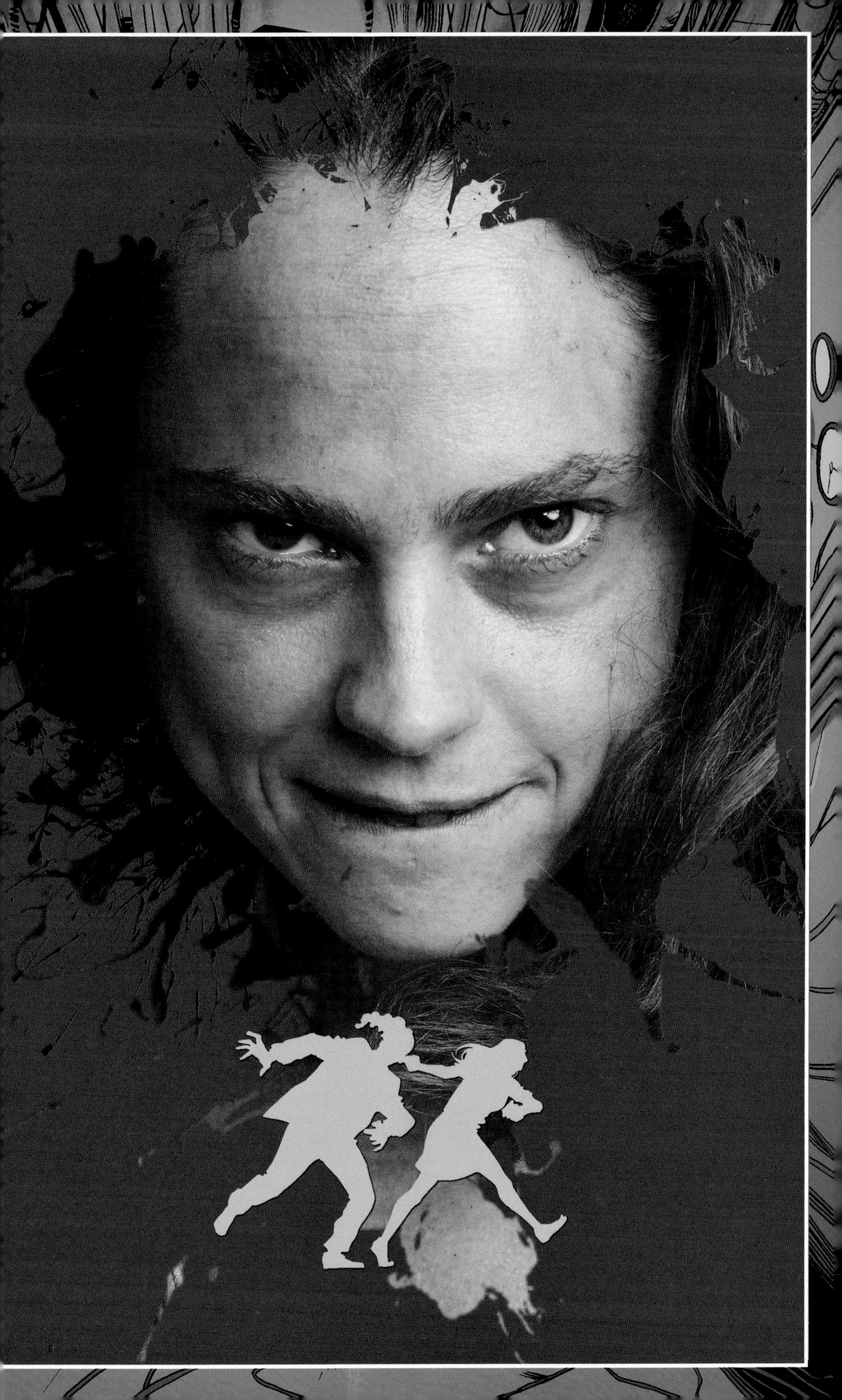

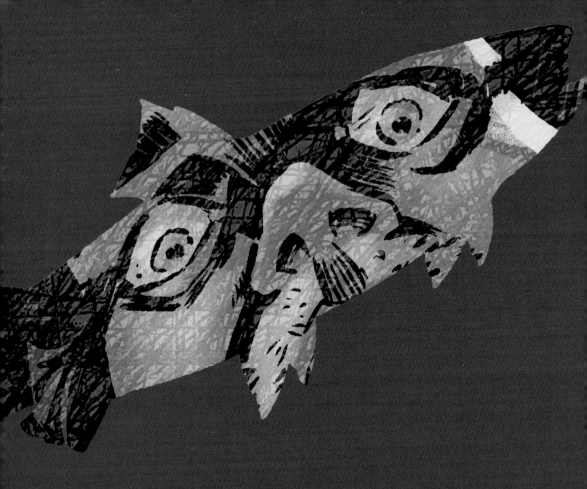

"Ken's Not a Hero"

Written by **Arvind Ethan David** · Art by **Dani Strips**
Colors by **Charlie Kirchoff**

Letters by **Tom B. Long** · Edits by **Denton J. Tipton** · Publisher **Ted Adams** · Executive Producer **Max Landis**

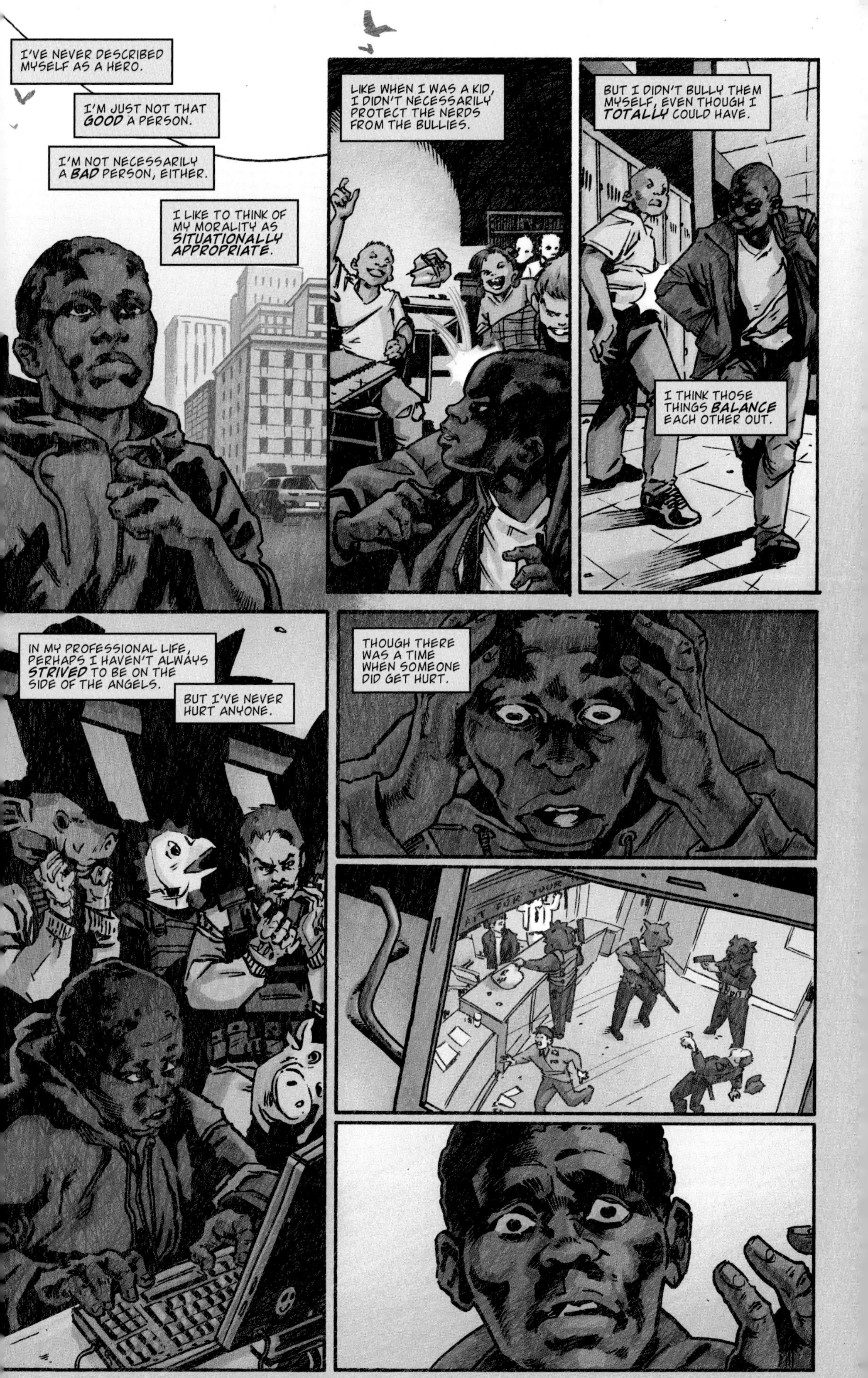
I'VE NEVER DESCRIBED MYSELF AS A HERO.
I'M JUST NOT THAT GOOD A PERSON.
I'M NOT NECESSARILY A BAD PERSON, EITHER.
I LIKE TO THINK OF MY MORALITY AS SITUATIONALLY APPROPRIATE.
LIKE WHEN I WAS A KID, I DIDN'T NECESSARILY PROTECT THE NERDS FROM THE BULLIES.
BUT I DIDN'T BULLY THEM MYSELF, EVEN THOUGH I TOTALLY COULD HAVE.
I THINK THOSE THINGS BALANCE EACH OTHER OUT.
IN MY PROFESSIONAL LIFE, PERHAPS I HAVEN'T ALWAYS STRIVED TO BE ON THE SIDE OF THE ANGELS.
BUT I'VE NEVER HURT ANYONE.
THOUGH THERE WAS A TIME WHEN SOMEONE DID GET HURT.

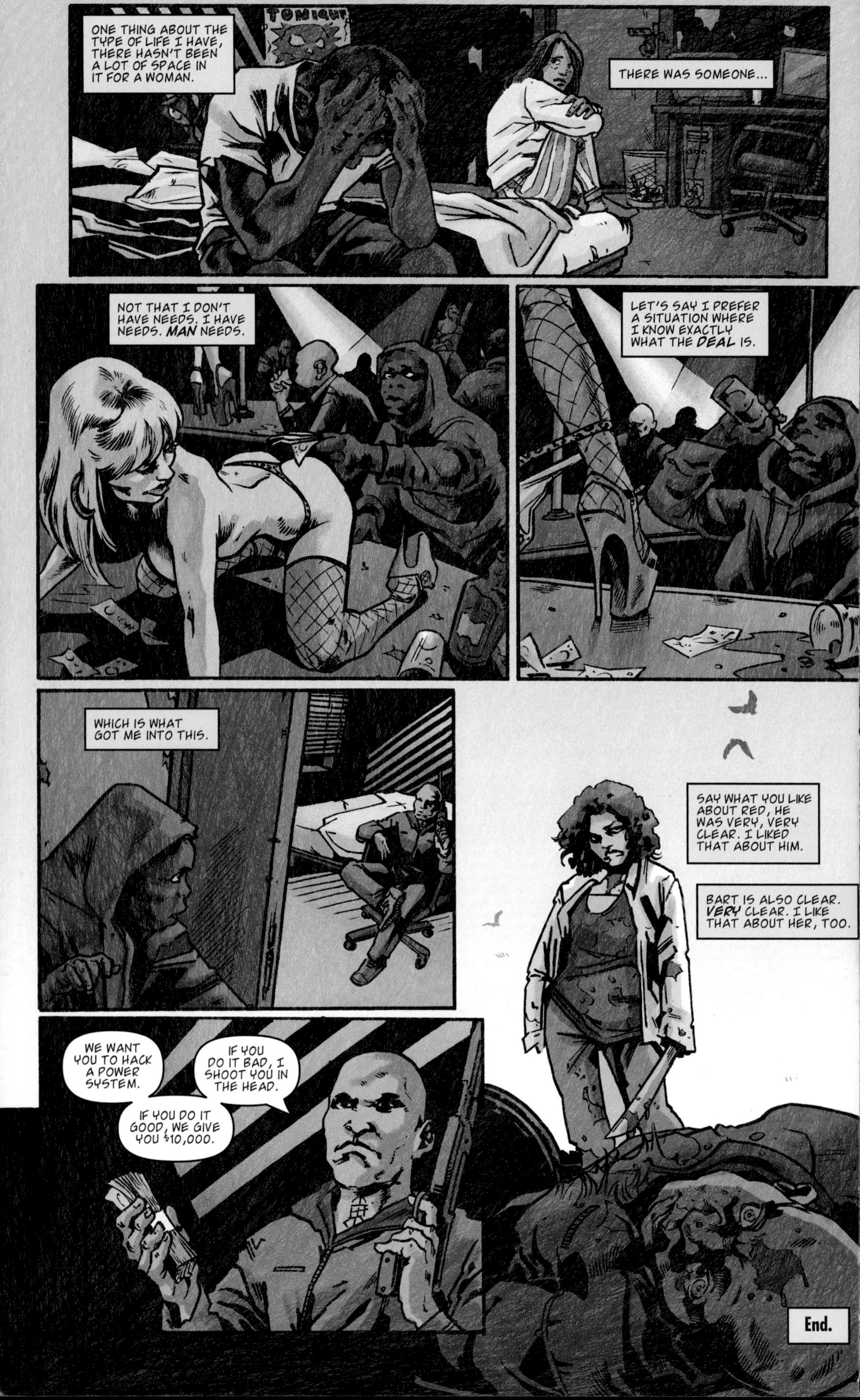
TONIGHT
ONE THING ABOUT THE TYPE OF LIFE I HAVE, THERE HASN'T BEEN A LOT OF SPACE IN IT FOR A WOMAN.
THERE WAS SOMEONE...
NOT THAT I DON'T HAVE NEEDS. I HAVE NEEDS. MAN NEEDS.
LET'S SAY I PREFER A SITUATION WHERE I KNOW EXACTLY WHAT THE DEAL IS.
WHICH IS WHAT GOT ME INTO THIS.
SAY WHAT YOU LIKE ABOUT RED, HE WAS VERY, VERY CLEAR. I LIKED THAT ABOUT HIM.
BART IS ALSO CLEAR. VERY CLEAR. I LIKE THAT ABOUT HER, TOO.
WE WANT YOU TO HACK A POWER SYSTEM.
IF YOU DO IT BAD, I SHOOT YOU IN THE HEAD.
IF YOU DO IT GOOD, WE GIVE YOU $10,000.
End.

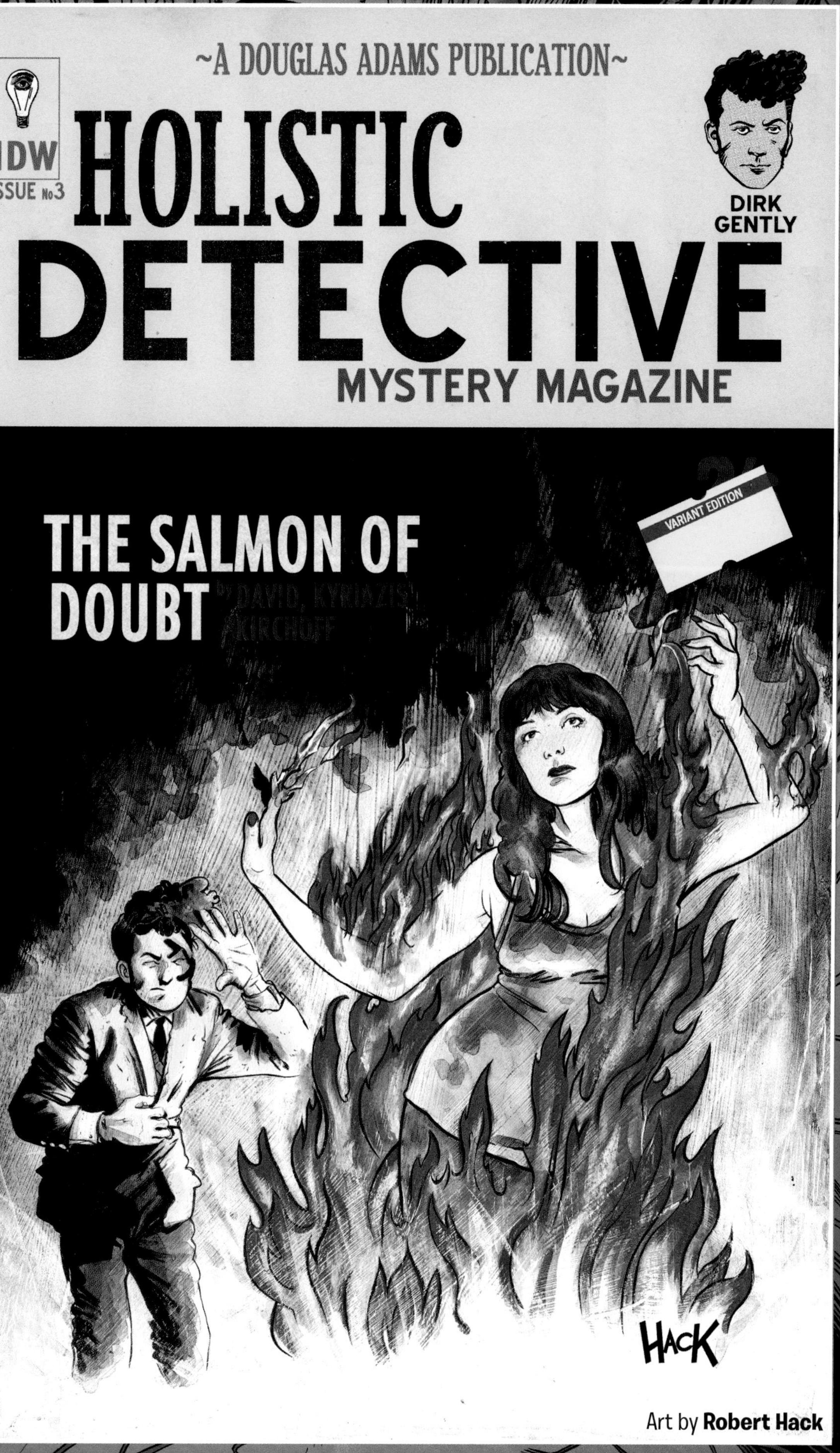
~A DOUGLAS ADAMS PUBLICATION~
IDW
ISSUE No3
HOLISTIC
DETECTIVE
MYSTERY MAGAZINE
DIRK GENTLY
VARIANT EDITION
THE SALMON OF DOUBT
by DAVID, KYRIAZIS, KIRCHOFF
HACK
Art by Robert Hack

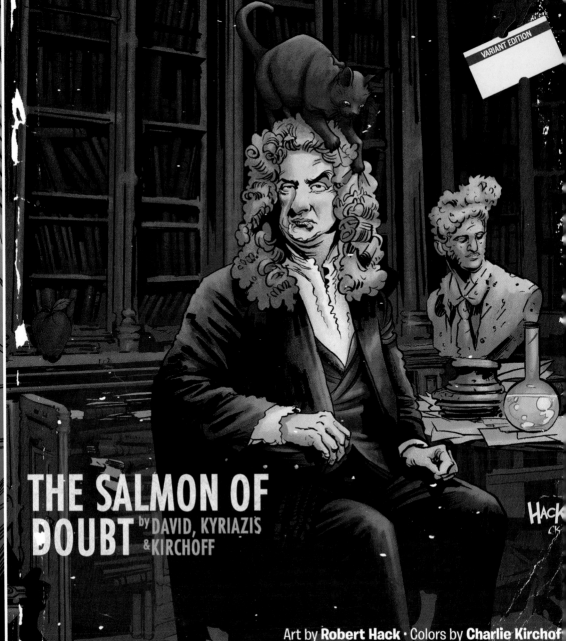

~A DOUGLAS ADAMS PUBLICATION~

IDW

ISSUE No 4

HOLISTIC DETECTIVE

MYSTERY MAGAZINE

DIRK GENTLY

VARIANT EDITION

THE SALMON OF DOUBT
by DAVID, KYRIAZIS & KIRCHOFF

HACK

Art by **Robert Hack** · Colors by **Charlie Kirchof**

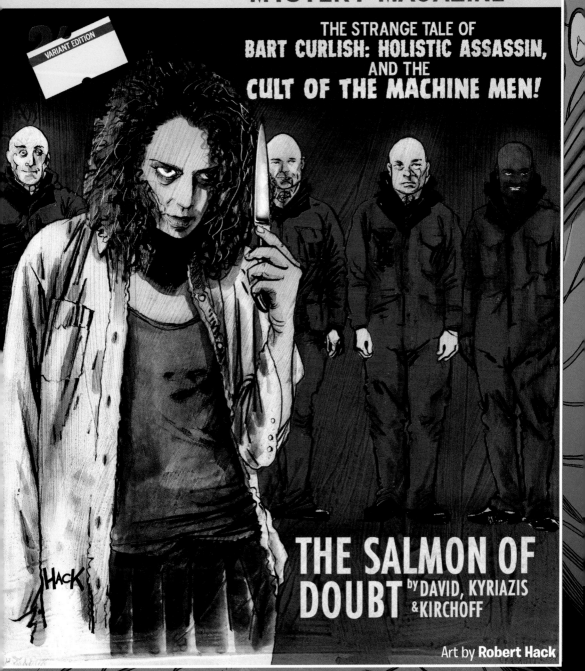

~A DOUGLAS ADAMS PUBLICATION~

HOLISTIC DETECTIVE

MYSTERY MAGAZINE

IDW
ISSUE No 5

DIRK GENTLY

THE STRANGE TALE OF
BART CURLISH: HOLISTIC ASSASSIN,
AND THE
CULT OF THE MACHINE MEN!

VARIANT EDITION

HACK

THE SALMON OF
DOUBT by DAVID, KYRIAZIS & KIRCHOFF

Art by **Robert Hack**

Dirk Gently Fan Art Gallery

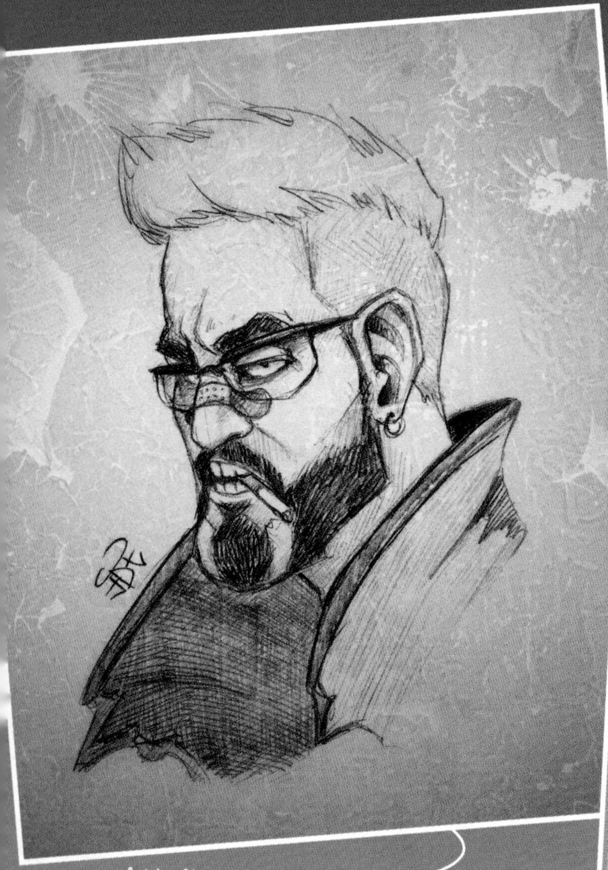

Art by Alymova Daria A.

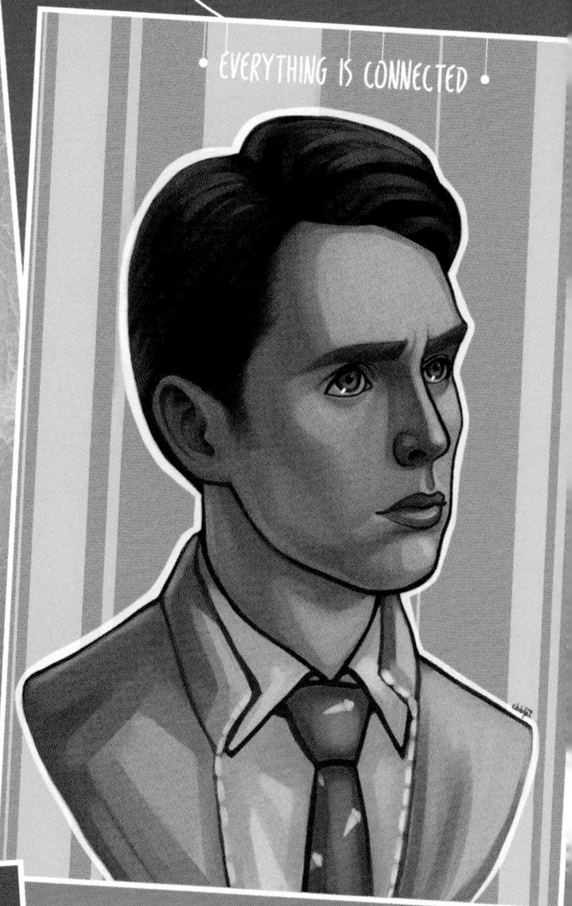
EVERYTHING IS CONNECTED
cbblpt

Art by cbblpt (Alina S.)

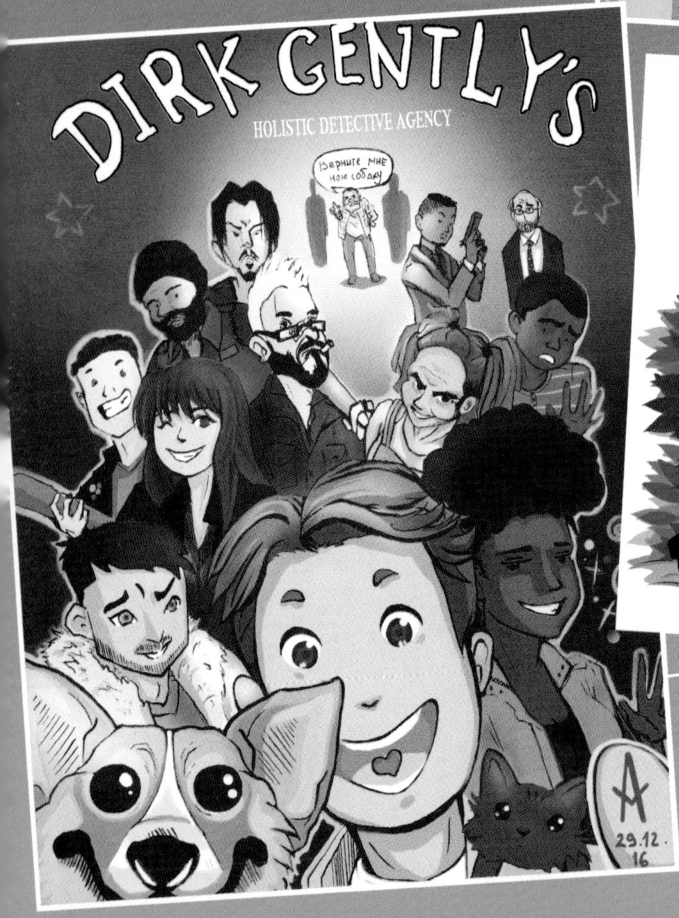
DIRK GENTLY'S
HOLISTIC DETECTIVE AGENCY
Верните мне мою собаку
29.12.16

Art by Ekaterina Orlova (Aliot)

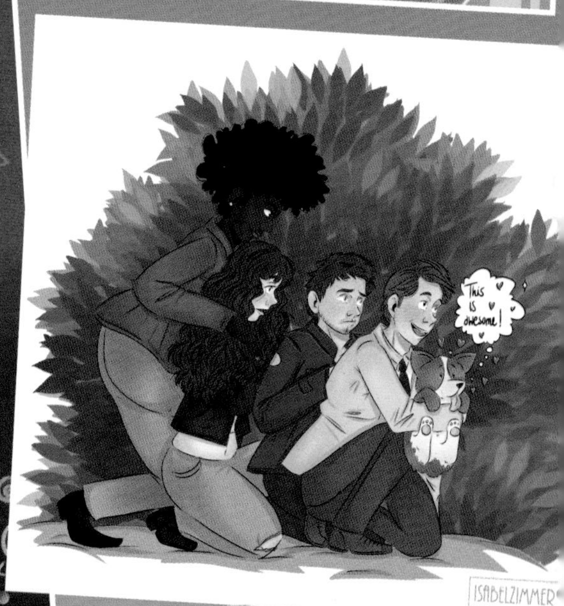
This is awesome!
ISABELZIMMER

Art by Isabel Zimmer

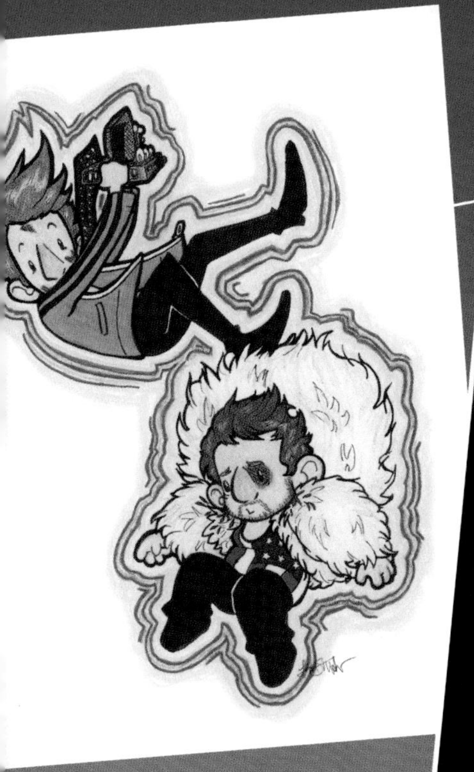

Art by Leah Snyder

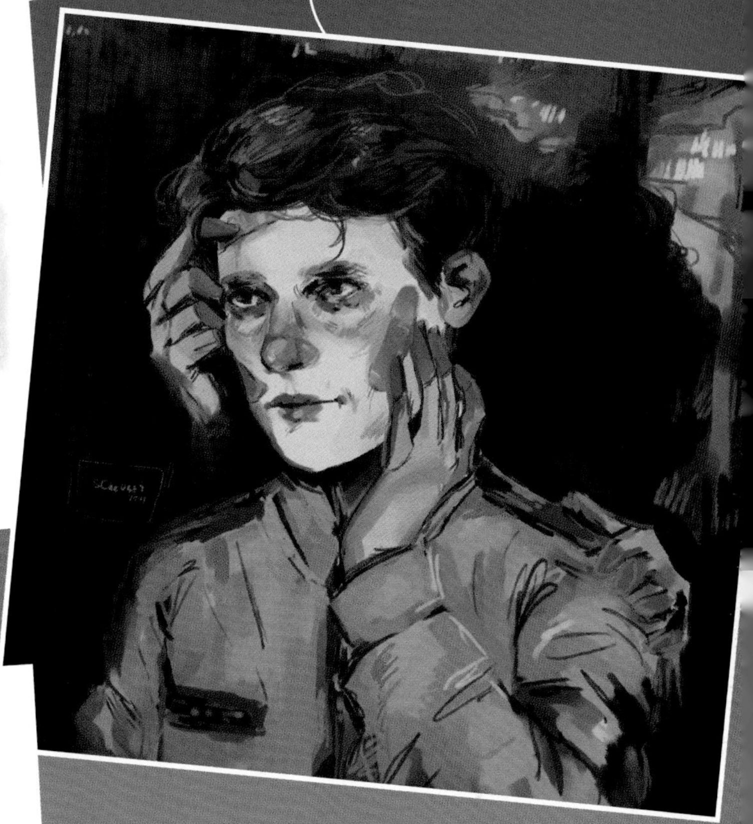

Art by Maria Fisik

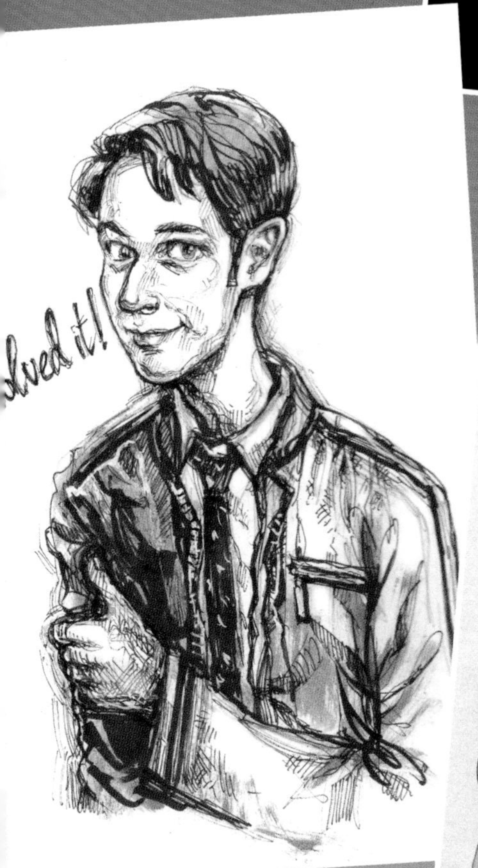
lved it!

Art by marizetta

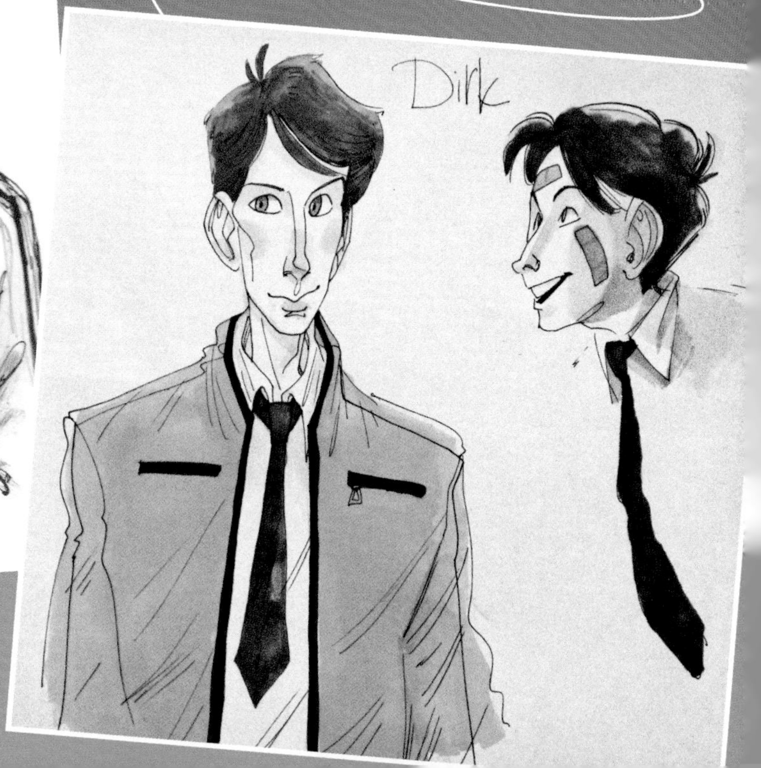
Dirk

Art by Polina Akhremenko

Art by Ilias Kyriazis

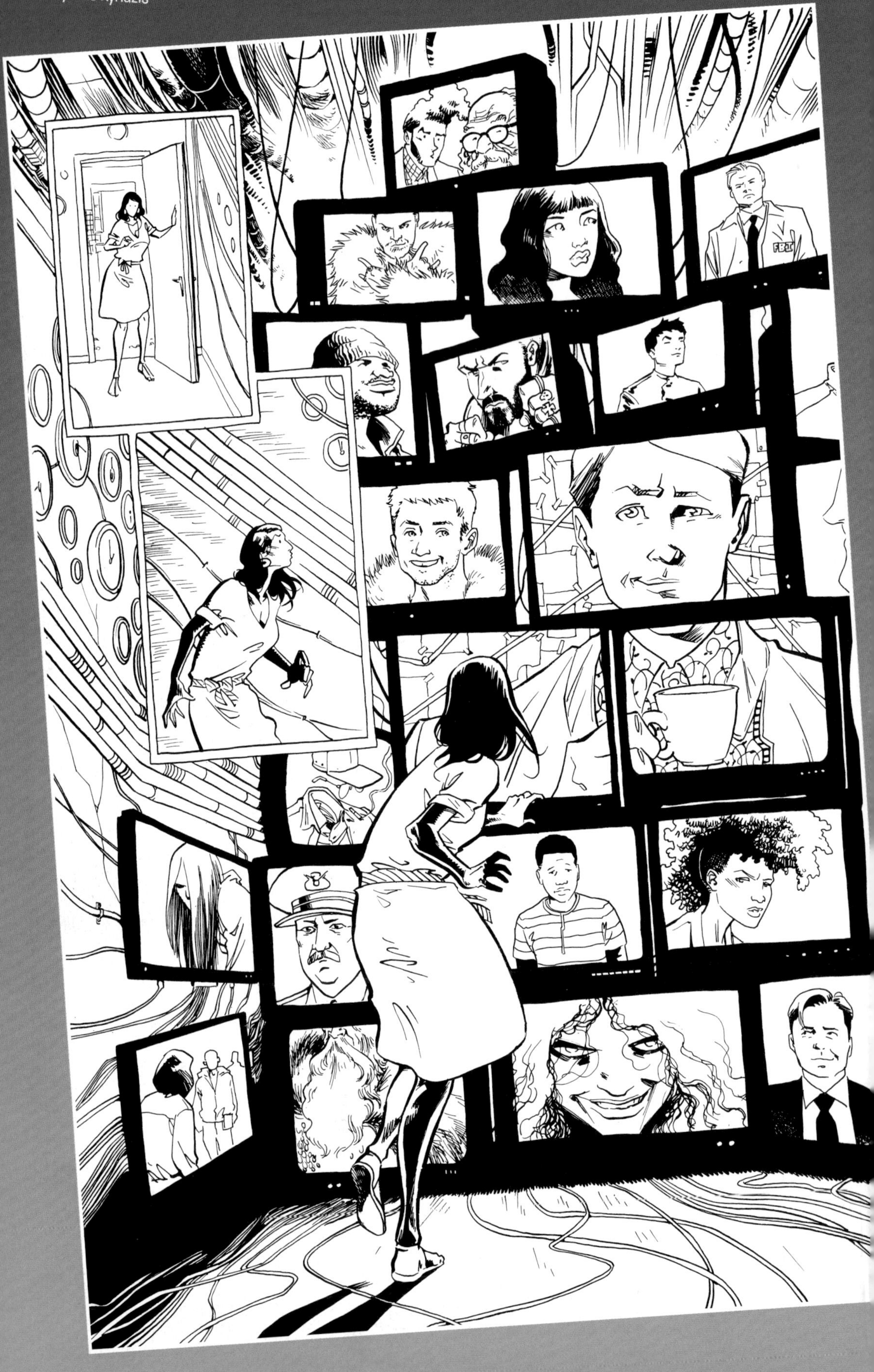

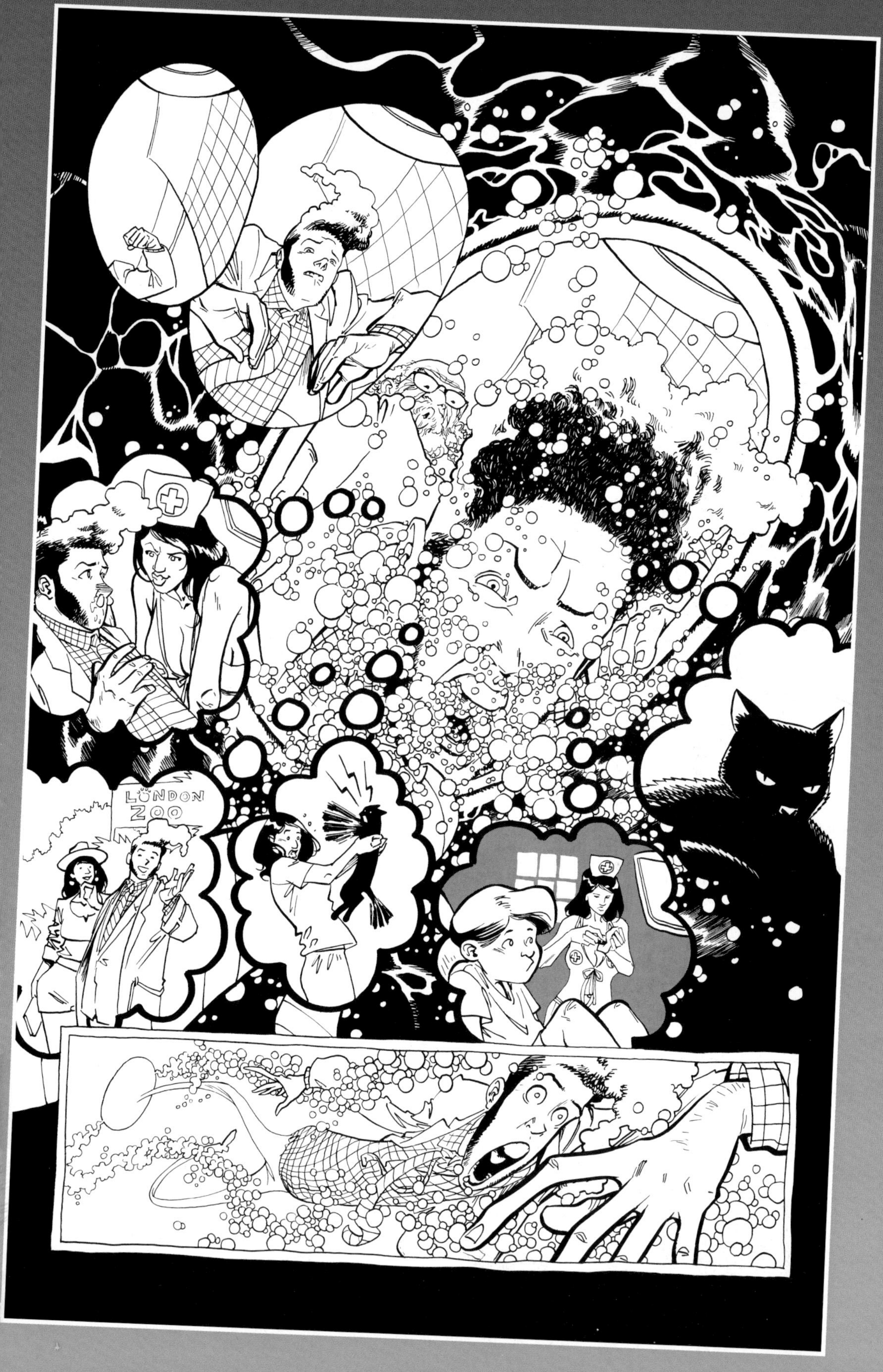
LONDON
ZOO

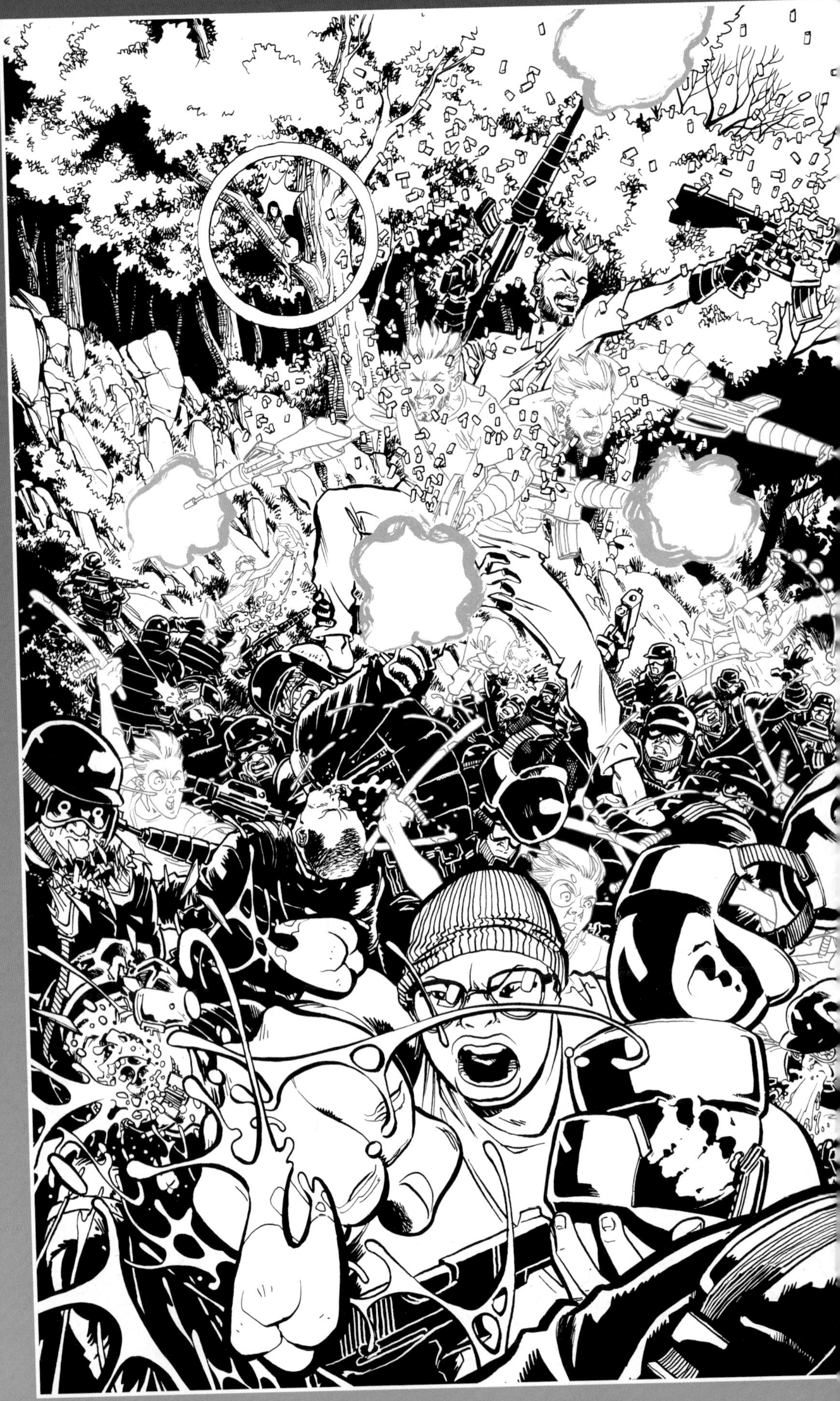

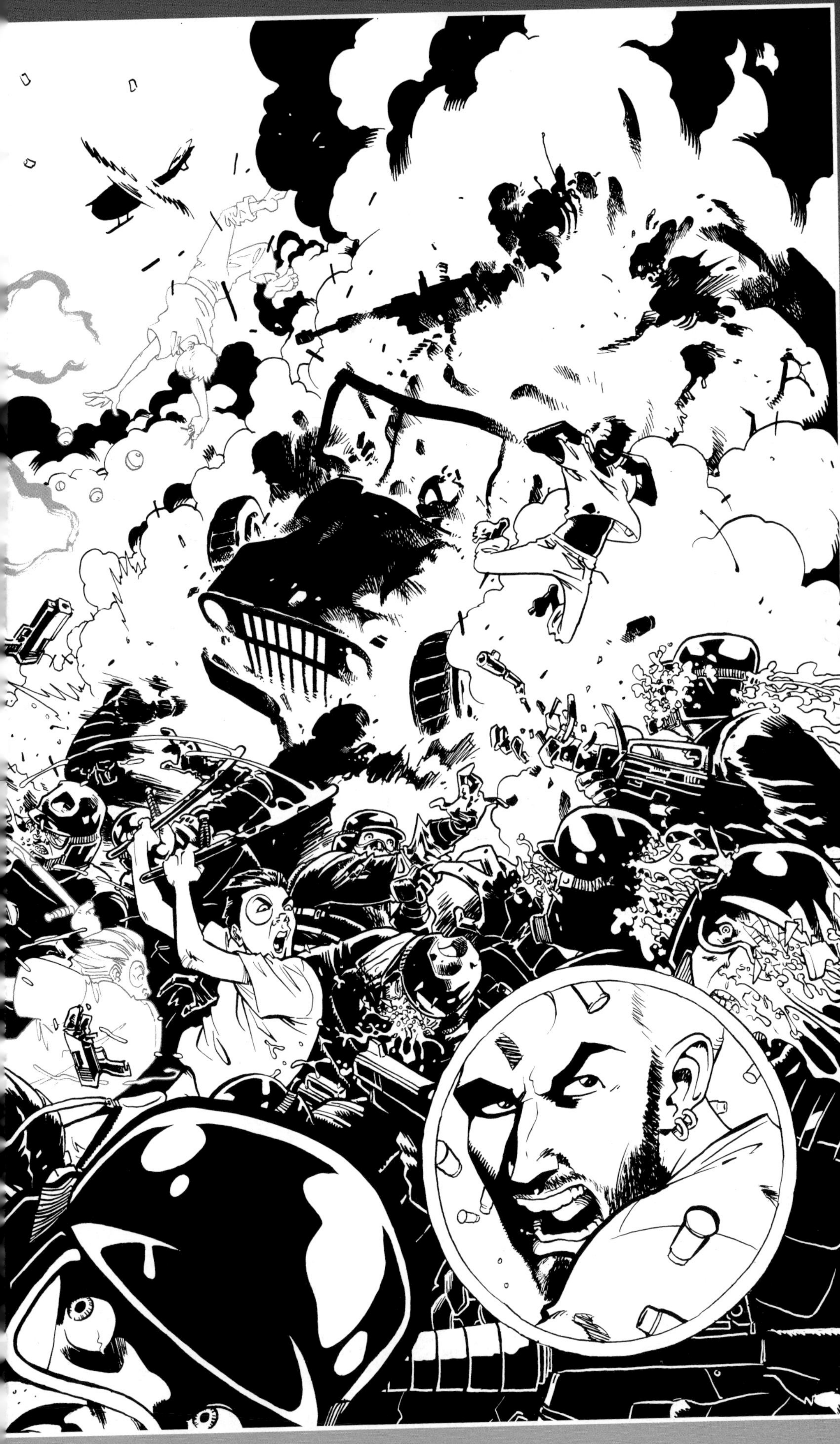

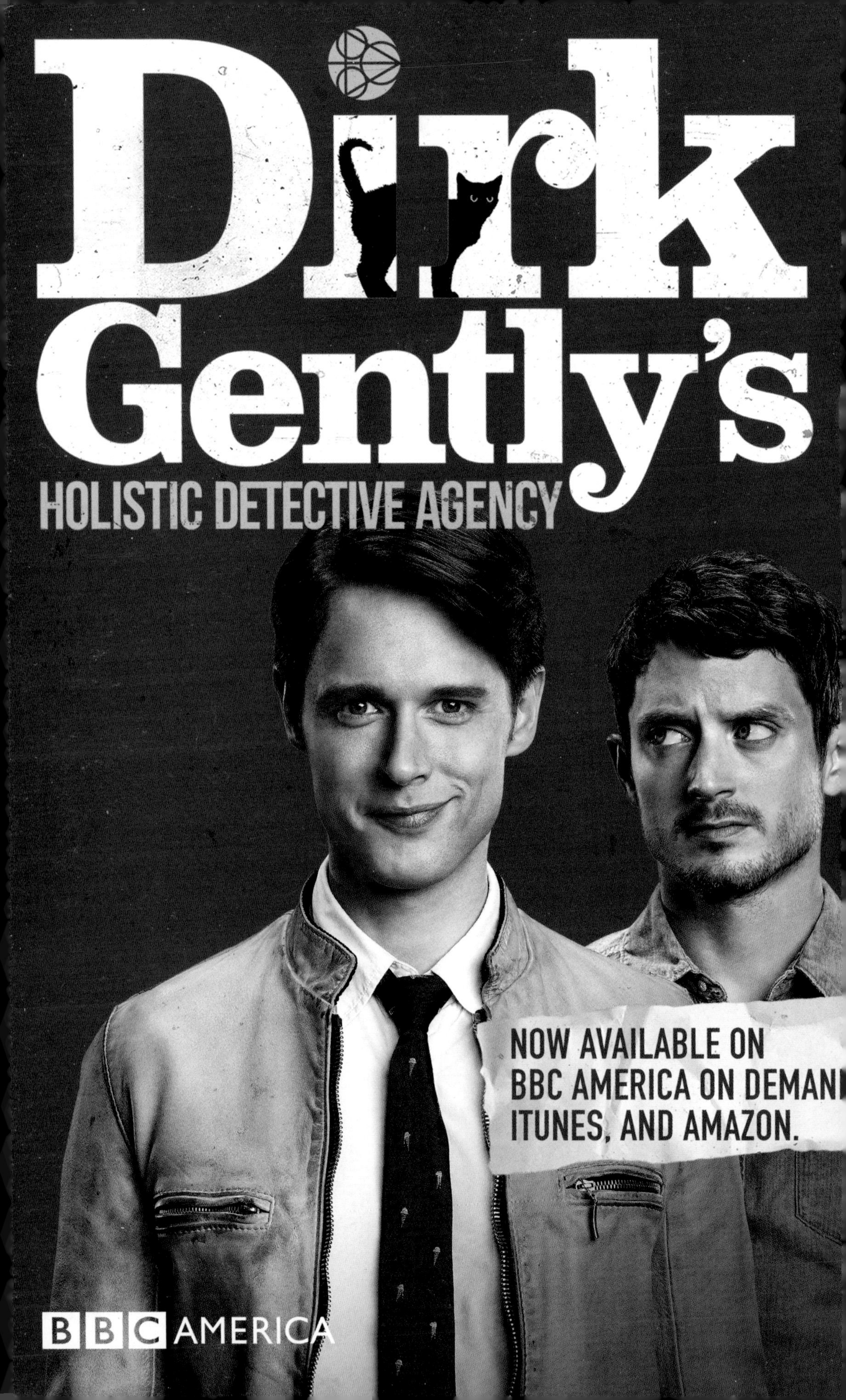
Dirk Gently's
HOLISTIC DETECTIVE AGENCY
NOW AVAILABLE ON
BBC AMERICA ON DEMAN
ITUNES, AND AMAZON.
BBC AMERICA